The Seventh Chamber

The Seventh Chamber

A Commentary on *Parmenides* becomes a Meditation on, at once, Heraclitean “Diapherein” and Nachmanian “Tsimtsum”

John W McGinley

iUniverse, Inc.
Bloomington

The Seventh Chamber
A Commentary on *Parmenides* becomes a Meditation on, at once, Heraclitean "Diapherein" and Nachmanian "Tsimtsum"

iUniverse books may be ordered through booksellers or by contacting:

iUniverse
1663 Liberty Drive
Bloomington, IN 47403
www.iuniverse.com
1-800-Authors (1-800-288-4677)

ISBN: 978-1-4502-9543-7 (pbk)
ISBN: 978-1-4502-9544-4 (ebk)

Printed in the United States of America

iUniverse rev. date: 3/30/11

With Gratitude and Profound Admiration
This Book is Dedicated to

Michele Geralyn McMahon

to put it simply,
she is the love of my life

Some say "the Seventh Heaven"; others say
The Seventh Chamber
["chambers" = heikalot]
*****

it is written here:

Sing to God; make music for His name. Extol the One who rides upon* ARBOT *with His NAME:* YAH. *And exult before Him.

[Psalms 68:5]

and it is written there:

He rides across Heaven to help you, and in His majesty through the Upper Heights.

[Devarim 33:26]

--- and the mountain was burning with fire up to the heart of Heaven: darkness; cloud; and thick clouds [surround Him].

[Devarim 4:11]

He made Darkness His Hiding Place, all around Him as His Shelter; the Darkness of Water, the clouds of Heaven.

[Psalms 18:12]

And can there be any darkness before Heaven!? Yet it is written:

He reveals the Deep and Mysterious [ameeyqata v-umsatrata <cognate to "mistarim"] ***; He knows*** [YADA] ***what is in the Darkness, and Light dwells with Him.***

[Daniel 2:22]

[[[A selective and orchestrated presentation of the Bavli commentary on Tractate Khaggigah.
Art-Scroll, 12b-iv--12b-v.]]]

One must seize the reality of one's fate and that's that

[V v-G in one of the Letters to Theo]

*****   *****   *****

an theos ethele

[Letter VI; 323c,7]

*****   *****   *****

"God," then, is at the head of the serious letters; but "Gods" of the less serious.

[Letter XIII; 363b,5-7]

{Socrates speaking}: *On the other hand, Parmenides, Forms* [***ei-don***] *(each one of them) may be thoughts* [**noema**] *and properly obtain only in souls* [*psukhais*]. *In this way each one of them might be a one* ***without*** *entailing the difficulties of which we have just spoken.*

{Parmenides speaking}: *Are each one of these thoughts* [**noematon**] *a one, but* [at the same time] *a thought* [**noema**] *of nothing?*

S: *No. That's impossible.*

P: *But, rather, of something?*

S: Yes.

P. Of something which is, or of something which is not?

S. Of something which is.

P. Is it not, some one thing which the thought [**noema**] *thinks obtaining over each and all* [[covered by that thought]], *being* [ousan] *some one* [mian] *idea* [idean]*?*

S. *Yes.*

P. *Is not* ***this****, then* <<i.e., what the alleged Form-as-thought **is referring to** rather than this alleged Form-as-thought>> *the Form* [eidos], ***itself*** [i.e., what the alleged Form-as-thought **is referring to** rather than this alleged Form-as-thought] *which, being construed* [**nooumenon**] *as a one always remains itself through all* [[the entities covered by that alleged Form-as-thought]]?

S. *That must be the case*!

P. *And here's another thing. Given your claim that the others* {talla; participants in a Form} *participate in* [their respective] *Forms* [**eidon**; i.e. these alleged Forms-as-thoughts in their referentiality to the one in question which is being referred to] *, wouldn't you also have to opine* [**doksei**] *that anything and everything at all (which is referred to) are composed of thoughts* [**noemato**] *with the consequence that all things are thinking* [**kai panta noein**] *or, that being thoughts* [**noemata**] *they are not thinking* [**anoeta**]*?*

S: ***That*** *contention, Parmenides, has no standing at all.*

[*Parmenides*132b,4--132d,2]

Headings.

*****

Codicil: **MAYA** (*tat tsam asi* <with a twist MAYA (*tat tsam asi* <with a twist>)

A. Introductory Remarks.

In 1976 I produced, in and as two slim volumes, a book titled *Commentary on Parmenides*. There were strengths and weaknesses in that production. I believe this production came to be included in the Library Collections of several institutions of higher learning.

I have now reprised that Commentary in the book you are now reading. It is my hope that the ratio of strengths to weaknesses of this book is better than the ratio of strengths to weaknesses which obtained in that production.

*****

So much, then, for those best laid plans of mice and men. What happened was not really an abortion, but rather more like *coitus interruptus* with a "conception" other than the "conception" which often accompanies a non-interrupted *coitus*. So be it. Let the work unfold itself to you much the same way as it unfolded itself to me.

All of my writings pretty much circle around the famous question posed by my dear friend Tertullian. Of course my response to his question (which, in his case, answers the question in the asking) is radically different from his. But my response is, as well and even more radically so, different form most accounts of how "Athens" and "Jerusalem" have formed a ***yikhud***. What obtains in my writings is a most idiosyncratic "union" of a most idiosyncratic "Athens" with a most idiosyncratic "Jerusalem." Let the reader beware, be aware, and warned.

*****

This 'Second Commentary' is totally predicated on and emerges from the themes, claims, and lines of argumentation which I developed in my 2009 publication, **THE DREADFUL SYMMETRY**

OF THE GOOD. [ISBN: 978-1-44016540-5; hereafter: **DSG**] Any putative reader of this 'Second Commentary' may very well find it difficult to follow the lines of argumentation of this 'Second Commentary' if she has not digested the themes, claims, and lines of argumentation of **DSG**.

*****

I have made extensive use of two translations of Plato's *Parmenides*. The first is the Gill/Ryan translation as contained in *Plato: Complete Works* edited by John M. Cooper (1997). The second is the Fowler translation as contained in the Loeb Classical Library [Plato IV; 1926/1939]. I have also consulted some other translations of *Parmenides*. It has been my habit to, more often than not, amalgamate these two (and other various) translations in accordance with my understanding of the Greek text. Pagination is virtually always given with reference to the Greek text as contained in the Loeb.

*****

The proofreading for **DSG** was atrocious precisely because about ninety percent of the proofreading was executed by me. More often than not my proofreading was merely a "skimming." I was emotionally exhausted as I did the proofing. Further, I find the task of making some remedy for such atrocious proofing to be beyond my present capacity.

Misspellings; lack of noun/verb agreement; using the wrong words; words out of their proper position or words in sentences which are in fact extraneous to the sentence in question; missing words; syntactical errors which skew the semantic flow; doubling certain words and phrases in certain sentences. All of this and more. Truly atrocious.

Even so, an intelligent and careful reader would be able, in virtually all cases, to correct, right while she is reading, all of these errors if the reader were reading carefully and empathetically.

While I hope the proofreading for this book will have been an improvement over that done for **DSG** (and I have reason to believe that such will turn out to be the case) it will remain the case that: *an intelligent and careful reader would be able, in virtually all cases which are mechanical, to correct, right while she is reading, all of these errors if the reader were reading carefully and empathetically.* But it is a different story when it comes to non-mechanical difficulties in my text. I have not made ease of readability a goal of my writing neither with regard to my lines of argumentation nor even with sentence structure (and length thereof). There is no perverse motivation in this.

The Divine Economy ((i.e., all that is the case; aka: "reality")) of its very nature exhibits itself according to the logic of the ***neither-nor-and-both-at-once*** paradigm with emphasis on the ***at once***. Such is in contrast to the simplistic ***either-or*** paradigm and the domesticating ***both-and*** paradigm. While these last two paradigms are compatible with a goal of ease of readability they inevitably fall short in the task of giving expression to "all that is the case;" aka "The Divine Economy;" aka "reality." More than that, these two paradigms channel, consciously and unconsciously, the expression of "all that is the case" into the "frame" of ontotheological discourse thereby falsifying "The Divine Economy" <aka "reality">.

Only a discourse which forces the reader to **struggle** [[think here of the Heraclitean **polemos** <and "The Greater Yihad" spoken of by Muhammod>]] in her reading will put the reader capable of such in touch with that which is to be thought. There is a paucity of such readers. Even so, if there is but one of you, my dear cherished reader, you are a co-creator of what this book can bring about. For *yikhud* between writer and reader can create a "conception" which the writer could never bring about by herself/himself.

B. More or Less Commentary on *Parmenides.*

A. Introductory Setting. 126a,1--127d,5.

Cephalus: When we came from our home at Clazomenae to Athens, ...
----- He himself, however, had heard Zeno read them before.

A-1. The first three names mentioned in *Parmenides* are Cephalus, Adeimantus, and Glaucon. Doubtlessly such naming at the very beginning of this dialogue was, at the least, intended to engender memory of the opening of *Republic*. My presumption is that in so doing Plato was signaling that *Parmenides* merited the degree of grandeur and honor which, even while Plato was alive, had been accorded to *Republic*. Even so, the opening of *Parmenides*, the first dialogue of the third tetralogy, shares, structurally and more subtly, a number of variables which tie *Parmenides* and the opening of *Symposium*, the third dialogue of the third tetralogy, together even though the cast of characters in *Symposium* does not include Cephalus or Adeimantos. There is however a reference in the opening scene to a certain "Glaucon" [172c,4] who may or may not be the Glaucon who was the brother of Plato. This is the only mention of Glaucon in the dialogue.

In *Republic* the *mis en scene* is quite clever, jocular, and entertaining. Through a chance encounter Socrates (who speaks in the first person and who is making his way back to Athens from attending an innovative religious festival held in Piraeus) is interrupted in his journey home. He is presented as being accompanied by Glaucon. They are more or less accosted by Polemarchus, who is accompanied by Adeimantus and a number of others. This playful interruption (which nonetheless "plays" on the possibility of force) orchestrated by Polemarchus has the net result that the parties to the encounter all end up at the house of Polemarchus, whose father is Cephalus. Polemarchus himself is to be hosting something of a soiree which includes some characters who -- along with Glaucon and Adeimantos, half-brothers of Plato -- will make an appearance in *Republic*.

The scene at the house of Polemarchus has Socrates initially questioning Cephalus about old age. This charming interplay leads into, almost accidentally it is made to appear, the question of Justice which is the major theme of *Republic*. Cephalus, citing his age, chooses to withdraw from the conversation at this point. But Plato by this time has now fully presented the dramatic setting for the entire rest of the dialogue. Note that the main part of the dialogue *directly* emerges from the scene of the opening conversation.

In contrast, with *Parmenides* and *Symposium* the scene setting mechanisms involve characters who were NOT at the original dramatic setting of their respective dialogue. However, one of each grouping had heard of it -- and the precise details of complex argumentation and/or speeches thereof -- from another who, each one of them (Pythodorus for the dramatic setting of *Parmenides* and Aristodemus for the dramatic setting of *Symposium*) are presented as having been present at the original scene. Further, each of the openings of these two dialogues call to mind dramatic settings which are presented as having happened *long before* the opening conversations of each of our dialogues. The suggestion being made here that Plato is, in effect, pairing off together the dialogue subtitled ***peri ideon**** with the dialogue subtitled ***peri agathon***.* I draw the reader's attention to the fact that in the tetralogical arrangement of the dialogues these two dialogues are mediated by the dialogue ***peri hedone*** * which, as is explained in great detail in **DSG**, functions as Plato's introduction to and grid of interpretation for that late-in-life radical revision of *Symposium*. The reader is also alerted to the fact that this *Philebus* has much to say about Form-theory, <Forms here being presented as "ones" and as "monads" most especially (but certainly not only) at 14c through 17>a.

*. [[The subtitles are contained in the collection of Thrasyllus. It is credible that the subtitles are the work of Plato himself. Indeed the subtitle for *Symposium*, "peri agathon" is, surfacely, counter intuitive and it is not likely that Thrasyllus himself would have taken it upon itself to assign such a subtitle to *Symposium*. On the contrary in his function of arranging for a fresh copy of this collection at all would entail that he would respect the text as he found it (inclusive of its tetralogical arrangement). On the other hand the descriptive categories ((e.g., "logical," "ethical," "tentative,"etc.)) which immediately succeed the subtitles are clearly not Platonic either in character or spirit. In assigning these descriptive categories Thrasyllus was trading upon a mix of an Aristotelian division of Philosophy combined with post-Aristotelian descriptive categorization of the Platonic corpus.]]

In the case of *Parmenides* a certain Pythodorus was the one present at the dramatic setting (invented by Plato) involving an intricate interchange between and among Zeno, Socrates (presented as a young man in this dramatic setting), Parmenides, and a certain "Aristotle" who is identified as one who later on would become one of "The Thirty." (127d, 2-3) Cephalus, the opening spokesperson in the *mis en scene* is the one who is presented as being very desirous of hearing about this most intricate interchange. He has heard that Antiphon -- the "half-brother-on-your-[i.e., of Adeimantus' who is being addressed and also, in fact, of Glaucon although he is not addressed] -mother's-side" -- was a close associate of this Pythodorus who himself was a consort of Zeno.

Adeimantus informs Cephalus that he will be able to lead Cephalus and his wisdom-loving companions to Antiphon's home where Antiphon has been for a long time devoting himself to horse-breeding. But Glaucon assures Cephalus that his half-brother (i.e., this Antiphon) has mastered the details of this intricate interchange from hearing it from the mouth of Pythodorus many times who and still carries it with him in his mind. Antiphon ((((interestingly only after first finishing up certain instructions for one of his workers on his horse-breeding farm <as an indication that necessary pedestrian affairs in life do -- and, really, should -- take a position of privilege relative to a dialogue subtitled "peri ideon)))) agrees to relate the intricate conversation. It is also interesting that Antiphon (and who was only a boy when he visited before) -- unless he is himself a Platonic-orchestrated stand-in for Plato tout court -- shares with Plato the status of being the "half-brother on your mother's side" of Adeimantus and, for that matter, Glaucon. Further, like Plato, this Antiphon is presented as clearly younger than his two older half-brothers. It is this Antiphon (aka Plato?) who relates the whole and most intricate "interchange."

In the case of *Symposium* Appollodorus, who describes himself as attending to Socrates in every way for almost three years, (173c, 6-8), is speaking with an unnamed companion. Appollodorus is responding to the unnamed companion's wish to know more about a most memorable "symposium" which brought together ["sunousian"; 172a,8--172b,1] Agathon, Socrates, and Alcibiades.

Appollodorus in his opening remarks is able to assure his unnamed companion that only recently he had occasion to sharpen up the memory of his conversation with Aristodemus who had accompanied Socrates to the drinking party. For it so happened that "the day before yesterday" [172a,2] he had been accosted by a certain "Glaucon" who himself wanted more, and more accurate, details about the drinking party and the speeches given at that drinking party. This Glaucon had recently heard a version of it from another but was skeptical of how accurate this version was. Glaucon is presented as sensing that Appollodorus might have had access to a better accounting of this drinking party. It is also pointed out that Glaucon is under the mistaken impression that the "sunousian" was of recent vintage when in point of fact Appollodoros makes it clear that the gathering was not at all of recent vintage.

This last set of observations may be Plato's sly somewhat sly and subtle manner of making reference to a version of this gathering produced by Xenophon and how that Xenophonic version can be compared to *Plato's* version. For while the *original* Platonic version of *Symposium* may well have been composed before Xenophon's production, Plato's significant revision late in life of *Symposium* post-dates Xenophon's composition. [[The reader must consult **DSG** concerning the argumentation for the thesis that Plato, late in life, revised an earlier version of *Symposium*.]]

It becomes clear from Apollodorus' report that Glaucon's dependency on this other accounting led to Glaucon's having had only a very inaccurate accounting of not only of when, but also of what, went on at that gathering. And in this vein Appollodorus relays to his unnamed companion how he corrected Glaucon on the spot with regard to Glaucon's egregiously erroneous understanding of the *when* of this gathering.

Apollodorus then relates to his unnamed companion that, between his encounter with Glaucon and the present scene, he himself *directly* questioned Socrates about some of the details from that long-ago gathering. Thus Appollodorus is now presented as being especially authoritative in the forthcoming account which he is about to give to his unnamed companion. Again, the subtext is that Plato's version, rather than Xenophon's, is the more authoritative accounting of what went on at the home of Agathon.

A-2.

When we came from our home at Clazomenae to Athens --- [126a,1-2]

The "we" of this statement refers to Cephalus, the speaker, and "these gentlemen, fellow citizens of mine who are very fond of philosophy." They remain unnamed.

A-2-a, Clazomenae.

Yes. Cephalus was said to have had his roots in Clazomenae. But he is also said to have spent most of his adult life in Piraeus/Athens where he raised his family and achieved a decent success in his business undertakings. He very well may have travelled back to the city wherein he was raised. But did he travel with "fellow citizens" who are "very fond of philosophy"? Certainly in the opening scene of *Republic* Cephalus is portrayed as withdrawing from the conversation just at the point at which the conversation turns to an overtly philosophical matter: Justice. True, in that scene Cephalus is portrayed as being a decent man of business with respectable ethical instincts. But in that same scene from *Republic* he hardly seems to be interested in a more theoretical discussion of living a decent life. So it is fair to ask: Why does Plato present him as being accompanied by the band of "fellow citizens who are very fond of philosophy"? And, further, is there any significance to the reference to Clazomenae?

A-2-b.

Virtually all commentaries on *Parmenides* make reference to the fact that Anaxagoras hails from Clazomenae. Noting this has become a commonplace and virtually *de rigeur* for those writing dissertations on *Parmenides*. And many of them claim that in opening up the dialogue in this fashion Plato is, so to speak, "tipping his hand." For the most famous son of Clazomenae, as far as Philosophy is concerned, is Anaxagoras. And the most famous teaching of Anaxagoras is the teaching that **NOUS** is the Divine principle which governs the Cosmos.

Just as is the case with Cephalus, Anaxagoras spent most of his adult life in the Athens/Piraeus locale. And the most famous episodes in Anaxagoras' life concern his life in Athens rather than in Clazomenae. He may have been senior to Socrates by about a decade or so, but he can hardly be called a "Pre-Socratic" the way that, say, Empedocles can be called a "Pre-Socratic." And famously (and as alluded to in *Apology*) Socrates shared -- albeit in a way different from what Anaxagoras had to say on this matter -- with this transplant from Clazomenae a reputation for not believing in "the Gods of the City." In any case, **IF** the opening sentence of *Parmenides* is trading on a teaching of Anaxagoras at all, it is not with reference to these matters of impiety. Rather, if this sentence is referencing a teaching of Anaxagoras, it is with reference to his teaching on Divine Nous. But not in an unambiguous manner, as we shall see below.

A-2-b-i. Nous and Anaxagoras. Nous and Plato. Nous and Aristotle.

Let us cite Aristotle on this to launch and contextualize this probing of Plato's intention in opening *Parmenides* with the reference to Clazomenae. His remark is clever and pithy:

> *When one man, then, said that reason* [nous] *was present -- as in animals, so throughout nature -- as the cause of order and of all arrangement, he seemed like a sober man in contrast with the random talk of his predecessors.*

[*Metaphysics-I*-3, 984b, 14-18. The Ross translation contained in the Mckeon edition of the works of Aristotle; 1941/2001.]

Interestingly enough Aristotle adds on an addendum [984b, 18-22] to the Nous teaching of Anaxagoras which, implicitly is in accord with his own Monistic view of Nous/Divinity contained in Chapters Seven and Nine of *Metaphysics-XII*, specifically with regard to the connection of Nous and motion and as well, allusively and indirectly, in accord with his brief allusion to the causal power of Beauty and its relationship to the causal principle of things given briefly at *Metaphysics-XIII*-3, at 1078a,32--1078b,6.

Ambivalence concerning the Nous teaching of Anaxagoras permeates both reviews given by Plato and Aristotle relative to this Anaxagorean Nous teaching. On the one hand, the electricity engendered by the Nous teaching affected both Aristotle (who probably came into contact with the teaching as a young man in Plato's Academy long after Anaxagoras and Socrates had died) and Plato. On the other hand each, effectively, dismisses Anaxagoras as a great thinker and, implicitly each claim that Anaxagoras never really got it right at all with regard to the critical question, *how and in what sense is* **NOUS** *a causal principle?*

Even so, Plato's dismissal of Anaxagoras is not softened with such pithy and clever characterization of this teaching which was offered by Aristotle. And the element of condemnation is far stronger in Plato's remarks than what is implied by Aristotle's remarks. But in condemning Anaxagoras Plato carefully explains why the rumor of the Anaxagoras teaching on Nous was so electrifying to him. For the rumor of this teaching, according to Plato's mouthpiece in *Phaedo*, conjures up the notion that all things are governed for "the best."* This would be an amazing break-through according to Plato's mouthpiece** in *Phaedo*. But, as it will have turned out, Anaxagoras does not, in Plato's review, really explain things in a manner which conduces why and how things are ordered for "the best." Pointing to "Nous" as a divine ordering principle is not at all to *explain* things according to Nous. For Plato, absent a **causal ACCOUNTING** of *how and in what sense* all things are ordered towards "the best" under the suasion of Nous, "Nous" becomes just a word. This highly critical review of Anaxagoras' Nous doctrine occurs on pages 96e--99d of *Phaedo*.

*****

*. Forms of *beltistos* and *beltios* are used frequently throughout this Phaedo passage. *Ariston* is used in conjunction with *beltiston* at 97d-3. *Ameinon* is used at 97e-2 and at 97e-3. Although *ameinon* is often translated as "best" in translations of this passage, it technically is better translated as "better." Interestingly, *agathon* is used [at 98b-3] when speaking of what all have in common immediately (and contrastingly, it appears) after *beltiston* is used [at 98b-2] when speaking of each thing.

Finally, it seems to be to be most interesting that in a plethora of languages, both classical and modern, the comparative and superlative forms of "good" have roots (or a root) quite different from "good." This is certainly true of classical Greek.

**. I am, of course, consciously passing over any speculation about "Socrates" and whether or not Socrates himself had such an experience with the Nous teaching of Anaxagoras and/or whether "Socrates" himself experienced radical disappointment with the Nous teaching of Anaxagoras. I rather doubt it on both counts. In this case, Plato, through the mouthpiece of "Socrates," is speaking of a stage in *his own* relatively youthful intellectual awakening. Socrates may have had -- late in life -- some interest in the impiety charge brought against Anaxagoras. Plato famously portrays such interest in *Apology*. Yet one must always keep in mind that while Plato's dialogues include historical information, he -- in general and in *Apology* as well -- always has a trans-Socratic agendum even when he uses the figure of "Socrates" for that agendum.

Plato the writer has several different presentations of "Socrates" in his various dialogues. Further, it must always be kept in mind that often enough -- particularly after Plato's return from his second voyage to Syracuse in 367/366 -- it is the rule rather than the exception that "Socrates" is relegated to a very secondary position in these "later" productions and completely disappears from some. In any case, in varying manners, the "Socrates" of any given dialogue is a dramatic invention of Plato. Through this varying "persona" Plato, dramatically, engineers an artistic manner by and through which HIS OWN teachings are presented.

Let it be re-stipulated for emphasis, then, that the Platonic dialogues are not intended to be anything like historically accurate presentations of the life and teachings of Socrates

> the actual man. Sometimes there may be overlap between the dramatic presentation of this or that "Socrates" in this or that dialogue and Socrates the historical figure. But such is virtually always incidental <<<yes, even in *Apology*>>> to what Plato is doing through the usage of his various and varying "Socrates'." The question is not at all whether or not it is possible to "disengage" the historical Socrates from the Platonic usages of "Socrates" in his various dramatic productions. Rather the task is really to "disengage" the teachings of Plato from the set of speculations about the "real and historical" Socrates from centuries-old-habit of reading Platonic dialogues as though *that* were something of primary importance in Plato's compositions.

*****

Then, most curiously, this expression of disappointment in the poverty of the Nous teaching of Anaxagoras glides into "Socrates' " decision to turn to what is, in effect, a "second voyage" [*deuteron ploun* at 99d-1] by which to give an accounting precisely for the realities about which the Nous teaching of Anaxagoras failed to deliver: how and in what sense things are ordered for "the best." This "second voyage" turns out to be an accounting, which is now going to be explicitly owned by "Socrates" (i.e.,Plato), is basically the theory of Forms. Plato gives an adumbration of this theory from 100b up into 105c. In referring to it Plato says:

> *It is nothing new, but what I have never stopped talking about, both elsewhere and in the earlier part of our conversation. I am going to try to show to you the kind of cause with which I have concerned myself. I turn back to those oft-mentioned things with which I have concerned myself. I assume the existence [ousia] of a Beautiful itself by itself* [auto kath'auto], *of a Good and a Great and all the rest.*

[100b-4--100b-5]

This "second voyage" analysis, as it proceeds up into 105c is remarkably similar to the presentation of the Forms/Ideas as introduced by the young "Socrates" to Zeno and Parmenides. It distinguishes between things themselves and the causes of those things. It speaks of things being what they are because they "participate"/"share-in" [*metekhei* at 100c-7] the cause by virtue of which the thing is what it is. But very quickly he goes oǹ to emphasize that he does not fetishize on this "methekhsis" language so long as one is clear that it is by virtue of the cause that the thing is what it is. [100d-1--100d-9]

Further on in this "second voyage" Plato makes a distinction between a true cause of something and those conditions without which the thing cannot be what it is even though these conditions, properly speaking, are not true causes. This is a distinction which will be reprised in *Philebus*. [Cf., for example, 27a.] In effect Plato is maintaining that what Aristotle would gather together, in *Physics*, under the headings of material and efficient causality, are not truly causal in the primary sense. I said, "in effect." Obviously it would have been impossible for Plato to have overtly been comparing his analysis of causality with the "four causes" discussed by Aristotle in *Physics*. Nonetheless, the Tradition, often enough, all too quickly (and misrepresentingly) brings *Aristotle's* accounting of the four causes to the discussion of "what Plato must have really meant, after all" when Plato spoke of causality. Such nonsense has been going on now for more than two millennia. But it is tragic nonsense in so far as it contributes to a whole nexus of filters and prisms which the Traditions unconsciously brings to the reading of Plato. Plato ends up not being read even when he is read.

Of course -- just as with the scene in *Parmenides* [130a-4--130e-5] wherein the young "Socrates" adumbrates (with a hesitancy for which Parmenides will chide this young "Socrates" [130c-7--130e-5]) his theory of the Forms -- this passage from *Phaedo* turns out to be a presentation which raises more questions than it answers. Even so, Plato is making it clear that any **CAUSAL** accounting of things must pass through the prism of the Forms/Ideas. The implied suggestion is that only by passing through this "second voyage" can one return to the accounting -- implicitly promised by Anaxagoras but never delivered in any way at all by the Nous doctrine of Anaxagoras -- of the cause which orders things for "the best." In effect, as we shall see, the dialogue which is subtitled *peri ideon* (which precedes *Philebus* <whose subject matter from start to finish is "the good"> in the third tetralogy) is, so to speak, the condition for the possibility of finally giving that wondrous account of how and in what sense things are ordered for "the best."

Finally, there are two observations about this "second voyage."

a). The tropes of "Being" and "Becoming" are noticeably absent in this passage. These tropes are very much at issue in Plato's presentation of the Forms in *Republic V* and also in Plato's Cosmology, *Timaeus*. The presence of this trope in such a late dialogue as *Timaeus* has been discussed at length in **DSG**. Its absence, however, in the relatively early dialogue (*Phaedo*) seems rather suggestive.

b). Our *Phaedo* passage is far more parallel to the way the Forms/ideas are treated in the interchange between Socrates and Parmenides at 130a-4--134e-9 of *Parmenides* wherein the Being/Becoming trope is also noticeably absent. In addition both passages center upon the formulation of hypotheses to be tested by argumentation. This "hypothesis" language is found in our *Phaedo* passage from 100a-4 onward. Such language, of course, permeates *Parmenides* both in the description of the proposal to be executed by Parmenides [135e-6--136c-7] and, of course, in and through the eight-plus-one hypotheses as executed by Parmenides with "Aristotle" as respondent.

From all of this, I suggest that what we have in this passage from *Phaedo* constitutes a post *Parmenides* doctoring involving an insertion or, more likely, an insertion which was an overwrite of what was contained concerning the Forms in the original text of *Phaedo*. It was, after all, the *Phaedo* which first introduced Form theory. And *Phaedo*, not *Republic*, is included in the first three tetralogies. [For information on the significance of the tetralogical ordering of Plato works the reader is referred to pages 37-43 of **DSG**.]

A-2-b-ii.

In all of this a pre-emptive observation must be made. It is only through the prism of Aristotle's system that Platonic Forms would be presented as (naively) ontologized "universals." Even today there is an ingrained, and mostly unconscious of itself, habit of presuming that Plato must really have counted his "forms/ideas" as universals. Nothing could be further from the truth. This topic has been carefully and at great length reviewed in several important sections of **DSG**. One must understand that the argumentation on this matter contained in that ground-breaking study is presumed as axiomatic in the book you are now reading. It is a theme in that book discussed all throughout the book. But, initially, one might refer to pages 1-17 in conjunction with pages 81-83.

A-3. The Nous teaching of Plato.

Let us begin with two citations (only one of which is from Plato) so as to set the tone. Through these citations we get an initial feeling for what this study understands as Plato's final position on ***his*** ultimate first principle. I am only setting a tone which introduces a complex causal frame of reference characteristic of the later Plato when he speaks about the ultimate first principle. To some extent the reader will have to make some incursions into **DSG** to fully understand this complexity. At the present time I wish only to set a tone. I hope it is clear that I am claiming that on this matter the Schelling of 1814/1815 and Plato are brothers although there is no extended thematic treatment of Schelling in this book. {{{Perhaps not "extended." But returned to and resiliated in "**C. *Coitus Interrptus and Beyond*.**" For now just relax and appreciate the suggestive tone.}}}

----- Everything depends upon comprehending that unity in God which is at the same time duality; or, conversely, the duality which is at the same time unity.

[Schelling; from *Ages of the World.* Written circa 1814/1815. Never published by Schelling although it was editorily worked over by his son. English translation, 1967.]

And then this from Plato himself.

Later on, some Ionian and Sicilian muses both had the idea that it was safer to weave the two views together. That say that 'that which is' is both many and one, and is bound by hatred or [[the "kai" has the force of "and/or" in this sentence]] *friendship. According to the stricter of these muses, in being differentiated they are* [at the same time] *brought together. The more easy-going muses, though, allow things to be free of that condition sometimes. They say that it alternates, and that sometimes it is one and friendly under Aphrodite's influence, but at other times it's many and at war with itself because of some kind of strife.*

[*Sophist*, 242d-243a.]

As **DSG** has established, Plato in *Timaeus*, suffered a lapse from his more stringent treatment of his first principle (which he developed dialectically in *Parmenides* and then dramatically in *Symposium*). In both dialogues Plato develops, without an explicit rubric, that duality-in-unity/unity-in-duality theme echoed in Schelling. [We shall return to this theme in the *Coitus Interruptus and Beyond* of this book.] In *Timaeus* however, Plato ends up following the more "easy-going" Muse from Sicily (Empedocles) by postulating **two** causes. Where Empedocles spoke of *philia* and *eris* Plato speaks of *Nous* and *Anankē*. But the causal structure each is quite isomorphic. And, quite obviously, *Nous* is on Plato's mind in that dialogue.

*****

We now prescind from Plato's reporting on the effect of Anaxagoras' Nous teaching on the young "Socrates" and turn to Plato's own teaching concerning Nous. In doing this we will, prudently, be on guard against the temptation (often enough unconsciously imported into Plato's Nous teaching) of reading Aristotle's overly famous Divinity-as-Nous passages from *Metaphysics-XII* (Chapters Seven and Nine) into Plato's account.

There are two places in the Platonic corpus in which a Nous teaching with cosmological import is presented by Plato. Famously in *Timaeus*; but also in certain circumscribed passages of *Philebus* and, in particular the passage running from 28d-7 through 30d-9. The passage from *Philebus* deals with the full implications following upon the fact that that the fourth class ((the class of causal combination)) is constituted by mind (Nous) and wisdom (Phronesis) and intellectual features akin to them. And in our passage, Nous is given position of privilege with these strong words which glorify Nous [emphases are mine]:

> *Socrates: Now do not imagine, Protarchus, that this is mere idle talk of mine; it confirms the utterances of those who have declared of old that* ***NOUS*** **always rules the universe**.

Nous/mind is in one sense supreme. But the discussion of the four (but really five; cf. 23d--9-13) "kinds" which ends up with this glorification of Nous is preceded by a sometimes jocular passage which, for the careful reader, radically limits this glorifying encomium of Nous. I am speaking of 21d-7 through 23a-6.

So keep this too in mind, if you will. The encomium of Nous has been preceded by this very passage which at once radically ***glorifies*** Divine Nous **AND**, at the same time, contextualizes the glorification of Nous in a manner which effectively precludes Divine Nous as the ultimate supreme principle. Please understand. Nous remains Divine, and unblemished. It rules in the sense that it is **A** causal factor in the make-up of things which works in concert with that heartbeat of reality which is always and of its nature **DifferENcing** allowing thereby for (((but does not make or produce))) points of recognizability and intelligibility <in things and in individual souls/minds>. There is no intelligibility without Divine Nous. But intelligibility -- and other key elements -- come into being (both in the timeless time of time and in the sequential timing of time) by virtue of that elicitative call of "the good." "The good" calls into being the very factors which, timelessly in time and in sequential timing, produce "the good." Of itself, this call OF (both senses) "the good" is radically impoverished in its own being and remains ever-fragile. Again, we remain now in 21d-7 through 23a-6.

In this famous passage Protarchus and Socrates -- in the context of determining what the good is and, ancillarily, what kind of life (the one of mind/Nous and other kindred intellectual activities championed by Socrates; the other the life of Pleasure championed by Protarchus) is closest to the good. This sometimes jocular exchange between Socrates and Protarchus does indeed insist on the Divinity of Nous and yet there are qualifications made about the hegemony of Nous which indicate that the true hegemonic factor in the make-up of things obtains in a wider and more subtle cosmic context. For this passage makes it clear that NEITHER the life of mind and wisdom [phronesis] NOR the life of Pleasure is "the good." Perhaps one or the other will win the crown of being closest to the good through the progress of the argumentation. But neither life can be considered the good. Thus our passage does indeed affirm the divinity of Nous and holds it dear. But it suggests that what is supreme about Nous is in the service of something even more fundamental. Listen to what our passage clearly affirms even as it also affirms the divinity of NOUS [emphases are mine]:

> *Socrates: And so I think we have sufficiently proven the Philebus' divinity is not to be considered as identical with the good.*
>
> ***Philebus*** [the one whom Plato has suddenly barge in usurping the role of Protarchus]*: But neither is your "mind" the good, Socrates, for it will be open to the same objections.*

> *Socrates: Such may apply to "my" mind, Philebus, but certainly not, I suspect, to the true,* ***divine NOUS****. It is in a different condition. I am not arguing that Nous ought to get the first prize over and against the combined life* [[which earlier <21a-11 up through 22b-10> had been stipulated as the class to which the good must belong and which is more complete and desirable than either one the other two causal classes <i.e., the fourth and implicitly, as we shall see, the fifth taken by themselves]] *but we must look and see what is to be done about the second place; for each of us might perhaps put forward a claim that Nous is the cause of this combined life, the other that pleasure is the cause.* ***AND THUS NEITHER ONE WOULD BE THE GOOD****, but one or the other of them might be regarded as the cause of the good.*

Dissertations could be written about the last sentence of this extraordinary citation. "The Good" is supreme yet "the Good" is not the cause of itself, but rather is caused by something else and in this "something else" is left undetermined in this sometimes jocular and playful 21d-7--23a-6 passage.

Finally, it should be noted, that at the very ending of the dialogue, in the final ranking of the variables covered in the dialogue, assigns Nous and wisdom (Phronesis) to the third place (which itself is intriguing given Plato's privileging of the third) and some limited pleasures as worthy of fifth place (which itself is intriguing given Plato's even greater privileging of the fifth). These kind of matters -- ultimately dealing with the causal paradigm in which the child (offspring) is father to the man -- constitute the major subject matter of **DSG**. And in that vein we now turn to that other major *locus classicus* concerning Plato's treatment of Nous. I speak of *Timaeus*.

In **DSG** there is extensive treatment of the conditions under which *Timaeus* was generated and produced. The major issue is that this dialogue ended up mostly as a rough draft to which Plato never returned. The contention of **DSG** is that in the midst of generating this dialogue the news from Syracuse about the assassination of Dion reached Plato. Plato, it is contended, was just initiating the second of three planned trilogies which would have been the final and supreme expression of his entire Philosophy. The first trilogy was *Sophist/Statesman/Parmenides*, all introduced by *Theaetetus*. Likewise, it is contended, the second of these trilogies was to be inaugurated by *Timaeus*. The case for these contentions is extensively argued for throughout **DSG**. Further, especially in pericope Three of that book, the case is made that Plato -- often enough relying on work already written (some of which were modified in and through the trying and depressed circumstances of Plato's personal life after the tragic news had reached him in 354/353) -- orchestrated a "make-do" final arrangement of his most fundamental and decisive philosophical works which ended up coming forth as the first three tetralogies in the set of nine tetralogies which was Plato's own arrangement of the works he wished to pass on to posterity.

In this regard, it is very revealing that the rough draft of *Timaeus* was NOT included in the first three tetralogies. Even so, there is much information -- about Nous and many other matters of the "late" Plato -- which are found only in *Timaeus*. It is a dialogue which neither can be ignored for those who wish to understand Plato's final philosophical position nor can it be taken unamended as being part of Plato's final philosophical position. Again, all of these matters are discussed at length throughout **DSG**. At this point I choose to adumbrate these matters (in the service of our "Clazomenae" reference from the opening line of *Parmenides*) by directly citing, with some minor amendments, the portion of **DSG** which most economically deals with Plato's own Nous teaching.

*****

From pages 220-222 of **DSG**:

Timaeus *as the Handmaiden to the Final project which Culminates in* Philebus *and* Symposium *(itself subtitled in its expanded and revised final form as* Concerning the Good*).*

Having noted the above, I do not give Plato a free pass. There is a struggle within Plato's own psyche which had been alive at least from the time when he first started to engage questions about Divinity in dialogues such as *Alcibiades II*, and *Theages*. In this struggle Plato never is in denial of the factor which ineluctably permeates the real: the positive (in the sense of not being merely a privation), active, and intractable unruliness in the make-up of things. This is to his credit. But a certain strain of piety seems always to tempt him to separate Divinity itself from this unruly and intractable character intrinsic to the make-up of things. Plato took this internal struggle into his great inaugurated project which he initiated after his return (367/366) from the second voyage to Syracuse. ((The project was to have been a trilogy of trilogies as his final statement of his philosophical teachings.))

The struggle in his later dialogues took on the contours of the tension obtaining in himself between following the stricter Muse from Ionia or the "easy-going" Muse from Sicily with regard to presenting the way in which the unruly obtains in reality as a whole. My suggestion is that -- albeit without explicit announcement -- the only trilogy completed as part of this grand final project <<i.e., *Sophist/Stateman/Parmenides* introduced by *Theaetetus*>> sided with the stricter Muse of from Ionia on the matter of what kind of ultimate causality governs the Cosmos and Reality as a whole.*

*. [[[[I did not pursue the following possibility in **DSG**. Perhaps, ab initio, this dualism of first principles which shows up so graphically in *Timaeus* was part of Plato's overall plan for the three trilogies. The initial one (completed; i.e., *Sophist/Staesman/Parmenides*) was to concentrate on unity <itself understood dialectically as a dyadicizing activity>. The second trilogy (*Timaeus/Critias/Hermocrates*) inaugurated but only partially and, in the case of the rough draft portion of *Timaeus*, desperately executed, was to concentrate on the terms of duality. The third trilogy (the planned names of which were never transmitted by Plato <<<<<although I suspect that "Philebus/Youth" would have been the name of

the first in a work whose contours would have been somewhat different from the "make-do" *Philebus* which was in fact executed>>>>>) would be devoted to the theme of that unity which is at once a duality and that duality which is at once a unity. But the great planned trilogy of trilogies was torpedoed *in medias res*.

So possibly the "easy going" Muse from was planned to be thematically honored as well. Possibly. It's a stretch. I still favor the conflict model of Plato's own psyche ((*Plato contra Plato*)) as the progenitor of the aberration which is *Timaeus*. Yes. Aberration, but one which, especially in the "dark middle" of that dialogue, has its own glory; an aberration which must be appreciated if one is to appreciate the full spectrum of Plato's genius.

Yes. All of that. But Plato was, in the final analysis, true to his deepest self by NOT including *Timaeus* in the first three tetralogies.]]]]]

With the *Timaeus* we get a glorification of what Plato counted as Divinity: *Nous*. Untrammeled. But -- in apparent alliance now with the more gentle Muse of Sicily -- we have *Ananke̲* as the resistant and "errant" cause. Yes, the words are *Nous/Ananke̲* rather than *Philia/Eris*. But structurally and functionally the two pairings are virtually the same. Even so, in the final analysis, this apparent bow to the Muse from Sicily really ends up anyway, ***through Plato's post-Timaeic machinations***, in the service of the stricter Muse from Ionia. Our guide for saying this is, as always when it comes to the final project (i.e., when it became impossible both emotionally and physically for Plato to carry through the original plan of a trilogy of trilogies) *Philebus*.

In that key dialogue *Nous* is the fourth "kind" [genos] of the four (but really five <cf. the remarks towards the end of 23d>) "classes"/"kinds" of *Philebus*. *Nous*, in this Philebean schema is, in effect, the cause of combination bringing together (but not producing) the first and second "kinds" <i.e., apeiron and peras> to form the Mixed/Third "kind" which is where ousia in general and the good in particular obtain. *Ananke*, in effect and by implication, is the fifth "kind" [referred to at 23d] and, in effect, functions as the cause of "separation" [diakrisin].

But it is in the third "kind," the class of the Mixture/Mixed, wherein the drama is played out. As mentioned, it is only in the third class that ousiai obtains. But more importantly, it is by the implied elicitative feature of this Third "kind" that the drama reverts back to the stricter Muse from Ionia with the fourth and fifth "kinds" playing causal-but-ancillary roles. [[What I am not supplying here is the overall argumentation for this which is brought out in **DSM**.]] And who is the star of the all-important Third "kind"? Here its Form-name is "One." There its name is "Good." Its secret name is "truth." ((And one is misconstruing the whole of this Platonic schema if one trades on the terminology, implicit in Aristotle and, terminologically made explicit by the Mediaval Scholastics, of the so-called "transcendentals of being." And an even more insidious is that Plotinian trope of "the ineffable One" which is often ***imported*** into the "one" of the first hypothesis and, as well, imported into the "Sun-as-image-of-the-Good towards the end of *Republic-VI*)) All of these matters have been explicated in and through pericopes sixteen through twenty (in **DSG**).

[[I use the translation of "kinds" instead of the more common "classes" to emphasize the structural isomorphism of the "five great kinds" of *Sophist* and the four-but-really-five "kinds" of *Philebus*.]]

The opening line of the dialogue *Parmenides* -- a grand project animated by the self-dyadicizing ***single*** first principle -- speaks of having "come from" <i.e., left it behind> "Clazomenae" the home of Nous/Anaxagoras. Perhaps something happened in that incredibly disappointing third voyage to Syracuse circa 361 (taken after the production of the first trilogy) which sapped his ability to stay the course achieved by that first trilogy (i.e., *Sophist/Statesman/Philosopher*<aka "Parmenides">). Perhaps the demon of melancholia pre-empted the best of him when the news came from Syracuse in 354/353. Who really knows? In any case, when he returned to writing again by filling out the contours of an artistically grand inaugurated opening of *Timaeus* with a long and very unartful rough draft, the daimon of the "easy-going" Muse came, for a while, to usurp the position of the daimon of "the stricter Muse from Ionia" in the creative impulses of Aristocles. Thus the second planned trilogy (abandoned as it would turn out) is launched with something of a reversal of a guiding principle. The words are *Nous/Ananke̱* rather than *Philia/Eris*. But it is the daimon of the "easy-going" Muse which prevails in this rough draft opening of the second planned trilogy. *Clazomenae!!! We have returned!* But this rough draft which will have become the "quagmire" named *Timaeus* (along with a severely truncated mytho-poetic introduction to what would have been *Critias*) and turns out to be the last <attempted> of the planned productions of this second trilogy. In effect this brutal interruption constitutes the abandonment of the grand project of those three planned trilogies. The grand project comes to be replaced <as he partially emerged from his crippling depression> by the first three tetralogies wherein Plato salvages some painfully produced simulacrum of the original grand design; a simulacrum produced by the creative melancholia following the dark depression in concert with the prospect of the grim-reaper completely taking over his heart and mind. And *Timaeus* does not gain entry into these first three tetralogies.

In the midst of writing *Timaeus* <<and having already finished the introductory backdrop of *Critias* {{an artist such as Plato surely had times when he couldn't help himself; having written the stupendously gifted story of Atlantis he was immediately driven to inaugurate (and that's all it would ever be) what would have been the stupendously gifted backdrop for the planned second dialogue of this planned trilogy}} the "bloody wounds" news [the "brotoi" found at 344d in Letter Seven] arrives and the whole second trilogy of the planned triplet of trilogies collapses. He does manage something of a retrieval of what would have been the all-important trilogy on "the good." As reviewed above, he does this with the catch-all dialogue *Philebus* which is the introduction to and guide for the reading of

the all-important third dialogue of the third tetralogy, namely the doctored-late-in-life *Symposium* <which, when doctored will have merited the subtitle *Concerning the good*>. [[Plato will have also, during this time period, "doctored" some of what he had said of "the good" in the famous "Sun passage" from 506d-6 through 509d-1. This last is covered in excruciating detail in pericope twelve of **DSG**.]]

In these final writings there is further evidence of -- and, at root, resolution of -- the internal struggle raging in Plato's own soul. The "truth"-imbued speech of Alcibiades brings the teaching on the good in line with the stricter Muse from Ionia. In *Philebus* Plato's love affair with a Divine Nous having nothing of the unruly about it still obtains. But if you read the two passages indicated above in conjunction with the ending of that dialogue <from 61e-4> carefully, the "truth" impetus of that dialogue wins out over that type of Piety which so often impinged on his writings. Plato's heart had fully returned to the stricter Muse from Ionia.

A-4. Antiphon Reports on The Gathering: Zeno and Socrates then joined by Pythodorus, Parmenides, and Aristotle.
127a-1--127d-5.

Antiphon, then, said that Pythodorus told him that …

He himself, however, had heard Zeno read them before.

There is nothing historical about this gathering. It is the creative invention of Plato who teases the reader by timing the gathering at a time when, "just possibly" such a scene might have occurred.

The ambience of the gathering maintains, but in a new manner, the trope concerning youth and old-age initiated in *Theaetetus*. Let us briefly recapitulate what was said above. We have the "regular" Socrates (((((((recall here that through various ploys Plato had orchestrated <through interpolations and other artistic strategies> an impossible backdrop for all of the entirety of this final setting of the first three tetralogies such that the "scenes" of *Euthyphro*, *Cratylus*, and *Theaetetus* <in this third case as remembered and edited by Euclides and read by Euclides' slave> occurred on the day Socrates was indicted [*Cratylus* 396d-e; *Theaetetus* 142d-c and, more especially, 210d] followed the next day by the scene of *Sophist*, followed in turn by on the next day [*Statesman*, 258a] by the scene of *Statesman* with the expectation that the next subject would deal with "the Philosopher")))))))) who is seventy or almost seventy is presented as orchestrating a discussion on knowledge in the presence of a "Young Socrates." This "Young Socrates" is said to be of the same age as Theaetetus [*Sophist* 218b] who himself is referred to as "a boy" as Euclides refers to the scene of *Theaetetus*. [*Theaetetus* 142c-d]. This "Young Socrates" thus is portrayed as being present in the dramatic settings of both *Theaetetus* and of *Sophist* but not at all as a significant participator in these intricate conversations. However, in *Statesman* Plato orchestrates a dramatic setting in which this "Young Socrates" replaces Theaetetus as the respondent to the Stranger/Visitor from Elea. [*Statesman* 257c-258b].

The trope being played upon in all of these dramatic settings is the trope of "old-age" and "youth" <<Recalling, also, that "Philebus" is a "name" which can be understood as "Youth" >> and its instantiations resonate with a famous comment from Letter II at 314c;

There is no writing of Plato's, nor will there ever be; those that are now called so come from and idealized Socrates rendered young.

[On this tangential matter of "Platonic" authorship of Plato's [i.e., his name was, in fact, "Aristocles"] writings as well as the correlative question concerning the so-called "unwritten works" the reader is referred to the discussions in **DSG** on pages 50-53 and pages 390-393.]

This artistically astute "old-age" and "youth" trope, is well established through the series *Theaetetus/Sophist/Statesman*. In *The-*

aetetus the Plato has the "regular" character Socrates playing his traditional role while this "Young Socrates"* is only alluded to. In *Sophist* as well, this "Young Socrates" tends to remain in the shadowy background. However in *Sophist* "Young Socrates" is joined in this shadowy background by the "regular" Socrates who withdraws from the role of *magister ludi* in favor of the Stranger/Visitor from Elea (with young Theaetetus playing the role of interlocutor). Finally in *Statesman* -- after making the requisite cameo appearance at the beginning of the dialogue so as to maintain the "Porch of Archon" setting of all of these dialogues -- the "regular" Socrates again withdraws into the shadowy background in favor of the Stanger/Visitor who once again takes on the normally Socratic role of *magister ludi*. However, unlike what occurs in *Sophist* and *Theaetetus*, our "Young Socrates" comes out of the shadowy background to replace Theaetetus as the respondent to the Stranger/Visitor from Elea. [[We shall revisit this trope of "youth/old-age" below.]]

> *. Some people tend to overly historicize the dramatic, inventive, playful focus of Plato's orchestrated dramatic settings. Yes. He often uses actual historical characters in these inventive and playful dramatic settings. And in some cases the identity of these characters based on "real" persons adds significant spice and flavor -- and sometimes irony -- to the dialogues in which these characters are present. Granted. But whether Plato uses the names of real historical personages or names which clearly are invented on Plato's part ----- so in BOTH cases ----- Plato is an artist first and foremost and only incidentally and happenstantially the bearer of some historical piece of information. Our "Young Socrates" is clearly a product of Plato's playful and inventive imagination in the service of artistically linking (with a backward look to the dramatic setting of *Cratylus*) our five dialogues (i.e. *Cratylus, Theaetetus, Sophist, Statesman, Parmenides* <with *Sophist* and *Parmenides* in third and fifth positions respectively>) together.

> Are you now going to bring up the "Socrates" who is referred to at 358e of what appears to be a merely mundane and happenstantial character of Letter XI? But why? Is it, after all, so strange that there may have been a real (and minor) person of Plato's acquaintance who was named after the figure of "Socrates"? And is not "strangury" a malady of old-age rather than of a youth? Whatever. The historisizing impulse in the reading of Plato bypasses the most important feature of Plato's casting of the "actors" in his dialogues whether the "actors" are assigned by Plato the names of real historical people or are the purely inventive products of Plato's literary imagination. This historisizing impulse relative to the "actors" and dramatic settings of Plato's dialogues is truly a case of not seeing the forest for the trees.

*****

A word, first, about the alleged missing *Philosopher* which, so the story goes, would have completed the trilogy quite clearly indicated by the opening of *Sophist*. Several hypotheses have been offered to explain this so-called missing dialogue.

a). It was lost.

Not likely at all. In the case of, say, Sophocles or Aristotle, there is reliable ancient testimony to works authored by these writers which did not survive. Most of these non-surviving works were lost in the great fire which destroyed so much of the great library of Alexandria. In contrast, there are no reports of dialogues authored by Plato which were lost. ((Lost; that is to say differentiated from the often cited plays he authored and whose burning *Plato himself* orchestrated since they were not worthy, in his judgment, of the heritage of Socrates.)) Indeed the problem in Plato's case is just the opposite. Spurious works were attributed to Plato which were not authored by Plato. Yet they too were saved and labeled as "spurious" (alongside Plato's own organization of the works which he wished to survive him in the nine sets of four) in the collection organized by Thrasyllus. [[It is credible to believe that Thrasyllus had access to the manuscripts saved in the Academy itself and that he orchestrated the production of good and accurate copies. If so, it was presumptuous of him to include in his collection the "spurious" works even though, to his credit, he labeled them as "spurious."]]

In this vein it is noteworthy that the Academy was continuously sustained up until the time of Justinian. This is surely a record for survival of an institution in the history of Ancient institutions. Doubtlessly, maintaining (and re-copying) the texts arranged by its founder would have been something of a sacred institutional duty.

b). A misreading of famous Platonic snippets concerning true Philosophy and committing certain things to writing leads to another false hypothesis concerning the so-called "missing" third of the inaugurated trilogy. This misreading of Platonic texts is often supported by an egregious misrepesentation of Aristotle's remarks at IV-2, 209b of *Physics*. Any fair reading of Aristotle's remarks here reveal that the "so-called" *unwritten works* were just that. "So-called." In other words, works available only to the inner circle of the Academy while Plato was alive and largely kept under wraps for about a generation after his death.

In this vein I also speak of the famous disquisition on writing from *Phaedrus* 274c-278d and the equally famous text from Letter Seven at 344c-d. In both passages Plato is playfully trading, *in writing*, on the dialectic of and between the playful/amusing and the serious which is the very condition for the possibility, according to Plato, of writing about the most important matters in Philosophy.

Doubtlessly Plato was painfully aware of how the written word cut free from the soul which produced it can be grievously misconstrued. They can become "orphans" whose parents are dead and thus not available to guide these "orphans" in what they say. Likewise -- let it be explicitly acknowledged -- Plato counted the direct mentoring of intelligent and younger mentees by bringing to birth in their souls great 'conceptions' and counted this as the highest and greatest gratification possible in the life of Philosophy. All of this is so stipulated and taken as axiomatic.

However, those two features which Plato so clearly articulated are, unfortunately, used in the service of misreading of Plato's subtle and self-referential teaching on writing, especially writing on matters which are of the highest concern to the philosophic life. This subtle concern animates the whole disquisition on writing from this passage in *Phaedrus*. And Plato, in Letter Seven, is trading on the memory of this Phaedric disquisition. Indeed!: written words always run the danger of becoming "orphans" when separated (which always will happen, death being woven into the very fabric of life) from the mind/soul which produced them. These orphans run the risk of being radically misunderstood when read and commented upon by people not equal to the mind/soul which produced them in the first place. And the most abused of all these "orphans" are the words written by Plato concerning his own writings.

In this regard one must shudder at the stupendously great and painful paradox in these matters involving Plato's written comments about his own writings. The received mantra on this is well known: the repetition, century after century, in the Tradition which grievously misreads those very orphans which playfully speak of the writing of the highest truths in Plato's philosophy. For, century after century the Tradition, in its mostly flat understanding of these passages, ignores -- indeed, for the most part does not even notice! -- those key, self-ironic, passages in which this dialectic of and between the playful/amusing and the serious by which Plato deconstructs his own teaching on writing.

Plato was the most compulsive writer ever. If it was important, he wrote it and he saved it.

Even worse is the Tradition's ***radical*** misconstrual of Aristotle's remarks at IV-2, 209b of *Physics* about the '**so-called**' [**legomenois**] "unwritten works." These points have been treated and adjudicated on pages 390-393 of **DSG**. The astute reader of *these* written words is referred to those pages.

In any case the Tradition's blindness on what Plato says and means about writing leads a fair number of commentators -- themselves unconscious of the blindness they carry within them in their contention -- to use this misconstrual of Plato's written words on writing as an explanation for the allegedly intentional decision NOT to have supplied any written version of *Philosopher*. They walk with blinders on as they pass through Plato's dialectic of and between the serious and the playful/amusing and claim that Plato must have made a conscious decision NOT to have the greatest teachings rendered in written form. For these foolish commentators the non-written character of *Philosopher* becomes the crowning glory of the Platonic corpus.

c). There is an interesting hybrid interpretation of the "missing" status of *Philosopher*. It is contained in FM Cornford's translation-with-interspersed-commentary produced under the title *Plato's Theory of Knowledge*. [pages 168-170]

Cornford pretty much adheres to that common misconception that the most important teachings of Plato were, intentionally, not committed to writing. And indeed, according to Cornford, such is validated by Plato's own seeding of the apparently false (in Cornford's view) expectation of the third dialogue of the inaugurated trilogy in the introductory conversations of both *Sophist* and *Statesman*. Even so such does not inhibit Cornford from -- quite thoughtfully as it turns out and in the spirit of Plato himself -- presuming to maintain that the artist in Plato was indeed suggesting, based on the dialogic structure of *Sophist* and *Statesman*, that the dialogic form of that intentionally missing third dialogue would resonate with what clearly is a major trope in many of Plato's later productions: the wistful trope of "youth" and "old-age."

Cornford suggests that the replacement of Theaetetus as the respondent to the Stranger/Visitor from Elea with the Young Socrates ((who was, for the most part, but quietly, present in *Theaetetus* <wherein Theaetetus shared the role of the respondent to the "regular" Socrates with Theodorus> and *Sophist*)) in *Statesman* would have given way in *Philosopher* to the replacement of the Stranger/Visitor from Elea by the very Socrates <i.e., an instantiation of the "regular" Socrates> who had withdrawn from active participation in the conversations obtaining in both *Sophist* and *Socrates*. Thus the missing <in writing> main conversation ((we are still enmeshed in the Cornford speculation)) which would have obtained in *Philosopher* -- had it been written -- would become what would have been, right there before the Porch of Archon two days after Socrates was indicted, a glorious conversation between Socrates and Young Socrates about the highest and most important teachings of Philosophy.

Cornford's suggestion falters, of course, by his adherence to the view that Plato did not commit his most important teachings to writing. But the suggestion is intriguing (and indeed can be construed as being implied by the dialogic structure of *Sophist* and *Statesman*) in so far as it may be an indication that Plato himself, at one point in his composition of this trilogy, did indeed entertain such a dialogic structure for the third dialogue in the trilogy <the trilogy itself introduced by *Theaetetus*> which would have in fact been titled *Philosopher*. We don't and cannot know for sure. ((My own guess is that Plato did entertain for some time that the climax of the trilogy would have Socrates and Young Socrates dancing such a duet. But before actually initiating *Philosoher* he came to understand that the symmetry involved was, so to speak, too good to be true; too cute and oh-so-symmetrical. He probably came to realize that the harmony which does not show itself is superior to the harmony which does show itself. Further, and in conjunction with the last observation, he came to realize that the real title for the allegedly missing *Philosopher* should carry the name of the one who elicited from Plato that stupendously honorific encomium given to this thinker at *Theaetetus* 183e,3--184b,2))

In any case *something* made him change his mind and, indeed, change the very title of the dialogue which, in historical fact, does complete this trilogy. The passage in *Theaetetus* ((which quite explicitly functions as the introduction to the entire trilogy)) just cited above involving that great encomium for Parmenides is weighty. For it includes, quite explicitly, the memory of the “regular” Socrates -- ***but when this ““““ real”””” and ““““regular”””” <u>was ‘ very’ young</u> thereby cleverly reprising the trope of this ““““other”””” ‘young Socrates’ who is present in*** **Theaetetus, Sophist, and Statesman** -- by way of the dramatic setting of *Parmenides* when Parmenides and Zeno visited Athens for a religious celebration. Thus this passage either substantiates the claim that *Parmenides* was already intended by Plato at least as early as the composition of *Theaetetus* OR that this encomium was ex post facto seeded into the text of *Theaetetus* in order to create the expectation of *Parmenides* (as the completion of the trilogy) instead of a written dialogue with the title *Philosopher*. One way or another, in any case, *Parmenides* becomes the crowning achievement of the trilogy. Let us turn to it now.

*****

The dramatic setting of our dialogue, *Parmenides*, both maintains, radicalizes, and changes this trope of “old-age” and “youth” established through the last three dialogues of the second tetralogy. There are two dimensions to this maintaining/radicalizing/changing <all at once> of the trope in our dialogue *Parmenides*.

In the first place it must be understood that in **DSG** and in other previous writings I have maintained that *Parmenides* is indeed the completion of the expectation of a trilogy dealing with “The Sophist,” “The Statesman,” and “The Philosopher.” In the all-important arrangement and sequencing of that all-critical grouping constituted by the first three tetralogies, *Parmenides* immediately succeeds *Sophist/Statesman*. Yes, we have something unexpected about this third entry of the indicated trilogy <which does in fact immediately follow upon *Statesman* appearing however in a different tetralogy from the first two entries of the trilogy> by virtue of the title “Parmenides.” Precisely. For so too, we have a whole complex of the unexpected in the not-obviously-symmetrical continuation of the "old-age" and "youth" trope inaugurated with *Theaetetus* and sustained through *Sophist/Statesman.* For the "real-and-regular" Socrates of *Theaetetus* recedes in favor of the visiting Stranger from Elea (((((and a further recession of the "real-and-regular" Socrates occurs de facto in *Timaeus* and whose Introductory Conversation indicates a continuing of this recession in the planned *Critias*))))) in *Sophist*. What happens, then, is the "real-and-regular Socrates" in *Theaetetus* has as his interlocutor the young Theaetetus whose interlocutory function, now as respondent to that visiting Stranger from Elea, is replaced by the metaphorical "Young Socrates" in *Statesman.* This amazing backdrop concerning Youth and Old-Age climaxes in *Parmenides* as the "real" Socrates, when his is "very young" mixes it up with an old Parmenides and a middle-aged Zeno and which backdrop, when it is time for naming an interlocutor for Parmenides, is replaced by Aristotle <<<!!!!! but see below>>> who is portrayed as younger than the "very young" 'real' Socrates.

A-4-a. The Setting and the Five Players thereof.

I suppose it is theoretically possible that Parmenides and Zeno travelled to Athens (lodging outside the Wall; 127c,1) around 450 to engage in a religious festival. Plato himself facilitates this only technically possible scene by arranging that his character, Socrates, was "very young" <127c,4-5> which implies a young man of about twenty. So yes. Theoretically possible. The dramatist in Plato does not want to create an absolutely impossible *mis en scene* for this dialogue. But that's all.

Certainly, given what is known about the background, development and education of Socrates, this "very young" Socrates would not have been drawn to the visitation of these two great minds. The Xenophonic and Platonic <excepting, of course, the scene of *Parmenides*> presentations of Socrates is one in which "Socrates" is well advanced into late Middle Age and, more often, in the last two years of his life. This "very young" Socrates invented by Plato for the dramatic setting of *Parmenides* does not correspond at all to any reasonable facsimile of the real Socrates when he was twenty. At that age, the real and quite mundane Socrates would not even have been capable of even being drawn to such a gathering. And most certainly of all such a "very young" Socrates would not have been credibly capable of presenting to ((or getting a hearing from)) these men of renown a version <albeit somewhat simplistic as per Plato's intention for this scene> of a "theory of Forms" which is first originated and then articulated in writings produced by *Plato* a decade or two after Socrates was put to death.

The general point is that in his written productions, artistry rather than history motivates our once and future dramatist. Egregious violations of history are avoided by Plato in his writings. And sometimes -- especially when referring to Pericles (and his associates male and female) and Alcibiades -- Plato does in fact, for dramatic effect, trade on definite historical happenings. But by and large even history itself is seldom anything but an incidental backdrop -- capable of being marginally manipulated by our Aristocles -- for dramatic and philosophic effect. Thus one is embarrassed for scholars who date the birth of Parmenides as "circa 515" predicated on the dramatic setting of this third dialogue of Plato's great trilogy. Again, it is theoretically possible to postulate a date of 515 for the birth of Parmenides. But one is foolish if one does this based on the dramatic setting of *Parmenides* . [[Yes. I know that the "forty-year" trope of when these various Presocratics allegedly "flourished" underwent a period of disfavor by those scholars who thought they were being very sophisticated in challenging that trope. But in the case of Parmenides there are strong reasons to believe that his birth was in fact close in time to the foundation of Elea.]]

Finally, one must continue to keep in mind that even on the dramatic artistic plane, Plato's appropriations of the "persona/mask" of the "regular Socrates" often varies, sometimes radically, from dialogue to dialogue.

*****

So. We have a “Socrates” who is “very young.” We have a “Parmenides” who is presented as “about sixty-five years” of age. Approximately the age of Plato himself when he started his first draft of this key dialogue. Zeno is presented as about forty years of age. It was understood that Parmenides and Zeno had been lovers when they were both younger. And finally there is “Aristotle.”

Socrates may have been portrayed in this setting as “very young.” But, later we will find out [137b-c], it is the case that a certain “Aristotle” (who was not listening to Zeno’s presentation but rather was outside the venue with Pythodorus and Parmenides, all three of them entering into the scene only when Zeno’s reading was almost complete) is the “youngest” of all. It is Parmenides himself who suggests that his respondent should be the youngest [137b] and Aristotle boldly steps up to the plate:

> *“I’m ready to play this role for you, Parmenides,” Aristotle said. “Because you mean me when you say the youngest. Ask away -- you can count on me to answer.* [137c,1-3]

Thus it came to pass that the most intense and dense of one of Plato’s most craftily-oriented presentations <<second only to the revised version of *Symposium* in this regard>> came to obtain as the exchange between “Father Parmenides” and the very young man whom Plato appears to have designated as the “Nous” of the Academy. And both in writing and in history, as it would turn out, this exchange is mediated by Plato himself.

Oh hush, you tired and worn-out skeptics. Yes. Of course. Plato was taking a huge risk. Would this young man somehow (even if not in battle) die young, as did that other promising young man named “Theaetetus”? Would this promising young man fail to achieve the stature which Plato imagined he would? After all this young man was still in his twenties when the final redaction of *Parmenides* was made. So, Aristocles hedged his bet by identifying him as someone who would **become** one of “the Thirty” almost a half-century after the dramatic setting of our dialogue. He is in fact making an allusion to the young Aristotle in the Academy in this passage and, at the same time, hedging his bet in case, for one reason or another, this young man does not become the one which he did in fact become.* In any case, what a grand and glorious "gathering" Aristocles has produced for us. Let us enjoy it to the fullest.

*. [[Well of course. "Aristotle" wasn't even a glint in his father's eye when the Thirty held sway for those short years as Athens was sliding rapidly off the radar as a credible military power. "The Thirty" was led by Critias, one who was admired by Plato. Apparently Socrates was able to challenge a ruling of the Thirty and NOT be held accountable by the Thirty. It was a desperate time in the life of Athens and desperate measures were called for. Doubtlessly it had the support of intelligent Athenians who understood that the "Glory Days" were over for good and that *drastic* measures had to be taken for the sake of coming out of the dire situation with any shred of genuine autonomy for the polity. Even that was not to be.

In any case it turned out that "rescue" orchestrated by the Thirty was also not able to prevail and even more blood was spilled as its relatively short reign disappeared from Athenian history only to be succeed by "democratic" (i.e., de facto another oligarchy with its own interests parading as a restoration) usurpation.

There is a charming naivete about how some people <<yes, even scholars who should know better>> fixate on this or that historical reference in the dialogues of Plato as indisputable guides for ascertaining what happened in Athenian history. My sense of it is that by and large the historical references in Plato's writings were fairly accurate. But always they are presented with a flavor which is Plato's own and which is in the service of his artistic motivation in setting the "stage" for his own Dramatic presentations. Was there in fact a "real" Aristotle who was a member of the Thirty? It is certainly not impossible. But to use this parenthetical remark made by Plato as "proof" for such is foolish.

Our only question is whether or not this "hedge" by Plato may have also have carried with it (i.e., in addition to the hedge factor) some negative connotation concerning this "Aristotle" who is portrayed as younger than the "very young" Socrates of this fictional setting which constitutes the "mis en scene" of our dialogue. Whatever Plato's own sympathies were at the time of "The Thirty," <<probably supportive of the Critias-led Thirty>>, by the time he was composing *Parmenides* the resonations of "The Thirty" probably were overwhelmingly negative. Indeed, four decades later, when Plato was composing *Parmenides*, "The Thirty" probably had been reduced in the public consciousness as something of a terrible aberration. ((((In fact, it had it succeeded in its goal would have been hailed as the salvation of Athens despite its responsibility for some executions which were perceived to be unjust. In any case, given the lack of nuance characteristic of any society's assessment of the generations of their fathers and grandfathers, by circa 360 it could easily be used as a credible vehicle by which to besmirch the reputation of this or that figure via guilt by association.))))

The return in 367/366. Getting down to business. Revising the Protagoras project inaugurated before the second journey and transforming it radically into the dialogue *Theaetetus* which would become the introduction to the great trilogy which comes forth as *Sophist/Statesman/Parmenides*. The actual writing and editing of *Sophist* and *Statesman*. One might intelligently surmise that, at the earliest, preliminary work on *Parmenides* was inaugurated, say, no earlier than 361 after the return from the third voyage to Sicily. Further, the very character of the eight-plus-one hypotheses probably reflected "exercises" for the Academy's "inner circle" which eventually would be filtered out by Plato and put into some final form in the service of producing the great "**peri**

ideon." It is likely that the finished product did not come into being no earlier than, say, 357. Further the making of this short parenthetical insert (and possibly other desired final changes) --((granted, we are not talking about computer technology))-- could have been accomplished even late in Plato's life when he was putting together the final versions of the first three tetralogies. Plato was a wealthy man and it would have been an honor to have been among those in the Academy allowed to generate these final drafts.

I bring this up -- this possibility of a late parenthetical insert concerning "Aristotle" with the possible motivation of besmirching him -- based on my hypothetical contention that Plato himself became somewhat discredited and dishonored *in the Academy itself* because of the Dion assassination which would come to pass in concert with Plato's correlative public "whitewashing" <via Letter VII> of his degree of responsibility in this horrible affair. Certainly Plato had nothing to do with the assassination itself. But he had everything to do with goading the young and mercurial Dion to go the route of a military coup (and correlative stringent-but-short reign). This last contention argued for especially in pericope thirteen of **DSG** on pages 366--372.

Further, the even more hypothetical case is made in that book to the effect that after this period of discrediting, by his own followers in the Academy, Plato withdrew from day-to-day leadership of the Academy due to his severe melancholy and his intense desire to generate some final version of the grand project which he had inaugurated upon his return from the second voyage to Syracuse and which came crashing down when the news from Syracuse arrived at the Academy. In other words, he was something of a recluse in his own Academy.

During this time his "sons" tended to become somewhat condescending to the "old man" and -- albeit inspired by what

Plato had accomplished in *Parmenides* -- they (Speusippus, Xenocrates and the relatively young Aristotle) already started down a path of, in their egregious presumption, doing "Platonism" better than Plato. The argumentation for these hypotheses are presented primarily in pericopes fourteen and fifteen of **DSG**.

Would these last developments have affected Plato negatively, especially with regard to Aristotle, the one whom he had honored by referring to him as the "Nous of the Academy"? Very possibly. Would these developments have affected Plato so negatively that he would insert the Thirty connection relative to Aristotle as something with a negative connotation? Possibly.

Please understand. I am not betting the mortgage that there cannot be a credible case made against my contention that the presence of "Aristotle" in *Parmenides* was in fact a masterly prescient intuition on the part of Plato of what would come to pass in history and thus validate the genius of Plato in making this choice of names for the role of the responder to Parmenides in the scene. Still less I am not betting the mortgage that -- after the assassination and in concert with this presumed reaction against Plato by his "sons" -- Plato, having already made Aristotle the respondent to Parmenides, inserted the parenthetical statement with disparaging intent concerning "Aristotle's " having become "one of the Thirty." I'll keep my mortgage, thank-you. But I certainly maintain the first contention and I do not automatically dismiss the second contention.]]

B. Plato's Retrieval of Parmenides: *peri ideon* as the Condition for the Possibility of Allowing the Poem of Parmenides to Say what It was always Meant to have Said.

127d,6-135c,8

Socrates listened to the end ---

--- "I don't think I have anything clearly in view, at least not at the present time."

B-1. Socrates Engages Zeno and Introduces the Subject-Matter of *Parmenides*: **peri ideon**.
127d,6-130a,3.

In the ancient world Zeno was well known for defending his beloved mentor through *reductio ad absurdum* argumentation. "Father" Parmenides was often castigated for his teaching concerning the motionless "one" which is said to imply the denial of both motion and plurality. To be sure it would take the fertile mind of a Plato to fully understand that the genius of Parmenides resides in the **belonging together** of "the way truth" and the **dupli**-citous "way of mortal opinion" with its dyadicizing structure. And, later, when we get to the description of the "training" which will become the intricate detailing and unraveling of a mystery, it will be the character Parmenides himself who will insist that the truth of anything can be revealed ***only*** through such a **dupli**-tous manner entailing the condition that the hypotheses dealing with anything's being are and must be complemented by the hypotheses dealing with that anything's non-being. [136a] But we are getting ahead of ourselves.

Zeno's lines of argumentation were twofold: i). To defend his beloved mentor Zeno initiated Philosophy's version of *the best defense is a good offense* strategy. So he subjects the implied hypotheses of his mentor's opponents <<that there is indeed motion and that there is indeed plurality>> by demonstrating that *their* common-sense hypotheses lead to absurdities more ridiculous than what they think his beloved mentor is saying. And ii). At least in the case of the motion-less character of the one, to mathematically expand upon his mentor's teaching thereby giving it credibility. We shall see that this mathematical expansion by Zeon of his master's teaching comes to animate the eight hypotheses, the truth and falsity of which is predicated on that "atopos" ["absurd"; "placeless"; "uncanny"; 156d,3] teaching of "eksaiphnes" contained in the insert hypothesis which occurs between hypothesis two and hypothesis three.* In our present text before us [127d,5-8 only "i" is at issue and even there only with regard to the hypothesis of plurality. We shall limit ourselves, here, to what is pursued just on these pages.

*. [[Concerning the motion prong this preliminary note will suffice.

Zeno's advance over Parmenides has to do with what today we would call "the theory of limits" and, had it been pursued as a model of mathematical thinking, it would have produced the beginnings of calculus. It is this Zenonian meaning of change which animates the eight-plus-one hypotheses of *Parmenides*. Real change -- whether one is speaking of a form or a participant in a form -- *without* continuous motion. Such a thinking is grand and glorious indeed and was caught in a work of fiction (often the hiding place of the deepest truths) by Joyce Carol Oates:

Like the flash of heat lightning that tells you all that is, is now.

[*I Lock My Door Upon Myself*; 1990]

However, it is Plato who is responsible for programmatically and thematically grounding these Zenonian insights (which themselves go beyond the Poem produced by Parmenides himself) in the " teaching" of the insert hypothesis.

This Zenonian thrust, expanded and adopted by Plato in *Parmenides*, was thwarted by the one who Plato planted as the respondent to "Father Parmenides." Aristotle. The Aristotle who was not in fact one of the Thirty <albeit he was the one so indicated by Plato as his hedge>. Aristotle's common sense presuppositions concerning motion -- which did not require arduous work to be comprehended -- were painstakingly marshaled into what he claimed was a point-by-point refutation of that Zenonian/Platonic mathematical model of the very nature of change. His orgy of common-sense mentality on these things is accomplished in his detailed review of Zenonian paradoxes of motion in *Physics* VI-9.

This thwarting had the unhappy effect in the philosophical tradition of postponing the serious mathematical accounting of change for almost two millennia. And even then -- Leibniz here, Newton there -- these Modern versions of calculus did not bring to this task the fertility present in Plato's appropriation of the Zenonian thrust. In **DSG**, pages 375-378, I have treated in some detail the egregious begging of the question orchestrated by Aristotle involved in the alleged "refutation" of Zeno in that long passage from *Physics* VI-9.]]

Continuing on.

As indicated, we will now return to the far more circumscribed reaction on the part of our "very young" Socrates to the "first hypothesis of the first accounting" offered by Zeno concerning the denial of plurality. [127d,5-8]

In this regard one must pause and mentally take into account that in our present passage and through the invented figure of this "real" Socrates-but-when-he-was-very-young Plato was putting forth the initial framework for an account of predication which involves the barest bones of his theory of forms combined with his notion of "participation." Keep in mind as well that *Parmenides* succeeds *Sophist* which itself puts forth fairly sophisticated accounting of the thorny matters dealing with the condition for the possibility of true and false judgments, [259e-264c]. My point is that Plato always, implicitly and explicitly, -- from the "second voyage" adumbrated in *Phaedo* {100b,1--102a,3} up through *Philebus* where Plato sums it up exquisitely and in detail at 15a through 17a -- joins Form-theory with predicational analysis.

In the overall schema of the eight-plus-one hypotheses of our dialogue we are going to find that the matter of predication becomes very complex and stratified and, as well, involves that contention that matters of being can be expressed only on the condition that non-being is recognized just as real as being, albeit in a *differing* manner. Such had already been adumbrated in *Sophist* at 257b-260a. In *Parmenides* what was adumbrated in *Sophist* is graduated to a whole intertwining complex which furnishes the guidelines for all questions of semantics and syntax and, at once, furnishes the skeleton for what later in the Tradition will be called "ontology."

It is a simple fact that in the history of Philosophy the decisive model for matters of predication is the model furnished by Aristotle in *Categories*. Aristotle's *Categories* was basically Aristotle's opening gambit to discredit the theory of forms and the complex model of predication made possible by {{{and required by}}} the theory of forms. The great but seldom acknowledged scandal of the Philosophical tradition is that this *Categories*-based "Frame" <<i.e., one generated to present Platonic Forms as "universals" and as less real than the individuals predicated by these alleged universals>> still remains the default meaning of predication and remains as well the mostly unconscious prism by which Platonic Forms are understood in the Tradition. A scandal which cries out for rectification.

These very matters have been thoroughly discussed all throughout **DSG**. Pages 1-17 of that book contains a précis of this claim which is then reprised and expanded upon all throughout that book. This book will not repeat the extended argumentation of that book. But please be advised. The unconscious presumption of the norms and vocabulary of *Categories* has been and remains the greatest hindrance both with regard to understanding Plato's theory of the Forms and as well the for understanding the correlative model of predication initiated in *Sophist* and carried through in *Parmenides*. Our dialogue is, at once, both the skeleton for what later in the Tradition will be called "ontology" and the "training" [*gumnasi* at 135d,4; *gumnasthe̲nai* at 136a,3] by which such is attained.

*****

B-1-a. **Excursus** on the Intertwining of Discourse/Predication and the Theory of the Forms.

In *Philebus* one finds a reprisal of what our "real" young Socrates is putting before Zeno and Parmenides. In both passages the issue revolves around the theory of the Forms as the condition for the possibility of there being the kind of predication required for true philosophical discourse and articulation. In the present passage under discussion from the bare beginning of *Parmenides* Socrates presents what is basically a circumscribed accounting of the Forms which, as our dialogue progresses, will be expanded by Parmenides into the theory of the Forms which animates *Sophist*, *Parmenides*, and the passages which we will be, forthwith, referring to in *Philebus*. In the passage from *Philebus* which follows, Plato refers to his forms as "ones" or "monads." We enter now into *Philebus* at 14c,6 and we shall be leaving it at 16a,5.

Of course in *Philebus* we find a *magister ludi* who is more or less the "regular" <albeit now weary (50d,7--e,3))> Socrates, in an unidentified setting, who is generally more self-possessed than the "regular" Socrates of most of those other dialogues wherein some version of the "regular" Socrates plays the role of magister ludi. The problem posed in our passage is the perennial problem of "the one and the many." Very quickly, the Socrates of our Philebean passages moves away from trivial manners of juxtaposing the one and the many in order to engage the question on a plane which is worthy of Philosophy; that is to say when the question is engaged with regard to the Forms themselves <which in *Philebus* are referred to as "ones" or "monads">:

> *I mean, young man, when the one is not taken from such things which come into being and perish, as we have just been doing in*

our examples. For that realm is where the sort of one belongs which we were just discussing and which we agreed is not worthy of our scrutiny. But when it is asserted that man is one, or the beauty is one, or ox is one, or the good is one, the intense interest concerning differentiation in these and similar such things becomes controversial. 15a,1-9]

Our Socrates then raises the serious question as to whether such unities even have being at all. [15b,1-2] This hint of skepticism is revealing in so far as such skepticism is both quite absent from Plato's other presentations concerning the Forms and seems to be a harbinger of how "that beautiful teaching of the ideas" [[Letter VI at 322d; i.e., despite the positive context there is a hint of wistfulness here]] seems to be withdrawn from the scene in works such as *Laws* and *Epinomos*. Be that as it may, it is clear that in *Philebus* the presumption of the reality of Forms is both operative and essential to all that he says in that dialogue.

This question about the very being of the Forms is followed by a number of "aporiai" concerning *how* the forms obtain. [15b,2-10] The "difficulties" raised here are very parallel to a number of <but not all> those "aporiai" concerning the Forms raised by Parmenides himself in *Parmenides* as he engages our young Socrates about the very theory introduced by the young Socrates. [130a,10--135c-5]. Just from the length of the pagination involved in these two passages from separate dialogues it is clear that not only are the difficulties reviewed by Parmenides <<who turns out in our dialogue to be the ever-staunch defender of the theory>> examined in much greater detail than this short review found in *Philebus* but that the review of the difficulties with the Forms by Parmenides in *Parmenides* includes lengthy discussions of difficulties not contained in our *Philebus* passage.

In any case, our present Philebean passage [15b,2-10] is but the first of two legs in our wider passage ranging from 14c,6 through 16a,5. As we pursue this passage we see that Form-theory and predication are inextricably woven together by Plato <emphases are mine>:

> ---- *By making the point that it is through statements* [logon] *always (both long ago and now) the one and the many are known by and through such utterances* [legomenon]. *Such will never come to an end, nor has it just begun. It appears to me that this is an 'immortal and ageless' feature endemic to statements* [logon].

This key excerpt is then followed by once again castigating the frivolous manner by which neophytes in philosophy banter about these things while ignoring the realm <i.e., the Forms > wherein the togetherness of the one and the many is both problematical and full of wonder at once. It is the space [khora] opened up by the postulation of the Forms which makes possible that ordinary things in our everyday experience can be rendered intelligible. But this last issue is also a matter for *Parmenides* itself. For now it is enough to note that for Plato matters of discourse and predication require Form-theory as the condition for the possibility of Philosophy. Indeed, in *Parmenides* it is Parmenides himself --- after orchestrating a relentless exposition of what appears to be devastating criticisms of Form-theory -- who is the one who insists that without Form-theory the very power of dialectic [dialegesthai] is destroyed. No dialectic, no Philosophy. Then the haunting question:

> **What will you do about Philosophy? Where will you turn, while these difficulties remain unresolved?** [135c,6-7]

*****

This excursus is in the service of showing that for Plato Form-theory emerges from and returns to the whole nexus of "statements" and predication. Form-theory opens up that space in and by which rigorous understanding of allegedly ordinary reality is made possible at all. In this vein there are three further dialogues which, one way or another, contribute to the task of gaining full access to the essential dimensions of the Platonic accounting of predicational matters. One of these has already been of service but it must be further pursued. I speak of *Sophist*. Another is the sister dialogue to *Sophist*, namely *Statesman*. For the third of these dialogues we must traverse backwards to the first dialogue of the first tetralogy: *Euthyphro*. Let us start with the sister dialogues.

Collection and Division is Plato's name for a certain kind of exercise by which any given "one" is iteratively and clearly separated from kinds and sub-kinds until the "one" in question stands by itself and is not confused with other "ones" which may indeed be akin to and or related to the "one" in question but which is in fact is different from those other ones. Collection and Division is itself a species of predicational analysis which exhibits a useful manner of clarification with regard to the broader category of "the one and the many" in any given one's many ways of being one and many. Collection and Division is quite useful in getting any given "one" separated from other "ones" (kinds/classes/genera and/or ideas/forms/monads) by which the "one" in question can (i.e., in the absence of a methodical Collection and Division) get confused with those others "ones." But it still falls short of giving an account [logon] since Collection and Division does not by itself entail a **causal** analysis of the "one" in terms of what makes the one this one and not that one. The dialogue *Euthyphro* <<albeit its aporetic status relative to the question posed by the dialogue>> is, more than any other production, as we shall see below, the dialogue in which a genuinely ***Platonic*** accounting of causality is brought to bear on this question of giving a proper accounting [logon] of any given one. {{{I typed "Platonic" in bold-face and italics to emphasize that we are NOT referring to the schema of the fours causes developed by Aristotle in *Physics*. Whenever -- consciously or unconsciously by virtue of the Tradition's engrained average tendency on this -- Plato's accounting of causality is forced to be conceived through the prism of the four causes of the *Physics* Plato's accounting is falsified and radically misunderstood.}}}

In both *Sophist* [i.e., with regard to the first five, of seven, attempts to define the Sophist] and, more especially, in *Statesman*, the "practicing/exercising" dimension of those dialogues (by which Collection and Division is exemplified) is both prominent and, as well differentiated from the proper subject matter of each dialogue. In contrast, the "practicing/exercising" character of the eight-plus-one hypotheses is fused with the primary subject matter of the dialogue. In other words, the "exercise" of the eight-plus-one hypotheses is, at once, both: a). a paradigmatic model for how the investigation of any conceptual term/reality is to be pursued so as to achieve a thorough and delineated accounting of what it means and what it does not mean; and, b). the supreme dialectical structure which exposes the "one," both and at once, as: b-i). grammatical place-holder for ANY Form <thus the subtitle "peri ideon"> and as: b-ii). the dyadicizing first principle of Form-theory. To be returned to.

Finally, the following note must be added concerning Collection and Division. In both *Sophist* and *Statesman* the various "practice" Divisions as well as the various "subject-matter-oriented" Divisions are always bifurcative in the various divisions which are executed. In *Philebus* Plato chooses to have his character (Socrates) not use the phrase "Collection and Division" although, in the Philebean treatment of the "one and the many," it is this procedure which is de facto being referred to AND expanded upon. The expansion entails the realization that it is not necessary to impose a strict bifurcative manner for the Divisions in question. This "gift of the Gods" <Plato's poetic phrase for Collection and Division in *Philebus*> is explicitly committed to the claim that at any level of a series of Divisions there can be more than simply bifurcative Divisions into the "ones" emerging from the "one" which is getting Divided in the procedure. This is a very important and necessary change which Plato addends to the method practiced and executed in *Sophist* and *Statesman*. The reader is referred to 16c,1--17a,6. The new wrinkle concerning Divisions is given at 16c,13--16e-3:

> *Since this is the structure of such things we have to assume that there is one idea* [mia idean] *for every one of them. And we must search for it (and we will find that it is there). And if we grasp this we must look next for two, if there be but two, or, if not, for three or some other number. And we must treat each one of these further "ones" in the same way until it is established concerning that original one not only that it is one, many, and unlimited/indefinite*

but also until we establish just how many "ones" obtain between the original one and the unlimited/indefinite ultimate particulars [which constitute our ordinary experience].

{{{The above is a relatively free amalgamation of the translations found in Copper and in the Loeb. The last clause in brackets is my addition.}}}

Now let us turn to *Euthyphro* and see how this early production (which does not trade on the refinement called "Collection and Division) nicely integrates a ***Platonic*** treatment of the causal factor in giving an account with the class and sub-class character of Collection and Division necessary for producing clarity and accuracy in one's giving of an account.

*****

So many things can and should be said about this singularly insightful dialogue. But I will restrict myself to two of them.

First.

Euthyphro, in its attempt to give an account of "osion" <<<"Piety" here, "holy" <or holiness> there, and all according to context; and yes, the one Greek word contains the common English denotations for both "piety" and "holy"/"holiness." That having been said, in the most important treatment about osion in this dialogue, osion is best translated as "holy" or "holiness.">>> Plato quietly integrates Platonic Form-theory into the discussion and makes Platonic Form-theory intrinsic for the project of generating a proper account of osion. As we have seen above (when we were still in *Parmenides*) it is precisely Form-theory which opens up the space by which predication can be understood in its proper function. Listen to the following passage <6d,8--6e,7>. The Greek words which are germane to understanding that Form-theory is at the heart of *Euthyphro* are given in bold-face. Any emphases in English are mine.

Socrates: Bear in mind then that I did not bid you tell me one or two of the many pious actions but rather that form itself [**auto to eidos**] *by which all pious acts are pious. For you agreed that all impious acts are impious and all pious actions are pious by one idea* [**mia idea**]. *Or don't you remember?*

Euthyphro: I do.

Socrates: Tell me then what is this idea [**ten idean**] *itself is so that I may look upon it, and using it as a model* [**aute pardeigmati**] *and say that any action of your or another's that is of that kind is pious, and if it is not that it is not.*

Form-theory quietly obtains in *Euthyphro* as opposed to it more overt and expanded treatment in, say, *Phaedo*; Book Five of *Republic*; and in our dialogue *Parmenides*. Nonetheless it is present in *Euthyphro* and the very logic of this first dialogue of the first tetralogy goes out of its way to draw attention to Form-theory as the necessary causal condition for the possibility of giving an account of piety/holiness.

Second.

Euthyphro offers an abundance of riches which have been, for the most part, either not noticed; or ignored; or poorly mined. Not all of these riches can be reviewed in this work. Our limited task in this present endeavor is to extract from several Platonic productions an exposition of the sense in which, at once, Form-theory entails, of its very nature, a properly Platonic accounting of predication and, in turn, the sense in which a properly Platonic accounting of predication entails Form-theory. In this vein *Euthyphro* offers an immensely important piece of the puzzle.

[[[I intentionally used the phrase "a properly Platonic accounting" as a way of indicating that, in the Tradition (with mostly unconscious pre-suppositions which are still maintained almost across the board today in Platonic scholarship) it tends to be automatically presumed that what Plato says about predication "must really mean after all" something akin to the accounting of predication matters as adumbrated in Aristotle's *Categories* and refined in Book IX of *Metaphysics*.

Aristotle's *Organon* came to be counted as normative in that greenhouse atmosphere (involving incredible cross-fertilization composed of Greek Philosophy, Judaism <as per the Alexandrian Diaspora>, and relatively early Christianity) from about 250bce up to about 250ce. The tragedy in this is that this cross-fertilizing spawning ground would become, in fact albeit not in intention, the source in the emergent Tradition for the almost knee-jerk (and most often not conscious of itself) tendency to read Plato through the prism of Aristotle's *Organon*. Such distortion came to be subtly-but-deeply ensconced in this amalgamative greenhouse atmosphere with the result, that -- again, mostly unconscious of what was going on -- this distorting prism came to be, in fact, *normative* in the reading of Plato, especially in those texts wherein Plato himself addresses matters of predication. With the passage of time this prism became radically sealed-in for the Tradition through the writings of Porphyry and, correlatively for the Latin world, the writings of Boethius who quite overtly leaned on Porphyry. Plato, qua Plato, comes to be entirely eclipsed through this horribly distortive, but deeply entrenched, manner of reading Plato. And this distortion (again, largely unconscious of itself as a distortion) remains normative even unto the present day.]]]

There is an important portion of *Euthyphro* which allows the careful and critical reader to access something fundamentally important about Form-theory in Plato which, if understood and properly appreciated, will allow for an unveiling of predicational matters on properly Platonic terms rather than through that *Categories*-based Aristotelian prism which, tragically really, came to be so radically ensconced in the tradition. The passage in question is 9c,1--11b,1 wherein Plato has his Socrates extract from Euthyphro a key modification of Euthyphro's second attempt to define piety/holiness. This key modification reads thusly:

Euthyphro: I would certainly say that the pious/holy is what all the gods love, and the opposite, what all the gods hate, is the impious/ unholy. [9e,1-3]

As veterans of the *Euthyphro* text will immediately understand, this modification is not at all a sufficient definition of "osion." Indeed, all the definitions of piety/holiness are orchestrated by Plato to fail in some essential sense in this dialogue which -- quite independent of the question of Piety/Holiness -- has as its primary purpose of vectorizing the discussion to the true character of a definition through these orchestrated failures. But this modification, itself orchestrated by "Socrates," of the second proffered definition points to the missing factor <<a factor which in the cases of "the good" and "holiness" [two names for the same] has a unique and idiosyncratic weight in Plato's accounting>> without which a definition (logon) cannot be a definition. More than that it points to a factor which is at the very heart of Plato's final treatment of the good through the Philebean introduction to that late-in-life re-write of *Symposium* <which, in its re-written form, merits the subtitle *Concerning the Good*>.

So what we have here is the revised version of the second attempt to give an accurate accounting of osion. As we have already seen above giving an accurate accounting [logon] of entails the grasping of osion in so far as it is **eidos** [6d,11], that **mia idea** [6d,12] in terms of which all instances of piety/holiness are indeed instances of piety/holiness. Arriving at such an **idea** [ten idean, 6d,17] will allow one to understand osion itself as the model/paradigm/standard [**aute paradeigmati** [6d,18] of all actions or states of being which can be called "pious" or "holy." By using this model/paradigm/standard one will be able to determine:

---- *that any action of yours or another's that it is of that kind is pious/holy, and if it is not that it is not pious/holy.* [6e,4--6e,7]

Now, with this priorly established meaning fresh on our minds of what kind of thing <<i.e.,the Form; the idea itself> we will be grasping if and when we arrive at a proper accounting [logon] of piety/holiness, we can return to that modification of the second attempt to give an accounting of osion. WE can return to that modification involving this critical causal factor which allows for an accounting of "osion" which our passage puts before us. WE, that is, can so return but not Plato in this dialogue. Plato, in writing this dialogue, has (as mentioned above) orchestrated things such that none of the definitions proffered achieves the implied standards of what a good definition entails. But -- and especially with this modification of the second proffered definition -- Plato expects the astute reader to maintain a memory of what was not only valid but critical in this failed definition in a dialogue intended to be, in a formal sense, aporetic from the very start. Let us now pay close attention to the critical and weighty feature ensconced in this modification (itself orchestrated to "fail") of the second proffered definition.

Euthyphro: I would certainly say that the pious/holy is what all the gods love, and the opposite, what all the gods hate, is the impious unholy. [9e,1-3]

After an agreement to use this modified version of the second attempt to give an accounting of piety/holiness Plato has his Socrates inserting a caveat which entails bringing the question of **causality** into this business of giving an account. It is noteworthy that in the case of Holiness, Plato orchestrates his characters in such a way that Euthyphro (presented as probably not sensing the immense import of what he agreeing to) affirms the caveat of Socrates which caveat initially hides itself as a mere question:

Socrates: Because we are in agreement that the pious/holy is being loved for this reason, that it is pious/holy and, as well, it is not pious/holy because it is being loved. Is this not so?

And Euthyphro consents: *You are speaking the truth.* [10e,6-8]

*****

In this passage as a whole [9e,1--11b,6] which engages the matter of causality relative to what it would mean to give an account of something, we must be on guard (-- yes it needs to be emphasized again --) against the entrenched habit of presuming that we can understand Plato's remarks through some sort of appropriation of the four causes worked out by Aristotle in *Physics*. As noted, this would perpetuate a common misreading of Plato. Our goal is to read Plato qua Plato rather than to read Plato through some prism generated by the man whose passion came to be the discrediting of Plato's Form-theory.

In this passage taken as a whole (and separable on principle from the question concerning the accuracy of this revised version of the second attempted accounting of piety/holiness) Plato plays upon two differing manners of causality. They do not necessarily preclude each other, but it is clear that Plato is insisting on a distinction between the two manners of causing.

The more obvious one is a model of causality which makes or renders something to be in condition it is in. So "x" is in such-and-such condition because something makes or renders "x" to be in that condition. The condition is visited upon the "x." In other words the range and domain of this model of causality is with reference to things which are in a certain condition only by being made or rendered to be in the condition it is in. This model of causality can be construed as what happens when a Form imprints itself on the something or other ((and/or some constellation of elements/stoicheia)) which obtains in the Timaeic hupodokhe̲ thereby rendering that something other to be in some condition. When such occurs the something or other is said to be "sharing in" the form.

Now holiness is certainly being construed as a Form/idea. But THIS kind of Form -- and it may be unique to this form -- does not do the imprinting. Its causal manner is elicitative, elicitating and drawing the desire of something other (((such a something other being conscious or unconscious of what is going on)) towards it, namely holiness.

These two models of causality do not necessarily exclude each other in the actual workings of any given concatenation of Forms. And indeed, in the case of holiness, holiness obtains as being lovED by all the gods and remains so affected; but at the same time holiness elicits that love and causes it to be lavished on itself by the Gods. In contrast, a suitcase, for instance, is rendered "carriED" but does not of itself elicit that condition to be rendered upon itself.

What is being established here is that Forms do not obtain at all without being causes of one type or another. It can be further hypothesized that if there are things in our ordinary experience which themselves elicit then, in this fashion, it would seem that they are, in some way, instantiations of holiness which is the elicitator par excellence given that it is loved by all the Gods. But just what is holiness? It remains true that it is loved by all the Gods, but such a feature would be something like a "***necessary*** accident" of holiness and not the same as the "ousian" of holiness. Is it possible that there is, so to speak, something sui generis about the Form/idea of holiness?

Before proceeding a bit further along this line of thought (and thereby bringing this excursus to a close) we must sum up the concatenation of these three: predication; Form-theory; and causality.

This or that Form/idea will utterly evade us unless our accounting of the Form/idea (or Forms/ideas) engages accurately the causal power of the Form/idea (or Forms/ideas) under discussion. Without an accurate grasp of the Form/idea (or Forms/ideas) under discussion there can be no reliable schema of predication dealing with the Form/idea (or Forms/ideas). In turn, without a reliable schema of predication there can be no accounting of the Form/idea (or Forms/ideas) under discussion. Predication and Form-theory are joined at the hip for Plato. We begin where we end and we end where we begin. This is the circularity -- which is not a begging of the question -- of "knowledge" which is always ahead of itself and behind itself at once. [[I refer here to that gloriously circular **gnonai ---- ten**

dapherote̲t̲a̲ < “that most beautiful accounting of knowledge”> at *Theaetetus* 209e,8-11 which is the *leit motif* of **DSG**.]]

*****

In **DSG** I often used a well-known formulation when speaking of the intricacies of Plato’s final teaching on the good:

The child [offspring; **tokos**] is father to the man.

It is, of course, a formulation ((by no means restricted to Philosophy and/or Plato)) used by many in many differing contexts and in many differing manners. I have appropriated it as a way of expressing, as a first approximation, how Plato’s final teaching on the good involves both the making/producing kind of cause and as well the elicitative kind of cause in their reciprocity in this particular case (i.e. of the good). The good, of all the Forms, is unique. The good, in a word, elicits that which produces it. The good is producED and what produces it (and makes it to be what it is) *is brought into being* by that elicitative call of that which would be the good. The good has no autonomy of its own but what ***would be*** the good calls into being the causes which ***births*** the good.

The good, of course, is a Form; but it is an utterly unique Form.

Three citations in this regard.

Protarchus: Of course! This is precisely that in terms of which the good differs [**diapherein**] *from all other things.* [*Philebus*, 20d,3-4]

This uniqueness is spoken of with regard to “completeness” [teleo̲taton, 20d,2] and with regard to being “ample-and-enough-unto-itself” [hikanon, 20d,3].

Later, the following is offered:

----- *Socrates: That the nature* [phusin] *of the good differs* [**dia-pherein**] *from all else in this respect.*

Protarchus: In what respect?

Socrates: That whatever living being possesses the good always, altogether, and in all ways, has no further need of anything, but is completely ample-and-enough-unto itself [hikanon teleotaton]. *Did we not agree to such?*

Protarchus: We did: [*Philebus*, 60b,11--60c,6]

OK. So far, it may seem, we have, virtually, an artistic presentation of what of what Aristotle says of both the human level of happiness and, in a fuller way, the divine level of happiness in Books I and X of *Nichomachean Ethis*. So it appears. However.

Philebus, the second dialogue of the third tetralogy <and preceded by our *Parmenides*, the first dialogue of that third tetralogy> functions as the introduction to and road-map of interpretation for <both at once> to the ***third dialogue of the third tetralogy*** whose subtitle is *Concerning the Good*, namely Plato's late in life radical revision and expansion of *Symposium*. In that third dialogue of the third tetralogy we find an interchange between Diotima and Socrates which -- when understood in its subtle complexity -- renders Plato's teaching on the "good" in terms of what is usually translated as "finality and self-sufficiency" to be on a plane of causal analysis which only intersects at one point with Aristotle's far less complex accounting of "that for the sake of which."

With these understandings we are now in the lead-up to what is not only the most important teaching in the revised *Symposium* but which is the most important teaching in the entire Platonic corpus.

Tes genneseos kai TOU TOKOU en to kalo.

[206e,6]

The birthing/producing, Indeed!, OF THE CHILD upon the beautiful.

The "kai" is, of course, the intensive function which this word sometimes has. Indeed, the "kai" must be so translated since, otherwise, both semantically and syntactically the phrase makes no sense given that "tou tokou" is in the genitive and is not in apposition with "genneseos" <even though many translators fudge this and make it appositional to "genneseos" (i.e., "birthing") because of their lack of understanding of how the esoteric in Plato's dialogues plays out. To be sure, and as we will see just below, "tokos" can properly -- by virtue of the verb root from which it is derived -- be understood as "birthing"/"begetting." But the genitive usage here both precludes that manner of translating it and makes it necessary to understand the "kai" in its intensive function.

In all of this Plato is trading on his prior <and radical> revision of the "sun/good" passage at 505a,2--509d,1 in *Republic-VI*. [[This last topic is discussed in excruciating detail in pericope twelve of **DSG**.]] So with all of this in mind, let us now turn to Diotima's critical lead-up to this ultimate teaching on the good. In any case we see the reciprocity between causality by way of producing/making and causality by elicitation in the case of how the good comes ((both eternally and in sequential timing) to obtain at all. It will be the logic of the lead-up to this supreme teaching of Plato which will enable us to see how radically unique "the good" is according to Plato in the two statements of its uniqueness already cited from *Philebus*. Listen [emphases, of course, are mine]:

"Now then," she said: "Can we simply say humans love the good?"

"Yes," I said.

"But shouldn't we add that in loving it they want the good to be theirs?"

"We should."

"And not only that," she said. "They want the good to be theirs forever, don't they?"

"We should add that too."

"In a word, then, love is wanting to possess the good forever."

"That is most true."

*"So. This then is what love is about," she said. "But HOW, in fact, do those in love actually pursue such? Just what is it that they actually **DO*** [praksei] *in their eagerness and straining? What **WORK*** **[ERGON*]** *are they actually engaged in? Can you tell me?*

*. [[The same word (preceded by the fertile qualification "pagnkalov"/"glorious"/"all-beautiful") used by Socrates in his attempt to elicit from the rather obtuse Euthyphro the task/work of the Gods which, when Mortals participate in such, would constitute the true definition of holiness. It is no secret that that the character "Euthyphro," according to the aporetic plan of the dialogue named after him, is orchestrated by Plat to beg off from this critical question. But the answer to this question is the very heart and soul of the Platonic undertaking. In **DSG's** analysis of *Philebus* and the late-in-life re-write of *Symposium* <which, in its rewritten form merits the subtitle "Concerning the Good"> this cooperation between mortals and Gods is precisely what sustains the good, indeed, in such a way that when such cooperation ceases, the good itself ceases.]]

"If I could," I said, "I wouldn't be your student, amazed at you and your wisdom [sophia]; *now would I be sitting at your feet to be enlightened on just these questions."*

"Well I will tell you," said she. For it [what they actually DO; the **WORK/ERGON**] *is a* ***giving birth*** **[TOKOS]** *in and around the beautiful both in body and in soul."*

Have you yet understood? This erotic loving of the good is the "doing" [*praxei*] of the "work/ergon" of Eros, namely the <producing>-***offspringING*** [*tokos*] of-the-offspring [**TOKOU**]. The good elicits what produces it.

[*Symposium*, 206a,207a. The reader is referred to the careful and detailed analysis of "tokos" as used by Plato in the Sun Passage of *Republic VI* as the key for understanding all of the birthing/offspringing/offspring language in this critical section of *Symposium* in **DSG**. Specifically the reader is referred to all of periscope twelve in conjunction with pages 525-527 of pericope twenty.]

*****

A suggestion and a clarification.

[[The argumentation in *Euthyphro* on this suggestion/clarification is to be found from 10a through 11b.]]

Euthyphro is the only dialogue of Plato's given over exclusively to this matter of Piety/Holiness. And *Euthyphro* is included in the first three tetralogies, indeed, as the first dialogue in the first tetralogy.

The dialogue does challenge, by way of skepticism, many of the stories told about the Gods which portray them as engaged in the most horrific of activities including parricide and, orrelatively, fathers having practiced castration on their sons. {{Such does indeed resonate with Freudian ruminations concerning the pre-history of our species; but such is tangential here.}} On the other hand -- unlike the portrayal of the Gods in most of the other Platonic productions -- God and Gods <<both terms are used in *Euthyphro* with a casualness which is lost in the ontotheologization of Judaism and

its two offspring>> . Plato's orchestration of *Euthyphro* requires a presentation of Socrates whereby Socrates simply "goes along" with the common meaning of "Gods," especially as used by Euthyprho

In any case, piety/holiness according to the analysis is not Piety/holiness by virtue of being loved by the Gods. On the contrary, the Gods love Piety/holiness **because** it is Piety/Holiness. Granted, it will turn out from the argumentation that being loved by all the Gods would still fall short of a definition of Piety/holiness since it does not, just by itself, supply the "what is" of Piety. Even so, this trait of Piety/holiness -- that it is loved by the Gods **because** it is what it is <i.e., rather than being made to be what it is by such love> -- suggests a status for Piety/holiness more fundamental <<and residing in the *third/mixed* class of those four-but-really-five classes of *Philebus* [confer, as always, 23d,9--23e,2]>> than the realm wherein the Gods obtain. In this sense Piety/holiness shares something in common <<perhaps even to the point of being the same>> with what will be said about "the good" in Plato's final productions.

Having said this I warn the reader against taking this the wrong way. Properly understood there is something *deinos* [**nora** in Hebrew] about Holiness just as there is something *deinos* [**nora** in Hebrew] about "the good."

*****

It is, of course <and as already briefly alluded to>, a truism that the words of classical Greek often can and often do have several valid English translations. Ideally, context determines what English word is appropriate as a translation in this or that passage. In actual practice however, conscious and unconscious presumptions, often based on "received traditions" of what the writer "must" have meant, determine the translation to the detriment of its true contextual function. It is not a truism, but it's no less true, that a wordsmith of Plato's caliber would choose to play on these multiple valid meanings for various reasons.

"<u>Osion</u>" is the word in question. "Piety" is a valid translation. "Holy" and "holiness" are also valid translations. "Piety" generally denotes an attitude (and correlative set of behaviors and practices) *towards* the Gods <or, if you prefer as Plato sometimes does, "God">. It is a human trait. On the other hand "Holy" and "holiness" are ambiguous. They, like Piety, can be construed as human characteristics denoting how people act towards the Gods and correlatively, in their own lives based on their relationship to the Gods (or, if you prefer, "God"). But "holy" and "holiness" can also denote the "object" ((The Gods? not really; God? Yes, with qualification; The Holy itself? **<u>YES</u>**.)) of such pious behaviors on the part of humans. [[In fact, -- the aporetic character of this dialogue being acknowledged -- both connotative features of *osion* are presented as complementive to each other in that decisive attempt to define piety/holiness as a subset to justice.]]

It is my suggestion that in the key text just cited <<10a--11b, and more especially 11a-b>> Plato has shifted gears, quite intentionally, from the human-based meaning of Piety to the more daunting meaning of "osion" as it functions as the *object* of human-based Piety. And, short as this part of the passage is, there is a grandeur about "osion" which Plato is playing upon. "Osion" is not what it is because it is loved by the Gods. Rather "osion" is "osion" because it is itself of nature to be Loved by Gods (and presumably, mortals). Granted, such is not, by itself, a definition of "osion." The dialogue returns to the fuller dimensions of the definition task immediately after this interesting interlude. In any case, this critical 10a--llb passage shows that this question of "Piety/holiness" has, so to speak, an ontological dimension which surpasses a set of practices and behaviors exercised by humans when they are "pious."

In this sense, "the holy" is an end beyond which there is no other end. In this sense "the holy" is another name for "the good." Ever since the time of Aristotle (at least if we limit ourselves to the arena of Philosophy) it has been presumed that such an end ((whether it be called "the good," or "God," or "Nous" (in the meaning given to it in XII-7 of *Metaphysics*)), or "the holy," is, in Aristotle's meaning of these phrases, something perfect and self-sufficient. Further, this *Aristotelian* meaning of an end beyond which there is no other end, has been read back into Plato's meaning of "the good" and the phraseology by which he presents "the good." Exposing the wrong-headedness of such a reading of Plato has been the main motivation of the book you are now reading and, as well, a main motivation in **DSG**. The paradigm of final causality as engineered by Aristotle when taken (consciously or unconsciously is of little significance since the result is basically the same in both cases) as the meaning of Plato's complex accounting of "for the sake of" utterly debases the subtlety of Plato's final, late in life, accounting of the good. Worse still such a prism (i.e. Aristotelian) when used to approach the Jewish Scripture's usage of ***qadosh*** keeps one radically alienated from God's Self-Revelation of God through Scripture.

***** ***** *****
***** *****
***** ***** *****

Holy are you to be,
for holy am I, Hashem your God!

[from *Leviticus*19:2; modification of the Fox translation]

***** ***** *****
***** *****
***** ***** *****

(end of excursus)

*****

B-1-b
127d,6-130a,3. (again)

Ton oun Sokrate akousanta palin ---

--- lambanomenois epideiksei

From **DSG**, pages 20-21:

Plato paid Parmenides the greatest tribute of all by NOT summarizing what the Master had to say <<<<and for all we know, Plato may have had less access to the actual text than we do today even with acknowledging all the sketchy speculation in our time of which fragments precede or succeed which fragments or, even, which fragments are authentic and which are not>>>>; in its stead Plato supplied, in a work named after "the one" from Elea, a ***khor***(a)***eographing*** *of what the Master had to say: "One" as virtually vacuous here; the same one as dyadicizing and full of life there. Whether the "one" is to be taken as a grammatical placeholder for any Form-as-a-whole ("****holon****" being a primary function of a Form in Plato's* Parmenides*) or as the name of the whole of all ----------, either way the one ends up with two faces of itself: one-as-vacuous and one-as-dyadicizing. And where there is dyadicizing there too there is, of necessity,* ***dupli-city, ITSELF A VARIABLE IN WHE WHOLE EQUATION OF THINGS WHICH THE GODDESS OF TRUTH HERSELF INSISTS <u>MUST</u> BE APPROPRIATED*** *as Goddess herself makes the transition to "*The Way of Mortal Opinion.*" This* ***khor***(a)***eographing*** *<<i.e., neither a summary; nor an analysis; nor a commentary>> of the Parmenidean one <<which is set in motion by* ***and as*** *form-theory>> through those eight-plus-one hypotheses, constitutes in its most glorious form what today we might refer to as the "retrieval" of the* ***entirety*** *of* The Poem of Parmenides*

*. [[This contention by the Goddess of Truth (as she guides the **young** man from The Way of Truth to The Way of Mortal Opinion) resonates strongly with what Plato will come to say in Letter VII, precisely in the passage in which Form-theory is at issue:

For in learning about these matters it is necessary to learn at the same time ***both what is false and what is true OF***

THE WHOLE OF BEING [te̲s holes ousias] *and that through the most diligent and* ***prolonged*** *investigation as I said at the beginning.*

[344b]

Yes. Reminiscent of the Goddess of Truth. Reminiscent as well of what Plato did when ***khor***(a)***eographing*** whatever he may have had at his disposal of The Poem of Parmenides: hypotheses [themselves set in motion by **and as** form-theory] **necessarily** dealing with the false as well as hypotheses dealing with the true.]]

My friends. The ***khor***(a)***eographing*** begins right here at 121d,6. This passage which we are about to review is part of that ***khor***(a)***eographing***. Of course, as noted above, Plato provides for a Parmenides who insists on the validity and necessity of Form-theory [confer 135b--135c for this claim of necessity] just before the "training/exercising" is to begin. This "choreographic" feature of Plato's undertaking is critical for the reader who wishes to understand *Parmenides* on Plato's terms. In this ***khor***(a)***egraphy*** Plato is effectively saying that it is ONLY through and by Form-theory that The Poem of Parmenides receives its validation AND AS WELL that it is only against the backdrop of The Poem of Parmenides that this now-mature version of Form-theory gets ITS validation. These two essential features of Plato's undertaking are joined to the hip in *Parmenides*. *Parmenides* is neither a summary nor commentary on The Poem of Parmenides. Technically, it is not even an interpretation of The Poem of Parmenides. *Parmenides* is the ***khor***(a)***eographing*** of The Poem of Parmenides.

*****

B-1-c.
127d,6-130a,3. (yes, again)

So. Our "real" (("real" that is, only by virtue of NOT being the Young Socrates circa 399 of *Theaetetus*, *Sophist*, and *Statesman*)) and totally fictitious ((by virtue of the setting involved circa 450 and presented as expostulating a version of Form-theory which Plato generated about a decade or so after the death of the "really real" Socrates)) Socrates kind of cavalierly engages Zeno on the first contention of the first argument in Zeno's reading. If beings are many than these beings would be both like and unlike. At the minimum they would be like in so far as any and all of these many beings all ***are***; and, at once, unlike in so far as any of these many beings ***are not***, <are different from> any and all of the "other" many beings. Such is presented as "imposssible." Fine. So we have here (in Plato's playful set up) our "real" and "very young" Socrates noting and reviewing Zeno's most primitive *reductio ad absurdum* as addressed to the opponents of Parmenides who claim <then as well as now> that it is ridiculous to maintain that "one is the all" [hen ... einai to pan] 128,9-10]. Further, our "very young" Socrates takes it upon himself to point out the obvious to the effect that the contention of Parmenides ["one is the all"] and the contention of Zeno ["it" <the all> ... "is not many"; 128,4-5] are two sides of the same coin.

Zeno agrees, but informs our "very young" Socrates about the original spirit of the treatise which, interestingly, was produced when Zeno himself was a young student of Parmenides. Among these clarifications is a Platonic-esque warning about the danger of the written word in so far as one does not have control, in the final analysis, of who gets to see such a production of youth and the correlative danger that these "orphans" will not be able to defend themselves when, as is inevitable eventually, when the parent is no longer able to defend them, [128d,7--e.6]. Fine.

128e,7--130a,c.

At this point our "very young" Socrates is portrayed as introducing into the discussion something totally absent from the cases and claims which, decades before Plato was born, were made by Parmenides and also by Zeno in and by Zeno's combative his defense of his lover as well as his own creative, thoughtful, and mathematically-oriented expansion of the teaching of the "motionless one." What Socrates introduces here is a version of Form-theory in many ways (***but not in all ways***) very much akin to the accounting of Form-theory in *Phaedo* to which we have alluded above [i.e., *Phaedo* 100b,1--102a,3]. In both cases we have an accounting of Form-theory which does NOT trade upon the heuristic trope of "Being" and "Becoming" as is found in Plato's presentation of form-theory in *Republic-V* and which trope functions as the backdrop for the cosmology found in *Timaeus.* We have likewise an accounting of Form-theory which allows that ordinary things in our experience [[["very young" Socrates will cite "stones and sticks and such-like" <129d,5>]]] can receive and be both "like" and "unlike" as well as "one and many." Indeed our rather confident "very young" Socrates displays his confidence ((in what is, in effect, a refutation of Zeno's first contention in the first argument of his treatise)) that it is virtually trivial *and, indeed, NOT surprising AT ALL* to recognize that such things are in fact "one and many," "*like and unlike*" at the same time.

On the other hand, the innovation which our "very young" Socrates brings to the table is to maintain that there is a Form, itself by itself [auto kath' auto eidos <as per Cooper and please note footnote #4 on pages 362-363>] of likeness, and as well, a form for unlikeness. As mentioned above, this distinction [*khoris* <shades of khora>; an opening up] between ordinary things and "forms"/"ideas" is not at all present in the actual teachings of either Zeno or Parmenides. We are already engaged in that ***khor***(a)***egraphing*** of The Poem of Parmenides in such a way that **Plato himself** *becomes* the Parmenides who is the magister ludi of *Parmenides* precisely in the service of allowing The Poem of Parmenides to say what it always was to have said. For Plato there is an implied genius-level contention involved in the belonging together (insisted upon by the Goddess of truth) of "The Way of Truth" and the ***dupli***-city of "The Way of Mortal Opinion." But Plato is just as equally sure that such genius can only find its validation in, by, through, **and AS** Form-theory which itself is to be graduated to ***ITS*** most refined expression in *Parmenides.*

It bears repeating. Plato is ***neither*** giving an analysis/exposition of The Poem of Parmenides and, still less, ***nor*** is he making commentary on The Poem of Parmenides. Rather (and it definitely bears repeating) he is -- by way of Form-theory -- allowing the genius of the Poem of Parmenides to say, properly, what it always was to have said and which it could NOT have said what it always was to have said without Form-theory.

So. With Form theory we find that while ordinary things can, at once, <<and *obviously* can as Plato makes clear>> be said to be "like and unlike" <or "one and many" and all in a multitude of ways at that> the contrary forms themselves which they share/participate in, it would seem, cannot ever be, become, or even share-in each other. So, it seems, such is put forth by our "very young" Socrates here in this passage which really is the presented teaching of our "old" Socrates on the day of his death as portrayed at 100b,1--102a, of *Phaedo*.

However, as we shall see just below, there is in fact a significant discrepancy between these almost parallel texts <i.e. the Form-theory text from *Phaedo* and our Form-theory text in from of us now from *Parmenides*>. It is a discrepancy orchestrated consciously by Plato in both passages so as to make it clear that Form-theory itself was but a genius level insight from Plato's early period of intellectual development which however, in its pre-367 incarnation, ***limped***. In and through *Sophist* and *Parmenides* Plato ceases to be a "friend of the Forms" (as that term is used in *Sophist*) in favor of generating a version of Form-theory which will allow Form-theory to say what it always was to have said but which it did not say until after 367. And we will find that **Plato**, <but not the character of this "very young" Socrates>, right here in this passage [128e,7--130a,] ((wherein our "very young" Socrates is presented as himself grounding the Parmenidean teaching on a grounds which will allow the genius of The Poem of Parmenides to be liberated and sustained)), is announcing that early Form-theory can only be liberated and sustained by becoming the Form-theory of *Sophist* and *Parmenides* (which is NOT the Form-Theory of "the Friends of the Forms"). In our present passage he only teases us into understanding this last point. But the project is launched right here in the passage before us.

B-1-b-i.
128e,7--130a,c. (yes. again)

For there is a ***pathos*****,** ***to thaumazein****, which is characteristic of a philosopher; and it is this, and nothing else, which is the beginning of philosophy. And it was no bad genealogist who made Iris* [the rainbow] *the child of Thaumus*. [*Theaetetus*, 155d,2-4]

thaumazein; what is that? "Wonder" is often, and not necessarily wrongly, used. Sometimes teachers of philosophy wax poetic and compare this to the endemic manner in which very young children experience the world. All that is fine and is a dimension of the equation which constitutes this ***arkhe̱ philosophias*** [154d,4]. But this association, while technically valid, tends to bring a dimension of domestication to what Plato is speaking about. Words and phrases such as "puzzlement" and "puzzlement-to-the-point-of-**consternation**" belong here as well. And let us not forget our strong word ***amazing*** with its connotation of "overwhelming" and as well let us keep in mind that the horrendous and dreadful is one of the things which elicits ***amazement.***

Nor should we ignore Aristotle here. He is not to be ignored precisely because he is the first to bring to this teaching of ***thaumazein*** as the ***arkhe̱ philosophias*** a kind of domesticating twist. This domesticating twist is not present in Plato. And all too often, on this matter, the tradition tends to presume that both of these accountings of ***thaumazein*** as the ***arkhe̱ philosophias*** are equivalent to each other. Such is not so.

The Stagirite starts out on the same note as Plato:

For it is owing to their wonder that humans both now begin and at first began to philosophize.

[*Metaphysics-I-2*, 982b,11-12]

But then he reduces the journey of Philosophy, birthed in wonder, to a journey which leads to knowledge and a correlative loss of wonder. [982,13-23 and then 983a,11-21]. For Plato, in contrast, Philosophy never can have finality. For Plato, wonder/puzzlement-to-the-point-of-consternation/amazement remains always the inevitable companion of the philosopher even after a lifetime of philosophizing. For Plato, ***atopos***, is the other face of ***thaumazein*** and the two go together and stay together forever.

Now let us return to our passage.

128e,7--130a,3.

Our "very young" Socrates is virtually mocking out the simplistic manner by which Zeno presents his *reductio ad absurdum* relative to the contention that there is a plurality of beings. However, it becomes quickly evident that there is nothing astonishing at all about anything being both like and unlike (or, for that matter, one and many) at the same time. As we have seen, such happens all the time and it is really trivial when the examples are taken from ordinary experience such as "stones and sticks and such-like" <129d,5>. In effect Plato, through our young Socrates, is making the case that only with Form-theory can there be any serious encounter with the hidden genius of The Poem of Parmenides when taken as a whole, when its ***dupli***-citous "Way of Mortal Opinion" is made to stand equal with "The Way of Truth." Lacking Form-theory any "defense" of the Poem of Parmenides by way of subjecting the contention that beings are many to a *reductio ad absurdum* (i.e., i.e. a kind such as Zeno is presented as attempting in his treatise) itself becomes a trivial argument lacking any substance. But Form-theory, as presented by our young Socrates does open up the possibility of how, on the level of Forms, questions dealing with the Forms themselves can lead to a serious engagement of how "like itself" and "unlike itself; or "one itself" and "many itself" are related to each other. Without Form theory any engagement of the Poem of Parmenides become trivialized, then as well as now.

Now we come to the moment of intrigue.

So far this passage we are in from *Parmenides* has been quite parallel to Plato's adumbration, already cited above, of Form-theory from *Phaedo*. Ordinary things from our experience < "sticks, stones, and suchlike"> can, at the same time, share in Forms which are contrary to each other (e.g. "like and unlike"; "one and many"). Yet, it appears to be contended that the contrary Forms themselves do not and cannot share in each other. *Phaedo* says this unambiguously. But I suggest that Plato has orchestrated the speech of our "very young" Socrates in *Parmenides* to be teasingly implying that, just maybe, contrary Forms can indeed and do share in each other. And as we shall see below, such is the explicit teaching of both *Sophist* and *Parmenides*. If this is true it would mean that not only is it the case that the genius of The Poem of Parmenides can be made to say what it was to have said only by virtue of Form-theory, ***but also*** that this task of allowing the Poem of Parmenides to say what it was to have said requires the radical revision ((which became distasteful to the "Friends of the Forms" cited in *Sophist* at 248c)) characteristic of Platonic Form-theory posterior to 367. And the "Dialectical Grammar" given in *Sophist* as well as the supreme Dialectical exercise of the eight-plus-one hypotheses both make clear that by way of the universal blenders (e.g., Ousia, Same, and Different) contrary Forms do in fact share in each other and must share in each other.

Granted. That case -- that somehow [cf. the ***pe*** of *Sophist* at 256b,6-8 which allows even **Rest Itself and Motion Itself** to share in each other]* or other contrary Forms do participate in each other -- is not directly being made in the passage from *Parmenides* before us. Indeed, surfacely at least, such sharing of and by contraries seems to be disallowed. But that is precisely where our present passage from *Parmenides* starts to part company with the Form-theory passage from *Phaedo*. Our present passage is only a suggestive tease; but it is a suggestive tease which becomes quite explicitly the case once we enter into our Dialectical exercise. Listen to the twice articulated repetition of the daring tease orchestrated by Plato and put into the mouth of our young Socrates. Emphases, of course, are mine;

---- *but if he shows that things which partake of both* [i.e., the Like Itself and the Unlike Itself] *themselves become both like and unlike, that seems to me, Zeno, not at all strange* [atopon]; *even if that someone were to show that all things are one by virtue of participation in the one and that these same things are also many by virtue of participating in multitude* [such would not seem strange]. *But if he could demonstrate that that which is Itself one is many, and conversely, what is Itself is many is one* ----- ***then I would be amazed!*** **[thaumasomai]**. *So too with all the others. If he could show that the kinds and forms themselves undergo and suffer these opposite conditions,* ***that would certainly be a foundation for amazement*** **[aksion thaumazein]**.

... ...

And Plato has our young Socrates repeat and emphasize the point:

But if someone first, as I was just saying, first opens and distinguishes as separate [diairetai khoris] *these forms themselves by themselves -- say, Like and Unlike; One and Multitude;* ***Rest and Motion*** **[stasin kai kinesin]**, *all such things -- have the power to mingle together as well as separate apart,* ***then, Zeno, my amazement would know no limits*** **[thaumastos, o Zenon]**.

So, OK. Let's cede that you have put up a manly enough display in your treatise [concerning how, say, a stick or a stone can be, at once both "like" and "unlike"; both "one" and "many"]. *But it would be orders of magnitude more impressive if someone were to display that in multitudinous ways the very strangeness* [aporian] *referred to above were to obtain for the Forms themselves (which are dealt with* ***only*** *discursively) in contrast to the merely ordinary things of our experience.*

[129b,1--129c,3; then 128d,8--130a,3. Amalgamation of the Loeb and Cooper translations along with interpretive phrasing not found in either.]

To me the tease is very clear. This post-367 Plato is indicating that the graduated accounting of the Forms (inaugurated in *Sophist* and painstakingly mapped out in the eight-plus-one hypotheses) is even more amazing than the already amazing hypothesis that there are Forms at all. The Poem of Parmenides not only requires Form theory as its condition of possibility, but requires the truly amazing graduation and expansion of Form theory as well as its condition of possibility. And if the recalcitrant and nostalgic "Friends of the Forms" (whether they are to be found in Plato's Academy itself or in Academia of the present day) cannot adjust to this, then they shall be left behind.

> *. [[[[Here is the story of how the most amazing and most perplexing <<i.e., that Motion itself and Rest itself can be construed as "somehow" participating in each other>> came to be understood as, when all the dust has settled, no-longer-perplexing. Listen carefully:
>
> *Stranger: Let me get this straight: Is it your contention that Motion and Rest are completely contrary to each other?*
>
> *Theaetetus: Most certainly.* [*Sophist* 250a,5-8]
>
> ***
>
> *Stranger: Well then, what if we ascribe to everything the power of having intercourse* [dunamin ekhein epikoinonias] *with everything else.*
>
> *Theaetetus: Even I can dispose of that contention.*
>
> *Stranger: How?*

Theaetetus: Because if Motion were permeated by Rest Motion would be resting and, in turn, Rest were likewise permeated by Motion Rest would be moving.

Stranger: So the supposition is that such is ruled out by a strict necessity that Motion would ever be resting and Rest ever be moving?

Theaetetus: Of course. [252d,4-11]

***

Stranger: So if it should turn out that somehow* [pe] *Motion does have a share in Rest, it wouldn't, after all, be so strange* [atopon] *to maintain that it was at rest?

Theaetetus: It would be completely right* [Orthotata]*, so long as we continue to maintain that some kinds* [genon] *mingle with each other while others do not.

[256b,6-11]

***

On one level one can have sympathy for Cornford's outrageous interpolation at this point in his translation [*Plato's Theory of Knowledge*, 1957; page 286] which effectively negates what Plato is clearly maintaining in that last text (256b,6-11). I say "outrageous" because there is no evidence in the manuscript tradition of any corruption of the Greek text at this point. Yes, surfacely, Plato appears to be contradicting himself. And even IF such were the case it would be far better to simply say *even Plato nods* rather than to presume to speak for and "save" Plato from himself.

The fact of the matter is that there is a suppositional quality about the interchanges between the Stanger and Theaetetus [both at 250a,5-8 and at 252d,4-11] which would prepare the acute reader not to be surprised by what is articulated at **256b,6-11**. Further, there is that all important "**pe̲**" at 256b,6 which reflects the intricacies <<<wherein nothing at all (not even a Form) is real unless it partakes of ***both*** Rest Itself ***and*** of Motion Itself {cf. the argumentation at 249b,1--249d,3 which is foundational although it will be subsumed into a higher level of overall organization}>>> of what Plato calls the science/knowledge most appropriate to "Free Men" at 253c,9 which is the very ambience within which these matters are articulated by Plato. In any case it is necessary to reprise this whole section of *Sophist* [248e,8--260a,3] as the condition for the possibility of showing the full significance of the Dialectical Grammar of this section of *Sophist* the intricacies of which animate Plato's way of "teasing" us through the repetitious trope of ***thaumazein*** in our present text from *Parmenides* [128e,7--130a].

***** ***** *****
***** *****
***** ***** *****

[[

Plato's Parallactic Vision

---

*Imagine, if you will, five spheres in space. These five spheres are all transparent although not all of them are transparent in the same way. Two of them, "**M**" and "**R**," share the same elliptically orbital plane, always being opposite to each other in their orbital journeys as they revolve timelessly-in-time around the empty space called "khora." "**M**" is a pulsating luminosity of white light. It is always pulsatingly showing. "**R**" is completely colorless and most times is so transparent that one cannot even see it. Even so, reflected light -- when the source of such is relatively near -- lets its always continuing presence to be recognized for a short time. "**M**" and "**R**" are the same* *size both of them are significantly smaller than the other three spheres.*

*The other three spheres, "**O**," "**A**" and "**Th**" are all the same size and, as mentioned, are larger by far than the other two. They share another elliptical orbital plane spaced in such a manner that imaginary lines drawn connecting them would look like a right triangle. In this orbit they too revolve timelessly-in-time around the empty space called "khora." Purest Sapphire is the color of "**O**." Bright yellow is the color of "**A**." "**Th**'s" color is a rapidly pulsating infra red. In this respect "**Th**" is somewhat akin to "**R**" insofar as its color is not seen under ordinary circumstances although it is see-able more often than what obtains for "**R**." So too "**Th**" is akin to "**M**" insofar as it pulsates.*

*The two orbital planes intersect each other in a way which is somewhat akin to the manner in which Pluto's and Neptune's orbital planes intersect. The spheres occupying the orbital plane which can appear as a right triangle is, most of this timelessly-in-time time, farther out than the orbital plane wherein "**M**" and "**R**" remain steadfastingly opposite each other in their elliptical journeys. On the other hand, however, there are timelessly-in-time times when "**M**" and "**R**" are farther away from the de-centering center than are "**O**," "**A**" and "**Th**."*

Of course there is an infinite amount of points from both within and without these orbital planes from which one might generate a projective light and to and from any of an infinite number of directions. If one can imagine a three-dimensional screen allowing for what might be called a three-dimensional Venn diagrams one would find -- in spectacular color mixes (some pulsating, some not) the sum-total of arrangements of how and in what sense these five variously transparent spheres are and are not superimposed upon each other. With reference to our Platonic text in question [254b,10--257b,4] *one finds that Plato's text heuristically furnishes the broad contours of how these five variously transparent spheres can and cannot be superimposed upon each other. However, there is no way at all to translate these results unto a Venn diagram projected unto a screen which is merely two-dimensional. The key word is* **pe** *at 256b,6. The "flat" version of this set-up (which has its own truth) never allows for intercourse between* ***R*** *and* ***M****. But parallactic vision can see things (including the intercoursing of* ***R*** *and* ***M*** *which two-dimensional seeing never does.*

***** ***** *****

***** *****

***** ***** *****

]]

]]]]]

Plato, via his character "the very young" Socrates, orchestrated that repetitious ***thaumazein*** trope in our present *Parmenides* passage <128e,7--130a,3>. But note again that there is a changing of the guard coming up. It will be Parmenides who not only ends up owning this graduated and expanded version of Form-theory, but who, via the eight-plus-one hypotheses, delivers the precise manner by which this "most amazing" [***thaumastos*** at 129e,5] degree of sharing-in/participating obtains. We now turn to the passage in which Parmenides takes on ownership of Form theory.

B-2. Parmenides wrests Form-Theory from Socrates.
130a,4--135c,8

Pythodorus said, that while Socrates was saying all this, he himself expected that at any time Parmenides and Zeno would get angry ---

------- "I don't think I have anything clearly in view, at least not at the present time."

B-2-a.

130a,4--131a,4

Remember. No such scene ever occurred. Plato is involved in an immense and subtle ***khor***(a)***egraphic retrieval*** of the entirety of the Poem of Parmenides. Further, it is a retrieval in dialogue form whose dramatic setting is fictitious. Again, this undertaking is neither commentary nor analysis. It is a strategy by which Plato is: a). allowing the Poem of Parmenides to say what it was always to have said but which, absent Form-theory <in its expanded and radicalized instantiation post-367>, could never by itself come to say what it always to have said; and b). This ***khor***(a)***eographic retrieval*** becomes Plato's own vehicle by which his treasured Form-theory comes to say what it was always to have said.

So. Pythodorus wasn't listening carefully enough as is evident from the way he reprises this scene. Plato's Zeno had already owned up to the fact this part of his philosophical endeavor <<i.e., his attempt at defending his lover by attacking his lover's opponents as opposed to his later-in-life mathematically oriented accounts of what might be called "motionless change">> was the all too quickly generated production of youth. Yes. Our young Socrates is, in effect, is presented as skewering Zeno's early endeavor, foolishly thinking that skewering such a naïve production of Zeno's youth somehow would give translate into kudos for our "very young" Socrates: The foolish young man of our invented dramatic setting. But anger is not at all what animates Plato's presentation of the reaction of Parmenides and Zeno to the young man's "tour de force." Yes, their smiles have something of a condescension towards the young fool whose "thumos" is so much on display. But not anger. Something far more essential is being presented by Plato through the smiles of Parmenides and Zeno orchestrated by Plato.

Indeed they are presented as paying close attention to this exposition of Form-theory. For only Form-theory can give the Parmenidean endeavor credibility. And in our passage we have a changing of the guard. Form-theory, first introduced by the young Socrates, is soon going to be owned by Parmenides himself as our young Socrates fades into the background. By the time this whole section [130a,4--135c,8] draws to a conclusion we have Aristocles *himself* quietly blending into the figure of Parmenides which metamorphosis represents the necessary reciprocity by which the Poem of Parmenides and the Poem of Plato (i.e. post 367 Form-theory) are both allowed to say what they always were to have said.

B-2-a-i. The Wresting Begins.
130a,10--131a,4

Parmenides starts out by articulating this paradigm of thinking which has been introduced by Socrates. Ordinary things in our experience are presented as being what they are by virtue of sharing-in/participating-in Forms which are separate from these things in our ordinary experience. Zeno, having corrected our young Socrates about the spirit of his own treatise, our young Socrates begins his own proposal about the Forms with the kinds of separate forms which Zeno had used in his treatises: Likeness separate from the likeness which we experience; and so too forms for "one" and "many" and in general forms of relationality, quantity, and other such "categories."

But wait! That is just the problem. To phrase it in this fashion -- which, in fact, is NOT the way that either Socrates or Parmenides phrase this connection between things in our experience participating in separate forms -- is to beg the questions in a common and widespread manner which nonetheless is an ***egregious*** falsification of Plato's Form-theory. There obtains, even among scholars and translators in general, an ingrained habit (sometimes conscious of itself; more often unconscious of itself) to read this relationship between things in our own experience participating in a separate realm of forms ***as though*** Platonic forms are "universals" predicable of subjects according to the schema first adumbrated in Aristotle's *Categories* and refined (and given ontological justification, at least from Aristotle's point of view) in Book IX of *Metaphysics*.

This habit of appropriating Platonic Form-theory through the prism of *Categories* tended to prevail in the schools of Philosophy in and around Alexandria soon after Aristotle's death. Eventually it spreads beyond Alexandria itself and reaches a defining crescendo in that small but incredibly influential work of Porphyry, *Isagoge*. In the Latin West, this Porphyryan frame of reference was adopted wholecloth by Boethius in his "Second Commentary" on *Isagoge*. In this fashion a radically distorting accounting of Platonic Forms became entrenched in European letters, becoming normative all through the Middle Ages and beyond. This radically distortive and all-permeating manner of understanding Platonic forms still dominates even otherwise sophisticated readings of Plato.*

*. [[[The injustice perpetrated against Plato in this fashion is multi-layered.

1. Already Porphyry's beloved mentor, Plotinus, -- the quintessential product of the Alexandrian greenhouse of intellectual and religious cross-currents -- generated an entire Metaphysics predicated on that Alexandrian amalgamation of Plato and Aristotle fused, in turn, to theological tropes from both Jewish and Christian theologies concerning the utter transcendency of God. So far, so good. Let Plotinus be Plotinus.

But Plotinus convinced himself that what he was generating in his own mind was also the true and hitherto unrecognized teachings of Plato. But in point of fact this amalgamated metaphysical salad can be called "Platonic" only in a very superficial way. Plotinus generated the supreme expression of the amalgamizing currents of the various Alexandrian schools. Fine. However, baptizing this amalgamated salad as "Platonism" was a huge, presumptuous, and fateful mistake. What came to be edited and presented as the "Enneads" by Porphyry is often referred to as "Neo-Platonic" precisely because that is how Plotinus understood his own creation. Such is, however, a slur against Plato. Traditions which look upon the Enneads in a positive light ought to be labeled as "Neo-Plotinian" rather than "Neo-Platonic."

In any case there is a more focused observation which has to be made here. Already what was called "Platonic" in the Alexandrian schools in general and, more specifically in what came to be called the "Enneads," was in fact -- and not without paradox -- an amalgamation having more Aristotelian elements in it than validly Platonic elements. This mixture was -- in fact but not as a program which was conscious of what it was in fact doing -- simultaneously grafted with theological tropes of radical transcendency from the Alexandrian-engendered ways of understanding Judaism and Christianity.

2. Porphyry was far better educated in the intricasies of Aristotelian Logic than his beloved mentor. The key for the entire Aristotelian *Organon* is that inaugural launching of the *Organon* through *Categories*. I have shown in excruciating detail<in **DSG**> how Aristotle, without mentioning Plato in that work, executes a pre-emptive blow against Platonic Form theory by treating what Plato counted as Forms as "universals" which do not stand by themselves but which have their very being ((and, indeed, only a secondary degree of being at that)) in their function of being predicable of individuals. The word which Aristotle uses for "universals" -- katholos/kathholon -- is not a word used by Plato as his meaning of Form. To be sure, Plato maintained that each and every Form was a "whole" <holon> of participating parts. "Kata holon" (with elision, "katholon") in the sense that "according to the whole (i.e., the Form)" would be the

Platonic meaning of these words, even when elided. But the predicational schema of *Categories* was totally foreign to Plato. Aristotle was indeed very clever in his generation of his neologism. Clever, but not fair. Aristotle also had the advantage of presenting his mentor's teaching without having to bother with what Plato would have said about his misrepresentation.

The whole point of the Platonic understanding of Forms was that the Forms were themselves are individuals ***with "kath'auto" free-standingness***. They could, in statements, function as either subjects or predicates, *but always as individuals*. By treating what Plato counted as Forms as "universals" (the being of which is contingent on and derivative from the being of individual hupokeimena of which these universals were but predicates), Aristotle was, in effect, preparing for the huge begging of the question which permeates his treatment of Platonic Form theory in his works subsequent to *Categories*. All of this has been covered in excruciating detail in **DSG**. ((This topic permeates virtually all sections of **DSG**. The reader is especially referred to the initial statement of these matters in that book on pages 1-17.))

Porphyry took Aristotle's *Categories* as normative in one sense. But he was astute enough to understand that Aristotle's implied treatment of Platonic Forms went against the grain of what Platonic Forms were presented to be (i.e., "really-real"; more real than virtually all the individuals of which these Forms were predicated). What Porphyry either did not see or chose not to bring into the discussion was the simple fact that Platonic Forms were not "universals" in any sense which could emerge from *Categories*. Had he presented this "bone-in-the-throat" of *Categories* for what it really was <a distortion>, the Tradition would have turned out quite differently and two millennia of misreading the Platonic text could have been avoided.

Instead -- probably in good <albeit ignorant> intention -- what he did was to "clarify" these matters by inaugurating an explicit discussion about the ontological status of these "universals." This discussion, in the Tradition, came to be called "The Problem of Universals." It turned out to be a discussion which assigned to Plato a certain meaning of a "universal" which was akin to assigning a species of color to sound.

3. Porphyry assigned to Plato a meaning of "universal" which often goes by the heading of "Exaggerated Realism" in the post Porphyrean/Boethian Tradition. This "Exaggerated Realism" came also to be referred to as "Naïve Realism" and was often contrasted to the "Aristotelian" position of "Moderate Realism" concerning the universals. Generally the Tradition credits "Moderate Realism" as the more sophisticated position on universals.

So the injustice to Plato is indeed layered: a). His theory of Forms comes into the Tradition through the prism of that Platonic/Aristotelian amalgamation fostered in the Alexandrian schools and then entrenched in the Tradition through the influential works of Porphyry and Boethius; b). In this fashion Plato's Forms come, axiomatically, to be counted as "universals" which is already and just by itself a de-naturing of Plato's theory of the Forms, especially in the teachings to be found in the dialogues post 367; and c). Having forced Plato's Forms to be perceived by the Tradition as "universals" at all, Plato then ends up getting assigned a meaning for a teaching, "Exaggerated Realism" (which begs the question in favor of assuming that a Platonic Form is a "universal" at all), which is counted as decidedly naïve and which suffers in comparison to the view of "Moderate Realism" which, in the Tradition is counted as the more sophisticated account. But how can a sound be a "better" color than another color?

> The whole development is both ludicrous and tragic. For, even today, with all of the supposed sophistication which scholars allegedly bring to their reading of Plato, this fundamental "frame" -- which radically distorts the meaning of a Platonic Form -- is taken as axiomatic.]]]

I am not at all suggesting that Plato himself never addressed predicational matters. He does so, precisely as a predicational matter and so labeled, both in *Sophist* [[260a,1—264d,7 <a discussion totally predicated on that most intricate passage which deals with "the free man's science;" "dialectical grammar;" ***and the real being of non-being as difference*** from 252e,10 up through259e,7>]] and in *Philebus* [14c,1--17a,6]. In addition predicational matters are systematically practiced in the grand and excruciatingly delineated "exercise" filled with ontological and not just logical significance in those eight-plus-one hypotheses of *Parmenides* wherein he systematically accomplishes a whole model of predication appropriate to genuine Platonic Form-Theory. But especially here we must be alert and on guard. If Plato's great predicational "exercise" (which at once furnishes the ontological scaffolding for Form theory as well as the scaffolding for the whole of all) achieved in these eight-plus-one hypotheses is filtered ((consciously or unconsciously, it doesn't matter; for that atrocious and sorry begging the question is the result in both cases)) through the prism of Aristotle's *Categories* <<animated by the presumption of certain Aristotelian ontological presuppositions and presumption as well concerning the manner by the which Aristotle will come to *present* Form-theory>> then Plato, qua Plato, slips through the cracks and is not being read even when he is read. It is a rather insidious habit which is still with us in our time even and especially in scholarly circles. Yes, even today, that Aristotelian "frame" functions as the automatic default for understanding Platonic Form theory and Plato's paradigm of predication.

These matters constitute what is a major theme to which I have referred and treated at length all throughout **DSG**. I have already referred the astute reader of this book to pages 1-17 of **DSG** for an economical introduction to this major hindrance to the understanding of Plato on Plato's own terms. I indulge myself here with two statements, in bold-face as they are on page 6 of **DSG**, as a brief and forceful statement on these matters. To wit:

---- there are NO "UNIVERSALS" AT ALL FOR PLATO. There are "ones" for "many" all over the place. BUT THERE ARE NO "UNIVERSALS" AT ALL FOR PLATO. PLATONIC FORMS ARE, FIRST, LAST, AND ALWAYS <u>INDIVIDUALS</u> [maintaining "per se" status whether they be in subject position or predicate position].

Then, speaking of Platonic accounts of predication (which is a major issue all throughout **DSG**):

It is a schema of predication ***in which "universals" DO NOT EXIST EVEN IN THE MIND.***

Continuing on.

130b,9--131a,4

So now Parmenides, taking the lead, turns to Plato's signature Forms, each one "Itself just by Itself" [130b,10; translation as per Cooper] of the Just, the Beautiful, and the Good. He easily gets our "very young" Socrates to agree to the existence of such Forms. I note here -- without making any final judgment about its significance -- that Plato seldom (if ever???) explicitly refers to "Truth" as a form. Let that pass for now.

Interestingly, Parmenides, now well established as the true *magister ludi*, draws our young Socrates' attention to Forms for species (e.g., man) and forms for the four elements (e.g., fire and water). Here our young Socrates wavers:

He replied: "I have often been in great perplexity [aporia] *whether I should talk about such things in the same way as the others* [i.e., Like Itself; Unlike Itself; One Itself; Many Itself; Just Itself;

> Beautiful Itself; Good Itself] *or whether I should treat them the same way.*

[130c,4-6]

No refuge for the faint/feint-of-heart. Parmenides senses the wavering and presses his point. What about undignified and worthless things such as "hair, mud, and shit"? Are there forms for these as well?

Our very young Socrates is portrayed at this juncture as being very confused. Like many academics even today he is extremely reluctant to speak of separate Forms of "hair, mud, and shit" and to do so seems absurd [atopon; 135d,5]. Yet our young Socrates is portrayed as being uneasy with such a dismissal. For he knows in his heart he is being inconsistent. If there are Forms for the Just Itself, the Beautiful Itself, and the Good Itself why shouldn't there be Forms for all things? He is in a quandary. If there are Forms for terms such as justice, beautiful, and good -- as well as likeness, unlikeness, one and many -- on what grounds can he justify his doubt about such terms as man, fire, and water or to justify his snappy rejection that, for sure, there are no forms for terms such as "hair, mud, and shit"?

Parmenides (i.e. Plato's character in this dialogue) shows that it is he, rather than this Socrates, who is the true champion of Form-theory. The young neophyte seems to be more concerned with not looking foolish rather than he is with the truly stubborn philosophical pursuit of truth irrespective of how he might look in the eyes of others:

> *"That's because you are still young, Socrates," said Parmenides, "and philosophy has not yet taken hold in you the way as, in my opinion, it will in the future. Then you will not consider any of these things to be not worthy of the same analysis which you now apply only to some. Now, however you are still overly concerned of what other stink of you by virtue of your youth.*

[130e,1-5]

This more radical notion of Forms -- which effectively says that if there is a name for "x" there must be a Form for "x" -- is what Plato re-affirms in the Seventh Letter. The context for this claim is Plato's example Form, "The Circle Itself," and how the grasp of any form involves a journey up and down through four stages by which the form, now designated as the "fifth" is grasped by the philosophical mind. Listen (emphases and interpolation are mine):

The same is true of straight-lined as well as spherical figures; of color; of the good, the beautiful, and the just; of all bodies ***whether artificial of by nature**** *(such as fire, water and all such things); of all living beings; of all states of soul, both doings* [poiēmata]e *and what is experienced* [pathēmata].

[342d,3-9]

*. [[I put the phrasing of "bodies both artificial and by nature" in bold-face (in the citation from Letter Seven just above) so as to distinguish it from a concept held by Aristotle and other young "sophisticates" who hailed from the Academy. There was a stage in his intellectual development when Aristotle still maintained Form-theory but -- in the company of other Academy sophisticates who felt that Plato had naively overstretched the range and domain of Form-theory -- excluded artifacts such as houses and rings, etc., as not covered by Form-theory. Cf. *Metaphysics-IX*, 991b,5-8. If that is being "sophisticated" I'd rather be "unsophisticated" with Plato. And indeed, even in today's "Academia" one will find Plato scholars so hyper sophisticated that they insist -- contrary to Plato's repeated practice -- that Plato did not apply Form-theory to everything which has a name.]]

[342d,3-9]

So our champion of Form-theory will now take our young Socrates through a critical review of a number of serious difficulties which are endemic to this postulation of Forms for anything which has a name. As it will turn out, these disturbing difficulties which Parmenides will outline to our young Socrates would, for some, be the occasion for jettisoning Form-theory. But not so for Parmenides who will turn out to be the ardent defender of Form theory as the very condition without which there would be no knowledge at all and no Philosophy at all:

"On the other hand," said Parmenides, "if someone, with his mind fixed on these difficulties and others of the same sort, were to deny that there are forms for all beings and won't mark off a form for each one, he won't have anywhere to turn his thought since he will not [[i.e., if these difficulties cause him to turn away from Form-theory]] *allow that for all of these various things which go by the same name there is one single idea which remains always the same. In this manner he will destroy the very power of dialectic entirely.* [135b,7-12]

So, as Parmenides, in our present text [130b,9--131a,4], prepares to engage these ultimately unavoidable difficulties, he gets the young Socrates to confirm the raw outline of Form-Theory:

So. This is the outline of your contention, no? There are certain forms which these other things [i.e., things other than what is contained in our ordinary experience such as "stones and sticks and such"] *derive their names, no? I mean, for instance, that they come to be like by getting a share of likeness; large by getting a share of largeness; and just and beautiful by getting a share of justice and beauty. This is your meaning, no?*

"It certainly is," Socrates replied.

[130e,6-131a,4]

So now we turn to a series of very profound difficulties with the theory. Our stalwart guide, it has now become clear, is Parmenides. Indeed, it will not be long before "Socrates," as was the case in *Statesman* which precedes our dialogue in the tetralogical arrangement, recedes from an active role in the dramatic setting in favor of a very young man, this time named "Aristotle." ((In the case of *Statesman* it is the "regular" Socrates (about seventy years in age according to the dramatic setting) who recedes in favor of a "Young Socrates" who was mentioned in *Theaetetus* and who had the slightest cameo appearance in *Sophist*. In contrast, in *Parmenides* it is the "real" Socrates presented as about twenty years old who recedes in favor of an even younger "Aristotle.")) Parmenides will subject Form theory to this critical review of difficulties not because he wants to discredit Form-theory but because he plans to put Form-theory on a foundation which can withstand these and any other "difficulties." In furnishing this foundation he works with the very young "Aristotle."

B-2-b. Journeying through the Difficulties.
131a,5--135c,8

<u>A</u>. Difficulties dealing with the nature of "participation."
The Whole/Parts Difficulty (131a,5--131e,7).
The First Infinite Regress Difficulty <and the only-apparent rejection of a proffered solution {{i.e., Forms as thoughts}}> (131e,8--132c-12).
Forms as "paradeigmata" and the correlative Second Infinite Regress Difficulty (132c,13--133a,11)

<u>B</u>. Difficulties dealing with the Possibility of Knowledge.
The Knowledge Difficulty on Its own Terms. (133a,12--134a,4)
The Knowledge Difficulty as an Indicator that Mortals are alienated from the God and Gods. (134c,5--135e,9)

B-2-b-i. Difficulties dealing with the Possibility of "participation."

> ***note bene:*** Now, back to our "difficulties." {{{{You will note that in this initial engagement of the "whole/parts" difficulty our perspective is generic looking at the whole field of difficulties in the service of giving an account of what it means to say that Plato is *choreographing* The Poem of Parmenides. The features of the difficulties -- particularly the inaugurating "whole/parts" difficulty -- are critical for this generic theme. I have taken the liberty of making some incursions into some early passages of the "whole/parts" difficulty which are in fact posterior to the very beginning passages of the "whole/parts" difficulty in the service of adequately dealing with this topic.}}}}

The whole/parts difficulty.
131a,5--131e,7.

So does each thing that gets a share get as its share the Form as a whole or a part of it? ---

--- "I don't think I have anything clearly in view, at least not at the present time."

This particular portion of our text is the occasion for some commentaries on *Parmenides* to make a very strange claim. Sometimes it is alleged that Plato is using a "physical/materialistic" model of the forms and that the meaning of "whole" and "part" in our passage is being used in such a manner. Often enough this claim becomes the occasion for dismissing this difficulty or of making some claim to the effect that some irony and/or satire is being orchestrated by Plato in these lines.

First of all, as we shall see below, the tropes "physical and non-physical" or "material and immaterial" are not at all put forth by Plato himself. We will pursue this matter just below. But even if we go with these tropes not articulated by Plato himself one would wonder WHY Plato would even get involved at all in such a distraction. One would wonder as well whether these same commentators would insist upon a disconnect between the statement of this difficulty and Plato's long and exacting treatment of wholes and parts in the eight-plus-one hypotheses and especially in the long and critical section in the service understanding the meaning of "metheksis" in Hypothesis # 2 at 142c,9--145e,7. If they were consistent they would have to insist on such a disconnect. But most of these commentators don't even bother to relate the passage in Hypothesis # 2 to the very difficulty which it is solving. Nor do they address the question as to *why* Plato would even bother with such a frivolous distraction in the formulation of this difficulty. On the contrary, there is no disconnect between the "metheksis" passage (the one just cited) based on whole/parts. Neither in the statement of the difficulty nor in the treatment of the response to the difficulty is there any whisper of understanding either wholes or parts according to the tropes of material/immaterial or physical/non-physical. Not at all. As per usual, such commentators, unconsciously for the most part, bring such Aristotelian "framing" to such passages with the consequence that they do not even come close to understanding what Plato is doing in such post-367 passages.

On the contrary, Plato very carefully sets up ***as a difficulty*** the variables which are being addressed in the eight-plus-one hypotheses in this "exercise" whose primary (but not only) function is to delineate what a Form (i.e., a "one") is and as well the schema by which accounts for what it would mean to participate in a Form and, as well, what it would mean for any of these "ones" to share-in/intercourse-with other Forms. In point of fact, there are many interpreters of *Parmenides* who do not have a clue with regard to what Plato is doing as he produces his dialogic listing of the difficulties. They remain in total ignorance of how and in what precise sense these difficulties are addressed in the hypotheses. To camouflage their ignorance they take refuge in cleverly orchestrated accounts by which our present text from the Introductory Conversation is made to say what it, the text, is so clearly not saying. Such accounts are, as we need to repeat often, radically entrenched in this misrepresentation. These are the interpreters who, early on in their careers, married themselves to a certain simplistic reading of Platonic Form-theory and who desecrate the post-367 dialogues by ramming through convoluted readings of *Parmenides* in the service of not having to give up their treasured certitudes about Platonic Form-theory.

So, let us begin with some preliminary remarks about the tropes actually used by Plato in stark contrast to the tropes often used in the Tradition starting with Aristotle which get read back into the Platonic texts as though they were articulated by Plato himself.

There is, first and foremost the validly Platonic distinction dealing with "sensible/intelligible." This distinction is analogous with another validly Platonic distinction <which is, in a sense, subset to his "sensible/intelligible" distinction> which is his usage of "somata/asomata"; "bodied and bodiless." This is his fashion of maintaining that nameable and identifiable bodies <as opposed to what might be called principles of body: "materiality" or "physicality"> involve *aisthe̱sis* as well as *noe̱sis* whereas entities lacking a body are grasped (but we are not speaking of intellectual intuition here which has no place in Plato post 367) by a species of *noe̱sis.* The "materiality" of things is not of interest to Plato. In the visible realm what catches his attention are always entities which can be *named.* Corporeality refers to **organized and identifiable** entities (artificial or by nature making no difference) which can have a name associated with them. Again, the mere "materiality" of the visible world is of no interest to him. "*Hule̱*" is not of interest to him either as a component of visible things or even as a construct functioning as the condition for the possibility of visible things insofar as they can be identified and named. For this latter -- a construct functioning as the condition for the possibility of visible things insofar as they can be identified and named -- he furnishes "*hupodokhe̱*" <the kissing cousin to "*khora*"> from the dark middle of *Timaeus* <48e,3--53c,4>. But unlike "*hule̱*" the *hupodokhe̱*, a cosmological principle for corporeal entities, is the condition for the possibility of entities to be perceptible things but not really part of the *composition* of visible things.*

*. [[[The emergence of those basically Aristotelian distinctions (physical and non-physical; material and immaterial) mentioned above <and then, often unconsciously, read misrepresentingly back into Plato> is a complex and intriguing question. Aristotle often takes his inspirational point of departure from concepts generated by Plato (especially in that dark middle of *Timaeus*) but then radically recasts them to fit the needs of what he is trying to express in *Physics* <<and then, further recasting them in the mature books of *Metaphysics*>> This is perfectly fine and, by itself, is completely fair. Plato is Plato and Aristotle is Aristotle. One may walk with either but one cannot, intelligently, walk with both. Unfairness and radical misrepresentation occur, however, from two derivative dimensions of how Aristotle (and the Tradition) emerge from Plato.

First is the case of Aristotle's ***presentations*** of Plato (in general and most especially with regard to Form-theory) which are, ostensibly, separable from his ***critiques*** of Plato (in general and especially with regard to Form-theory). For what Aristotle does, time and time again is to egregiously beg the question by ***presenting*** Plato's contentions through the prism of conceptual frames of references ***generated in the first place*** as alternatives to Plato (especially with regard to Form-theory). Thus, even before the critique of Plato is stated, the critique of Plato is, in effect, already decided as valid by this subtle pre-emptive move on Aristotle's part by accomplishing the begging of the question in Aristotle's ***presentations*** of this or that teaching of Plato's <and especially with regard to Form-theory>. (((((Conscious? unconscious? on Aristotle's part? It matters little since the terribly misrepresentative result, which comes to be largely ensconced in the Tradition century after century, is the same in either case.)))))

What I have adumbrated in the above two paragraphs I have treated in excruciating detail in **DSG**. For the benefit of the astute reader I hereby list the most salient relevant headings (and correlative page-numbers) by which this duplicative Aristotelian procedure scenario Aristotle not only emerges from Plato but emerges in such a manner that he falsifies Plato's teaching as he generates an alternative to Plato. Such could have been accomplished without misrepresentation. Aristotle's guilt is that he customarily generates, trading on Platonic frame of reference as his point of departure, a conceptual alternative to Plato (i.e., completely fair taken by itself) AND, at the same time and quite unfairly, radically misrepresents this or that Plato's teaching (especially on "Form-theory") by ***presenting*** Plato's teachings through conceptual prisms ***brought about in the first place by Aristotle's own alternatives*** to the Platonic teaching under discussion. Aristotle's critique of Plato ends up being validated in advance by virtue of his presentation of this or that Platonic teaching, a presentation permeated by his own conceptual ***alternative*** to the Platonic teaching in question. The begging of the question involved is breathtaking but largely goes unrecognized in the Tradition.

Have I repeated myself? Is that what you are saying? I certainly hope so. It takes emphasis to awaken people to these misrepresentations of Plato which have been taken as axiomatically true of Plato by the Tradition for more than two millennia. The most relevant generic argumentation for this claim of mine is to be found on pages 137--139 of **DSG**.

I will now list, in staccato fashion, several of the most prominent examples of this bedevilment of Plato by Aristotle with references to the accounts of such in **DSG.**

a). Aristotle's explicitly announced domestication of **dunamis** in Book Nine of *Metaphysics* which domestication is often (and mostly unconsciously) is read back into Plato's far more "dynamic" usage of **dunamis** such a "dynamic" usage of the word being true to its ordinary meaning in classical Greek. **DSG**, pages: 30--31; 160--163; 186--192.

b). Related to the above and derivative from the above. Based on such a domesticated and passive meaning of **dunamis** Aristotle (in accordance with his ontological presuppositions) transforms the "paskhein/poiein" pairing thematically used by Plato with his "dunamis/energeia" <<sometimes a "dunamis/entelekheia" pairing>> using, of course, his artificial (in the sense that it goes, by Aristotle's own admission, against the ordinary meaning of "dunamis") domestication of **dunamis**. Incredibly even fairly good English translations of Plato's dialogues generally translate the Platonic pairing of "paskhein/poiein" in a way which not only reflects the Aristotelian flavor but also ignores the richness of Plato's own flavor. "Paskhein/Poiein"///"Undergoing/suffering//Making" terminology tends to be translated with "passive/active" tropes more reflective of Aristotle's potency/act trope, itself the vehicle by which Aristotle, often enough with clever sarcasm <<especially in Book Nine of *Metaphysics*; confer. Chapter Eight, 1050b,35--1051a,4 especially>>. For **DSG's** accounting of this matter you may start with pages 113-114.

c). Aristotle's various inspirations from terms and themes taken from the "dark middle" of *Timaeus* [47e,4--53c,4] even as he transform these terms and themes into something radically different from how they are used by Plato. Pages 47e,4--53c,4. <<<Confer the detailed treatments of this matter in **DSG**, pages: 335--353.]]]

With these clarifications, it is now safe to return to our present text and attempt to explicate it on its own terms rather than from a conceptual prism unconsciously maintained in the Tradition when it comes to understanding Platonic Form-theory.

B-2-b-i. The whole/parts difficulty. (again).
131a,5--131e,7.

So, keep this in mind. **NEITHER** the materiality **NOR** immateriality of "Forms, "wholes," and "parts" are at issue. Not at all. Likewise keep in mind that we are dealing with the post-367 version of Form-theory in contradistinction to Form theory as once maintained by Plato himself and which certain recalcitrant "Friends of the Forms" in the Academy wished to still maintain. [*Sophist*, 247d,9--249d,4 with special attention to the case concerning Knowledge Itself <i.e., itself being a Form even as it knows the Forms> relative to "poiein" and "paskhein" occurring on the level of Forms]. In *Sophist*, time and time again (including most especially the Form of Knowledge Itself) Forms were presented as subject to *paskhein and poiein* ***just as much as are all things which obtain in the visible realm***. [[*Sophist,* 247d,9--247e,4; 248b,6--245d,5 with, again, special attention to "poiein" and "paskhein" relative to the paradigm Form for all of this namely "Knowledge Itself" at 248c,1--248e,7*]] Even if Plato had presented the materiality of visible things and the immateriality of invisible Forms ((and such is NOT Plato's language at all) it would still remain the case the Forms, **just as much as visible things in our ordinary experience of things,** would equally be subjected to the play of *paskhein and poiein* **and in innumerable ways** as are the things which obtain in our ordinary experience. Indeed, even moreso.

*. [[The boilerplate is given at 248e,8--249a,2:

> *But for Heaven's sake! Are we to let ourselves be persuaded that it's true that motion and life and soul and wisdom are present in that which is most completely real* [to̲ pantgelo̲s onti] *and that it remains without motion, solemn and awe-full devoid of mind?*

]]

So. Let us indeed turn to this network of the whole/parts difficulty on **its** terms as presented by Parmenides in his interchange with our young Socrates free of prisms which distort the dynamic that is going on in our passage.

B-2-b-i. The whole/parts difficulty. The actual launching of the "Dance-Writing."
131a,5--131e,7. (yes, again)

alef.
What evidence do we even have that Plato intended a "choreography" of the Poem of Parmenides? I believe the answer is given in the dialogue whose very first line is a hailing of a certain figure with a playful moniker: "Terpsion." I am referring, of course to that spectacular encomium for Parmenides at 183e,3--184a,4 found in *Theaetetus*. In this passage, as you will recall, our Socrates is presented, at age sixty-nine/seventy, as bearing witness to a meeting he had with Parmenides and Zeno when he was a "very young" man. Of course, as it always is with Plato, it is Plato himself who is inventing the scenes of both the remembered story-within-a-story which is the final form of *Theaetetus* as well as the remembered story-within-a-story which is *Parmenides*. As we have seen above, most certainly the interchange of and between Socrates, Zeno, and Parmenides which launches *Parmenides* is the product of Plato's fertile literary imagination. In relating what never took place Plato reveals some of the overall architectonic of that masterful trilogy of dialogues which is introduced by *Theaetetus*.

First of all, towards the end of this encomium [183e,3--184a,4], we find Plato's concern that we not just allude to what transpired in that fictional encounter <<since the subject matter is so critical>>. On the other hand, to attempt to scrunch it in as a "side-show" in the dialogue *Theaetetus* would be to add insult (i.e., turning what was covered in *that* incredible encounter into being merely a handmaiden to *Theaetetus*) to injury (i.e., the "handmaiden" is so all-encompassing that it would drown out the issue being discussed in *Theaetetus*). [184a,5-9] It is true that the fundamentally aporetic character of *Theaetetus* is, and can only be, adjudicated through the frame of reference provided by *Sophist*, and more especially, *Parmenides*. But the detailing of the choreographed Eleatic content of such should not be introduced in the midst of a dialogue which is delineating the layers of the "aporiai" of Knowledge which is, in effect, the sum total of *Theaetetus*.

Secondly, and in the service of revealing ***Plato's own*** agendum for what he has in mind when he gets to *Parmenides* (i.e., which is more than just getting to *Parmenides*) Plato has Socrates give the following two-edged warning in this same encomium passage:

I fear that we may not even understand his actual words and even at a farther remove would be our ability to understand at all the thinking expressed therein.

[184a,1-2. amalgamated translation from Cooper, Loeb, Cornford, and McGinley.]

Plato is here alluding to two separable issues. First of all Parmenides himself was sparse and cryptic in his Poem (which, additionally, was forced into a further economy of expression by the hexametric constraint of his form of expression). But further, in some way, Plato seems to be suggesting, the Poem cannot really speak for itself. It does not unpack itself and it needs to be ***made*** to be unpacked. Plato, daringly, takes up the implied challenge in the dialogue with the sub-title "peri ideon." The stupendously presumptive implied claim of Plato is that the Poem of Parmenides can only say what it was always was to have said by and through Plato's (post-367) Form-theory. He is not writing a commentary on whatever shards he may have had access to of the original writing. Still less is he writing something like a philosophical analysis on whatever of those shards he may have had. Rather, he takes it upon himself to ***choreograph*** (by way of and through his now revised accounting of Form-theory) what was always to have been the true meaning of the Poem. The project is indeed stupendously presumptive on the part of Plato. And that's why Plato is Plato; the shoe fits.

beit.
We're so sorry, Uncle Alfred. The History of Philosophy does NOT consist of a series of footnotes to "Plato." The formation of "Plato" is largely forged through two overlapping and eventually amalgamated dynamics.

a). We need to remind ourselves. The most decisive and most subtle wave of this formation of "Plato" in the Tradition comes from Aristotle. In his ***presentations*** of "Plato" Aristotle is seldom faithful to the teachings of Plato. That he would engineer alternative conceptual frames of reference to his mentor is to be expected. The problem is that more often than not Aristotle **presents** (i.e., prior to his critique) Plato's teachings through a conceptual prism *generated in the first place as an* ***alternative*** to this or that Platonic teaching. The begging of the question involved is breathtaking but largely unacknowledged in the history of Philosophy. By virtue of such question-begging Aristotle's *critiques* (which ordinarily immediately follow upon those presentations) of this or that Platonic teaching come forth as virtually validated as soon as they are expressed. It is a fault which sloppy philosophers with poor training in Logic are often guilty of. It seems, then, totally out of place in the thinker most responsible for generating Formal Logic. So out of place is such sloppiness in a mind as exact and precise as the Stagirite's that it raises the possibility that Aristotle may have been conscious of what he was doing through his malappropriations of Platonic teaching. But consciously orchestrated or unconsciously orchestrated such an unfair picture of Plato's philosophy has all too often become, from the centuries immediately following upon Aristotle and onward from there, something taken as axiomatic even by Plato scholars. Plato ends up falling between the cracks in the history of Philosophy in favor of a "Plato" created by Aristotle's **presentations** of Platonic teachings.

Of all of these misrepresentative "presentations" of Plato it is Aristotle's presentation of Platonic Forms as "universals" which is most egregiously misrepresentative and, at once, most ensconced in the Tradition affecting, even today, the presentation of "Platonic" Form-theory even by those who call themselves "scholars" of Plato. [Confer the entirety of "pericope one" in **DSG**; pages 1-17]

b). The "greenhouse" germination period in the history of Philosophy from about 150bce up through 300ce which emerged and obtained in Alexandria and its environs during this time period.

These currents and cross-currents generated models of philosophical speculation which we might call "Aristotelian-esque" (which means heavily Aristotelian without being "pure" Aristotelian) and what was becoming "'Platonic'-esque " (which means, in this case emerging from the growing influence in this Alexandrian hothouse of "Platonism" (largely influenced by and through Aristotle's question-begging *presentations* of Plato), tended, on the average, to amalgamate into a species of "Platonism" which owed more to Aristotle's *presentations* of Plato than to Plato's own writings. The great irony here is that "Platonism" generally was honored more than Aristotelianism in the Alexandrian hothouse based on a meaning of "Platonism" only made possible by the way Aristotle *presented* Plato's teachings.

These Alexandrian currents and cross-currents came to be extremely influential for subsequent ages of Philosophy even when "Alexandria" itself had ceased to be the dominant center of learning. But the influence of that Alexandrian "greenhouse" had another huge variable which was also grafted unto that view of "Platonism." Largely in a non-systematic way this (already false) "Platonism" comes to be grafted upon new conceptual models God/Divinity from Jewish and Christian sources active in that centuries-long "greenhouse"

> and which came to be over time (here consciously; there unconsciously) grafted onto both “Aristotelian-esque” and “‘Platonic’-esque models of thinking. Clearly the allegedly “Platonic” teaching of Plotinus (saved for history by Porphyry’s editing and presentation of Plotinus’ lectures which became the hugely influential *Enneads*) concerning the “beyond being” Ineffable One constitutes the crowning achievement of these false meanings of “Platonism” emanating from these amalgamating greenhouse centuries.
>
> And Plato, qua Plato, became lost to the Tradition. Worse than that, key phrases in Book Six of *Republic* in its treatment of “the good” came to be subjected to this Plotinian/Porphyrean invention of “The Ineffable One.” And this subjection maintains its strength even unto the present time. Yes. There is much which is truly “mystical” in Plato. But these mystical strains in Plato come to be radically misunderstood and misrepresented when they are subjected to and filtered through (consciously or through the unconscious habit of the Tradition) the Plotinian/Porphyrean frame of “the Ineffable One.”

gimmel.
So, keep in mind that Plato is involved in *Parmenides* in the task of his recasting of his own Form-theory (such recasting being accomplished schematically in *Sophist*, and with greater and exacting rigor in *Parmenides* <and finessed, just a bit, in *Philebus*>) and as well, by and through that recasting, he engages the correlative task of *choreographing* (i.e., “dance-writing,” especially in the eight-plus-one hypotheses) the shards of the Poem of Parmenides available to him. In this fashion he is orchestrating/choreographing the Poem of Parmenides so that it can say what it always was to have said. As I pointed about above: a stupendously presumptive undertaking on Plato’s part. But the shoe fits.

In this undertaking Plato had to walk away from a vision of Form-theory wherein “Forms” stood eternally in themselves, by themselves, quite independent of there being "Knowledge" (a more technical phenomenon for Plato post-367 than it had been for him and certainly more technical than how that word is ordinarily understood) of said Forms. In this vast undertaking Plato had the great fortune to be doing Philosophy before Philosophy became "ologized." <e.g., "epistemology"; "ontology"; "theology"; "psychology">. Although this model of doing Philosophy originated in Aristotle's Lyceum, Aristotle himself did not use these exact rubrics. But the very spirit of Philosophy as it would be practiced over the next two millennia started to be hinted at in Plato's Academy. For example, surely there were lectures on Mathematics and other "sub-divisions" of Philosophy. And indeed Plato himself towards the end of his life refers to the work of the coterie in the Academy which followed Speusippus' concentration on "ta phusika." But the thematic and somewhat rigid systemization of Philosophy was, overall, largely foreign to Plato. The thematic systemization of Philosophy which came to govern the Traditions was hinted at in the Academy but was birthed at the Lyceum and not in the Academy.

Doubtlessly there are thematic treatments having an overtly "epistemological" and/or "ontological" character all through *Theaetetus*, *Sophist*, and *Parmenides*. But, as we shall see, each (i.e., the unlabeled "epistemology" and the unlabeled "ontology") entails, includes, and **PERMEATES** the other in these three key dialogues. One cannot take the prisms generated from the time of the Lyceum and up through Medieval Scholasticism and apply them to Plato's achievement wherein nothing whatsoever stands by itself. Plato neither is nor could be a "Realist" or "Idealist" ((still less for that matter what in theory could be called an "'extreme/exaggerated Realist'" or "Moderate Idealist" or perhaps even "Moderate Realist" as those terms are bandied about in the post-Aristotelian/Alexandrian Tradition meditation on "universals*)). What we have in the later dialogues is Form-theory which, to use the language of the Tradition as a first approximation, is ontology only on the condition that it is at once epistemology and is epistemology only on the condition that it is at once ontology. ((Precisely in this belonging together of ontology and epistemology his undertaking is and is not similar to some aspects of what is said in "Quantum Theory" all depending on which accounting of "Quantum Theory" one is married to. But let that point pass for now since there are radically differing accountings of what "Quantum Theory" even entails.)). In this Plato seems to have been inspired by a closer appropriation and appreciation of shards of the Poem of Parmenides which came to be at his disposal when he was not attempting to make peace between the younger Dionysius and his beloved Dion. So, let us now turn to some of these shards which appear to have so inspired Plato during that from the time of the "second voyage."

> *. [["Uncle Alfred" again with a slightly different, and more accurate, twist. The history of Philosophy is not a series of footnotes to Plato. Plato got lost in that Alexandrian "greenhouse." Indeed, the History of Philosophy is de facto a series of footnotes to what emerged and coalesced in that Alexandrian hothouse.]]

dahlet.

Interlude on the Poem of Parmenides. (All references are taken from the 1960 hardcover edition of *The Pre-Socratic Philosophers* by Kirk and Raven. Please understand that in making these references I am not necessarily endorsing -- or for that matter not-endorsing -- interpretations of the Poem made by their joint undertaking. I sometimes take liberty with the translations used by K&R.)

From the outset we can dismiss a common, but not universal, approach to the parts (however incomplete they may be) of the poem often referred to as "The Way of Truth" and "The Way of Mortal Opinion," this latter, also and properly, often referred to as "The Way of Seeming/Appearing." One common approach, first articulated by Aristotle in *Metaphysics* I-5, 986b,28--987a,1 and which has its adherents in the Tradition even today is to maintain that in the Way of Truth one is speaking of noetic intellection of some kind while in the Way of Seeming/Appearing one is speaking according to sensation/perception. This distinction ((not at all isomorphic, it should be noted, to the tropes of "material/immaterial" and "physical/non-physical" which are also NOT employed by Plato)), however, is NOT in any way used as a guide for Plato's *choreographing* of the Poem of Parmenides by way of his revised Form-theory.

Yes. To be sure. The distinction between visible things which can be perceived and non-visible things which cannot be perceived is deeply ensconced in Plato's frame of reference both pre-367 and post-367. Let that be stipulated. Even so, his de facto treatment of participants in a Form ----- (((**Only SOME classes of participants are visible and perceptual, BUT BY NO MEANS ALL.** An individual "like" <or "likeness"> which is what it is only by virtue of participating in "The LIKE Itself" is just as invisible as "The LIKE Itself." And there are myriads of other possible examples. For in the Platonic schema the "like" character of a participant simply does not function as an implied universal functioning as a predicate.))) ----- in the dance of the eight-plus-one hypotheses Plato treats both the "ones" (i.e. Forms) and the "others" (i.e. participants in Forms which he also designates as "ones" and, when necessary for accuracy, as the " 'not-ones' of a 'one' ") exactly in the same way without thematically using an aisthesis/noetic distinction. Indeed, the only thematic distinction between Forms and participants used in those eight-plus-one hypotheses is "khoris" (separate) which, of course, necessarily resonates, intentionally on Plato's part, with the "Khora" from the dark middle of *Timaeus*.

Of course, throughout the Tradition it is often enough presumed in the history of commentary on the Poem that this Aristotelian understanding of the two parts of the poem (i.e., along noe̲sis/aisthesis axes) is the meaning intended by Parmenides himself. Such is a silly proposition which again reveals how deeply entrenched are the tropes, themes and philosophemes invented by Aristotle which, having their origin in Aristotle, came to be expanded upon about and taken as axiomatic in the centuries which I refer to as the Alexandrian greenhouse. These orientations bypass both Plato and the Poem he is choreographing. I mention it so as to note explicitly that such a frame of reference is not operative in this book either for the understanding of the Poem itself or for the understanding of Plato's grand *choreographnig* of the Poem.

dahlet-i.) What truly is difficult is discerning what status obtains **for Parmenides himself** as the intended meaning of "The Way of Seeming/Appearing." There is, no doubt, a stern rebuke by the Goddess of Truth for those who follow this path. On the other hand the Goddess --((and here we have the problem concerning the fragmentary character of some of these statements and, as well, the sequencing of these collections of fragments))-- is adamant that the truth of the whole ***requires*** that this ((two-headed)) way **must** be pursued. Listen to Her cacophony of statements on this tension. It is a tension which is NOT resolved in the extant fragments of the Poem itself. Further, it is, as we shall see, a two-tiered tension which animates Plato's *choreographing* of the Poem.

First, it is to be noted since we are speaking of Plato's orchestration of the Poem, that it is the Goddess (not named in the Proem as "the Goddess of Truth") who welcomes "Youth" (a theme decisively dear to Plato's heart in many of the post 367 dialogues). [K&R, 267]

It is the Goddess who announces that right and just that our "Youth" come this way [hodon], a way which is portrayed as:

> *Far indeed does it lead from the beaten path of humans.*

[267]

Immediately upon designating the journey which our Youth is to be on, the Goddess tells him that it is just [dike̲] that he learn all things, BOTH:

> *the unshaken heart of well-rounded truth in conjunction with the seemings/opinions [doksas] of mortals in which there is no true trust.*

[267; slight amendment of the translation].

My claim (which, a fortiori, is my claim about Plato's *choreographing* of the Poem) is that THIS COMBINATION [*the unshaken heart of well-rounded truth* ***in conjunction with and ultimately not separable from*** *the seemings/opinions [doksas] of mortals in which there is no true trust*] is that which "lies from the beaten path of humans." To be sure, "the beaten path of mortals" is ubiquitous. But what is not ubiquitous -- indeed, quite, quite to the contrary -- is the sealing together of BOTH of these accountings as the "way"/path which must be followed by the Youth for the sake of truth.

[267. Emphasis is mine.]

dahlet-ii). Immediately after what was said in # i just above, the Goddess states the deepest mystery of the entire Poem.

Yet nonetheless, you shall have to learn these things as well: how things-which-appear, as they be through [peronta] ***in every way through everything, of necessity MUST genuinely achieve the appearance of being.***

Or:

Even so it behooves you to learn **{you are to learn}** ***such things as well, to wit: that appearing things MUST BE in an appearing manner, as they be through everything in every way.***

[267; translations somewhat amended from Kirk and Raven in conjunction with the McKirahan translation and its footnote # 5. Emphasis was mine, of course.]

This extraordinary and agendizing statement which brings The Goddess' précis of just what is to follow sets the parameters of what the careful reader is to find in the rest of the Poem. Any accounting which is not in tune with this agendizing statement is one which is out of tune with the Poem. Since the shards left of the Poem <<and it seems clear that Plato only had access to shards and likely fewer

shards than are available to us>> tend to emphasize but one pole of this dyadisizing program <<<a “dyadisizing program” which is the whole, this very whole then containing within itself a sub-dyadisizing program in one of its parts, i.e. “the Way of seeming/appearing”>>>. And that is the point which even many scholars of the Poem have not appreciated. There are **TWO** non-symmetrical dyadisizing axes which animate this Poem. If this key insight is not recognized, it becomes most difficult for readers to catch the spirit of the whole of the Poem. Further, to merely make commentary or analysis on the Poem in its sharded form is to misrepresent the Poem of Parmenides. Only a ***choreographing*** of the Poem ((provided that such ***choreographing*** is produced prior to the distorting “Frame” brought to these matters from the time of Aristotle onwards)) remains as the best possible hope of understanding the Poem as a whole.

In any case, these considerations are very much reflected in Plato’s discussion of the long and arduous “training” which is the condition for the possibility of successfully dealing with the enumerated “difficulties.” In describing the elements of this “training” Plato has the character Parmenides formulate a remarkable requirement about the training. It is first established that that whatever is to be discussed is to be discussed on the plane of the Forms and not from the visible realm of ordinary experience. This does not entail that the treatment of visible things in the eight-plus-one hypotheses in so far as they are participants in an invisible Form will be treated any differently than the Form itself. Rather the point is being made that the serious kind of training must take as its point of departure something worthy of such “training” whereby the network of what participating entails can be displayed. When one is dealing only with the visible things of ordinary experience discourse about “the one and the many” is either trivial or, as practiced by some, sophistical.

Then, with that clarification having been stipulated, Plato’s Parmenides is presented as making as a further key requirement of such training something which mirrors the dyadisizing tension in the original Poem of Parmenides:

But you must do the following in addition to that: if you want to be trained more thoroughly, you must not only hypothesize, if each thing is, and examine the consequences of that hypothesis; you must also hypothesize, if that same thing is not.

Plato then requires his character Parmenides to convey more concretely what he is trying to indicate with several examples all of which examples emphasize that it is just as important to examine from every perspective not only the hypotheses which presume that *the-x-under-discussion* IS, BUT ALSO AND EQUALLY AS IMPORTANT, to examine from every perspective the hypotheses which presume that *the-x-under-discussion* IS NOT.

All this you must do if, after completing your training, you are to achieve a full view of the truth.

[Taken from the translation in *Cooper*. 135e-136a; 136c; and all in-between.]

A number of years later Plato -- reacting to the trauma of Dion's murder (perpetrated, it is said, by two members of Plato's own Academy) -- briefly returns to this theme in Letter Seven in a passage which immediately follows upon his adumbration of the four stepping stones which lead the soul to the "fifth" which deals with that sudden (eksaiphnes) grasp the Form itself. In what is sometimes referred to as the "epistemological digression" of Letter Seven Plato is at pains, as we shall see from the citation below, to maintain that acquisition of **that** kind of knowledge is simply impossible unless the person involved has certain character traits, the chief of which would be "quick of learning and remembering" combined with the person's affinity to justice. That having been stipulated Plato adds on that being "akin to justice" is not by itself sufficient to be proficient in the great task:

-----nor any man, who, though akin to justice, is slow at learning and forgetful, will ever attain the truth about virtue. Nor about vice, either, for these must be learned together, ***just as the truth***

and falsity about any part of being must be learned together,
through long and earnest labor, as I said at the beginning.

[Taken from the translation in *Cooper* slightly modified. 344a-b. Emphasis is mine.]

dahlet-iii). The boilerplate. In the concluding passage of *Parmenides* Plato give his parallel wording to how the Goddess of Truth insisted that BOTH parts of the Poem -- the true and the false; the real and the unreal; being and seeming -- MUST go together if truth is the goal. Listen.

Plato's astounding boilerplate ending of *Parmenides* climaxes with this pregnant comment: ***ALETESTATA!*** For Plato, this double entwining summary -- which would be paradoxical only to someone who consciously or unconsciously has a mind bounded by the "Frame" of the Tradition which was set in motion by Aristotle and ensconced through the centuries of the Alexandrian greenhouse -- is literally true for Plato and, at once, is Plato's final choreograph for how the two parts of the Poem inter-penetrate each other. Listen:

Parmenides speaking: *If we were to summarize with one expression, "the one; if it is not, then nothing is," we would be speaking correctly, no?*

Aristotle speaking: *Without any doubt.*

Parmenides speaking: *Let us, then, also say: "As it appears, the one, whether it is or is not, the one and the others both with respect to themselves and with respect to each other in every possible way both are and are not and both appear and do not appear,*

Aristotle speaking: ***ALETESTATA!***

[166c,1-7]

*****

The journey into and of truth MUST INCLUDE the journey into appearing; appearing which MUST achieve the genuine appearing-of-being and indeed "is," in this sense, as well. The deceitful character of appearing -- and travelling through all its vicissitudes -- is part and parcel of the journey into and of truth. And as we shall later on [in the Goddess' transition to the Way of mortal Appearing/Opinion <278-279>] this journey into and of truth, which entails BOTH ways as intrinsic to itself, will keep our Youth from being outstripped by those who ONLY taste the fruit of Appearing/Opinion and, by implication, all those who, foolishly, ONLY taste the fruit of the Way of truth:

The ordering of all these appearings which I convey to you will insure that the [limited scope] of merely mortal learning [gnome] will not outstrip you.

[279. I have amended the spirit of the translation.]

Finally, let us note that the Goddess, via her "daimon" (no?), reigns in the ever-swirling Way of Appearing/Opinion just as much as She reigns in the Way of Truth:

The narrower rings were filled with unmixed fire, those next to them with night, and after them rushes their share of flame; and in the midst of them is her **Daimon** *who steers all; for she it is that begins all the works of hateful birth and begetting, sending female to mix with male and male in turn to mix with female.*

[page 283; translation ever so slightly amended]

hey.

hey-i). We now come to those statements in the Poem of Parmenides which have a profound double effect on Plato's *choreographing* of this Poem. These are statements which -- and to use time-worn labels for OUR heuristic purpose which neither Parmenides nor Plato would have used -- maintain in effect that any epistemology must be at once ontology as the condition for it to epistemology at all and, as well, any ontology must be at once epistemology as the condition for it to be ontology at all.

My suggestion is that, while on the "second voyage" to Syracuse, Plato discovered these and other statements in the Poem *and awakened to their significance for his own Form-theory.* Such awakening led his radical revision of Form-theory away from being merely "paradigms in nature." This emergence away from *that* true but simplistically incomplete accounting of Form theory is executed by Plato through, primarily, *Sophist* and *Parmenides* <along with some finessing, late in life, in *Philebus*>. At the same time Plato *awakened to the possibility of, at once, using his revised Form-theory as the vehicle by which he could allow for the Poem of Parmenides to say all that it was to have said.* And it is only in this context that one can make sense of the "whole-parts" difficulty as the vehicle of entrance into the a final orchestration of Form-theory and, at once, the vehicle of entrance to the project of allowing the Poem of Parmenides to say all that it was to have said through Plato's ***choreographing*** of what was indicated by the surviving (yes, even then) parts of the Great Poem. So let us examine these pregnant gems of Father Parmenides which so radically affected Plato. Plato would mid-wife them to their proper expression.

hey-ii). The phrases and statements are cryptic, allusive and difficult to translate. They all, one way or another speak of an indelible and inextricable togetherness of thinking and being. There is no one without the other. They are the same even as they remain different. [[Warning: there are two major ways in which these phrases and statements can be radically misconstrued. One manner is the Hegelian take on these phrases and thoughts. The other manner -- so very different from Hegel but just as misrepresentative if not moreso -- is the Heideggerian take on these phrases and thoughts. Burn your books by Hegel and Heidegger if you would understand Parmenides.]]

to gar auto noein estin te kai einai

the same: thinking as well as being

[269; translation slightly amended]

*****

khr<u>e</u> to legein to noein t'eon emmenai

that which can be spoken and thought needs must be

[270]

*****

ou gar aneu tou eontos, en <u>o</u> pephatesmenon estin,
enuresis to noein

for you will not find thought without what is,
in relation to which it is uttered.

[277]

hey-iii). As we attempt to return to a "parmenideanized" Plato we must come to understand that the Platonic teachings of the "parmenideanized" Plato not only "translate" those cryptic statements to the field being tilled by Plato. More than that they allow Plato himself, relatively late in his life, to have become and to be Plato at all.

So, we begin in the first place with something not taken directly from the Poem but rather a Platonic phrasing from the ending of *Theaetetus* the dialogue which first introduced us to the scene of *Parmenides*. [[Cf. the encomium of Parmenides in *Theaetetus* which includes an allusion to the very scene of the dialogue *Parmenides* at 183e,3--184b,2.]] What we have here is that "most beautiful" [209e,7-8] proffered definition of knowledge from the climax of *Theaetetus* which reprises a major, albeit subtle, leit-motif of the dialogue concerning the birthing of "episteme" from "**gnonai**" and its various linguistic derivatives.

gnonai ----- te diaphoroteta

[*Theaetetus*, 209e,7-8]

It is true that a technicality in this accounting [[this whole accounting itself presented as the **third** possibility of a **golden dream** <<<I have bold-faced these two markers of the playful/esoteric in Plato>>]] of three final attempts to define "episteme.," It is the formulation of this technical circularity ((a merely semantical technicality which, in another context would point to the ***pregnantizing*** role of **gnonai** relative to the birthing of "episteme")) which allows *Theaetetus* to remain true to its aporetic and vectorizing (i.e., to *Sophist* and *Parmenides*) function and which presents this formulation as a technicality which allows the dialogue to remain aporetic. Thus by virtue a mere ***orchestrated-for-this-purpose*** technicality, this "most beautiful" accounting of episteme" is disallowed from being endorsed as the true accounting of "episteme." Yet a careful reading of *Theaetetus* reveals the theme and fundamental teaching of *Theaetetus*: the never-completed nor complete-able emergence-from and return-to on the part of "episteme" relative to "**gnonai**" <and its various linguistic derivatives>. This constitutes the sustained and fundamental theme of *Theaetetus*, a theme well delineated and analyzed in detail and great length all throughout **DSG**. The reader is referred to that book.

Secondly, we have this profound, pregnant teaching of the visitor/stranger from Elea in *Sophist*:

Strnager/Visitor: It appears that the nature of the different is all cut up into little bits, as is the case with knowledge [episteme].

Theaetetus: How so?

Stranger/Visitor: Knowledge [**gignomenon**] *as with the other* [i.e., the “thaterous” at 257c,8], *is indeed one, but each delineated part of it is an idea* [idian] *with a name peculiar to itself. That is the reason why there are said to be many arts and kinds of knowledge* [epistemai].

Theaetetus: Yes, of course.

Stranger/Visitor: And the same obtains by nature for the shares of the different [thaterou] *as well even though the different is a single being* [[[“ouses.” Forms of “ousia” are used in *Sophist* and *Parmenides* as Form-terms <<often displacing the usage of “eidos” and “idea>>.” Linguistic variations of “ousia,” as with Forms themselves, are likewise often used in these dialogues to designate participants in a Form by virtue of the fact that in sharing in a Form they take on the structure of the Form. The reader is referred to the heading “The Platonic Manner of Privileging “ousia” on pages 234-239 of **DSG**.]]] *in its own right.* [[The reader is also referred to Aristotle’s helpful testimony that Plato counted sensible substances as having ousia-status. *Metaphysics* VII-2;1028b,19-21]]

[257c,8--257d,5]

In the Platonic ***choreographing*** of the shards (then as well as now) of the Poem of Parmenides Forms are stable nodal points of reference for thinking and speaking obtaining in a sea of ***diapherein*** [differENcing/differencings]. Such differeENcing and differencings, obtain both on the side, so to speak, of the mind (or soul, if your prefer) as well as on the side of the real obtaining as differentiated patterns which are then crystallized by our “Forms-AS-thoughts.” And of course such crystallization can become more refined as the person with these “Forms-AS-thoughts” advances in his epistemic/scientific education.

Forms really **DO** obtain as objective even as they fundamentally obtain only as thoughts or as thoughts articulated in speech.* Platonic Forms may be compared to mapping nodal points in the great sea of

diapherein. And maps can always be improved and, indeed, MUST be improved as that sea of ***diapherein*** evolves and/or devolves.

Here the mind wonders to one of the more intriguing observations brought up in the listing of the difficulties. I speak of a proffered solution [132b,9--132c,8] by Socrates to Parmenides's articulation of the **first of two** infinite regress difficulties. The first of these infinite regress difficulties has come to be known in the tradition according to Aristotle's way of referring to it: "The 'Third Man' Difficulty." The expostulation of this first infinite regress difficulty ((In Plato's de facto text it would be have to be referred to as "the Third Great")) which leads to the central thesis of the book you are now reading. Because the manner in which the treatment of this first infinite regress leads to the most important teaching of our dialogue in concert with the need to address this central teaching without interruption, I will, now, insert [with indentation] our treatment of the ***second*** infinite regress difficulty (and its resolution) so that the key matter of this dialogue -- [[which key solution <<i.e. to the "Third Man/Third Great" difficulty>> central to the main thesis of this book comes up de facto posteriorly in the text after this additional infinite regress matter <concerning participation> is adumbrated and then disposed of]] -- can be unfolded in its proper continuity. Thus herewith the treatment of this **second** infinite regress difficulty followed upon immediately by the treatment of the **first** infinite regress difficulty (("the Third Great")) the expostulation of which deals with the secret of *Parmenides* and the central teaching of the book you are now reading. So:

> **. [[*The second infinite regress matter.* There is an other and quite separable, infinite regress argument which is NOT "the third man" infinite regress. As we shall have seen, the solution to the "third man" infinite regress <i.e., to the effect that Forms are thoughts> is to be effected by the "thought"-passage <132b,4--132c,12>, the analysis of which leads to the major point of both *Parmenides* and the book you are now reading.

This **second** "infinite regress" occurs at 132c,13--133a,11. It is an infinite regress with regard to the presumed difficulty of an infinite regress with reference to the participation [say, between a horse and the Form Horse Itself] wherein such participation is understood as a relationship of "Likeness." The presumed difficulty here is that one would have to generate a second form of Likeness to account for the Likeness which obtains as the participation between horse and Horse Itself. But then yet another form of Likeness would have to be brought in to explain both the original Likeness between horse and Horse Itself as well as the Likeness which had been brought in to explain and account for the Likeness which allows the original Likeness between the horse and Horse Itself and as well that Likeness which had been brought in to explain the immediately prior Likeness so generated.

Structurally and, so to speak, mathematically, this second infinite regress difficulty is not at all isomorphic with the first infinite regress difficulty. This second infinite regress is with regard to the ***sharing/participating itself*** which already makes it a different KIND of infinite regress compared to the first (i.e., the matter of "the third Great"). Further, the very fact that it is the participation-as-Likeness itself (i.e., being **neither** the original Form **nor** the original participant) the number of Forms which would need to be generated would, mathematically, double each time since this infinite-regress solution always brings with both a new Form ***and a new participation itself requiring yet another Form for ITS accounting***. In contrast, "the third Great" infinite regress only adds on one Form at a time as an accounting of what preceded it.

Plato address this difficulty in hypothesis two wherein: a). Likeness is shown not to be the primary "stuff" of participation and that the Like Itself <as well as the Unlike Itself> is derivative from a complex set of relationships between Sameness and Difference whereby the Unlike Itself is grounded in the Same Itself and the Like Itself is grounded in the Different Itself. [147b,2--148d,5], **And** b). The interplay of Sameness and Difference is shown to obtain as a kind recursive and self-limiting interplay wherein Sameness of the Form with the participants <referred to as "others" and also as the "not-ones" of a one> turns out to be animated by Difference <<<<<***although not for any stretch of time***; this key stipulation by Plato through his character Parmenides is a reference to the ubiquity of the "eksaiphnes" teaching of the insert hypothesis which will be discussed below. [cf. especially 147c,3--148a,3 for this "stretch of time" business.]]>>>>>. It is precisely this self-limiting interplay of Sameness and Difference which constitutes the dialectical meaning of participation in the post-367 dialogues. As mentioned before, "Likeness" itself is derivative from that interplay. Form and participant are in fact Like each other (and, just a forcefully, Unlike each other) ***incidentally***. Again, the participation itself comes from the self-limiting interplay of Sameness and Difference with "Likeness" and "Unlikeness" alike being derivative from that interplay.]]]

We now return to that first infinite regress difficulty which, in its treatment by Plato, is countered by way of an amazing contention which is, at once, the major point of *Paremenides* and, at once, the major point of the book you are now reading. The proffered solution by Socrates is to treat Forms as "thoughts" [132b,4--9]. In so doing he proffers, in effect, the very persuasive suggestion that this conceptual move [i.e., Forms as thoughts] vacates the need for the "third Great." And as you know it is the introduction of this "third Great" in the formulation of the difficulty which inaugurates the infinite regress, just adumbrated in the text [132a,1--132b,2]. This very pregnant hypothesis that Forms are thoughts (functioning initially as a way out of the dilemma of the first infinite regress) turns out to be the great breakthrough of this whole dialogue. But the treatment of Forms as thoughts appears, superficially, not to have been vindicated. This apparent lack of vindication will be addressed just below. For now it is sufficient that a short-but-incisive case has been made by this young man named "Socrates" to the effect that if Forms are indeed entities "***which properly occurs only in our** souls.*" [132b,5-7; translation slightly amended from the one in *Cooper*; emphasis is mine] ***Then "the Third Great" objection VANISHES and stands in no need of adjudication.*** Remember this. Retain it in your mind as we go through this.

Curiously-but-insightfully Plato's Parmenides does not counter with the obvious observation that doing such would only generate a parallel infinite regress in the mind the solution to which would be the generating of a parallel infinite regress procession of thoughts for thoughts which would lead to absurdity and triviality. For the real issue is that, qua thought, a Form is different in kind from that which participates in it. Two things different in Kind -- Form and participant -- having the same structural character and same name even as they remain **identifiably** different in Kind. Thus this "second-Great" [i.e., the Form "Great"] of this first alleged infinite regress is not a kind of Great commensurate with the participant which is what it is by participating in this "second Great" ***since this "second Great"*** [i.e., the Form] ***is a thought obtaining quite differently*** [and identifiably so] ***in the soul/(mind) whereas the "first Great"*** [i.e., thing (e.g., a big horse; a big house; etc.) ***obtains outside the soul/ (mind) even as the two "Greats" share the same structure, character, and name***. Thus a "third Great" is not at all necessary to explain the "Greateity" of the two Greats (i.e. the original participant and the Form by which the participant is what it is) since the two "Greats" in question obtain in identifiably different manners.* The "third Great" (as well as a putative fourth, fifth, etc.) is superfluous since the second Great supplies sufficient accounting for the first Great yet, being **different in kind** from the first Great, does not constitute the kind of "second" whose status would require a third Great as the accounting for the two. Thus a *different-in-Kind* second "Great" <i.e., "Great" as thought"> is brought in to account for the original "Great." The series therefore stops and there was no infinite regress to begin with.

> [[Here we would do well to keep in mind the "solution" to that second infinite regress which explicitly deals with the nature of "participation." In the texts cited from hypothesis # 2 [i.e., 147b,2--148d,5 and 147c,3--148a,3] that the very "Likeness" obtaining between Form and participant is grounded in Difference. In the same vein Plato is equally insistent upon maintain that there equally obtains an relationship of Unlikeness between Form and participant which is grounded in Sameness. Thus it is Difference which sustains the Likeness between the two. Participation *itself* is a ***differentiating*** process. Likewise it can be noted that the Form and participant share the same structure, character, and name by virtue of an Unlikeness which is grounded in the Same.]]

But please note. While hypothesis # 2 (i.e., of the eight-plus-one) will have adequately dispensed with this second infinite regress dilemma (and Plato knows this solution even as he expounds the difficulty) Plato, here in this presentation of the first infinite regress dilemma, does have his character Parmenides counter with a variable which is over and above the solutions to **both** of the two infinite regress difficulties. I speak here of the factor brought up by Plato's character "Parmenides" concerning the endemic **referentiality** of thoughts which introduces the key point of this whole mini-pericope. Surfacely these remarks by Parmenides have been taken by some to mean that with this factor of referentiality the infinite regress is re-instated. But listen carefully with your third ear as these matters are carefully and subtly articulated by Plato and you shall hear something quite different. You will hear the "keystone" which holds together Plato's nuanced Form-theory post-367. It is an amazing edifice.

{Socrates speaking}: *On the other hand, Parmenides, each one of these Forms* [***eidon***] *are may be thoughts* [**noema**] *and properly obtains only in souls* [*psukhais*]. *In this way each one of them might be a one* ***without*** *entailing the difficulties of which we have just spoken.*
{Parmenides speaking}: *Are each one of these thoughts* [**noematon**] *a one, but* [at the same time] *a thought* [**noema**] *of nothing?*
S: *No. That's impossible.*
P: *But, rather, of something?*
S: *Yes.*
P. Of something which is, or of something which is not?
S. Of something which is.
P. Is it not, some one thing which the thought [**noema**] *thinks obtaining over each and all* [[covered by that thought]], *being* [ousan] *some one* [mian] *idea* [idean]*?*
S. *Yes.*
P. *Is not* ***this****, then* <<i.e., what the alleged Form-as-thought **is referring to** rather than this alleged Form-as-thought>> *the Form* [eidos], ***itself*** [i.e., what the alleged Form-as-thought **is referring to** rather than this alleged Form-as-thought] *which, being construed* [**nooumenon**] *as a one always remaining itself through all* [[the entities covered by that alleged Form-as-thought]]?
S. *That must be the case*!

[132b,4--132c,1-8. A Mcginleyized amalgamation of the translations in the Loeb and in Cooper.]

This is a most extraordinary passage. On the one hand there is no direct objection raised at all against the proposition to the effect ***FORMS REALLY ARE THOUGHTS.*** [[Indeed, this notion that

Forms-as-thoughts obtain "in souls <<*en psukhais*>>" {and thus not reducible to "paradigms fixed in nature} squares with Aristotle's own testimony concerning Plato at *De Anima* III-4,3-6, a text which we shall unpack below]]. The very terminology being used here [*mian idean*; *eidos*; being <*ousan*>; *a one* <***hen***> *being maintained throughout* ***is the very vocabulary which Plato uses when he speaks of Forms***] is maintained throughout, here referring to the alleged Forms-as-thoughts, there referring to what this alleged Forms-as-thoughts refer to. This **knot <<**Forms being presented as thoughts obtaining in the soul {mind} on the one hand and, on the other hand the "ones" outside of soul/mind which are the referents of these Forms-as-thoughts>> is nothing less than the spectacular secret of Plato's accounting of the Forms post-367. **These alleged Forms-as-thoughts are indeed Forms and, at once, are the very condition** for any objectivity and any science of being precisely in their **intrinsic** character of **referentiality**. This dyadic structure -- in the soul <mind> **and** as such (i.e., being thoughts in the soul <mind> which only obtain by referring to what these Forms-as-thoughts refer to outside of the soul<mind>) -- is the key by which even the most obtuse passages of the eight-plus-one hypotheses are rendered as both intelligible and necessary. Again, all of this is to be parsed out below. Yet it must be pointed out that our passage is immediately followed by a deflective side-issue, appearing as an objection to the Forms-as-thoughts which brings us back to the infinite regress matters which both precede and succeed this most fundamental of all Platonic teachings. What point is Plato making through the proffering by Young Socrates of the contention that Forms are thoughts in the soul <mind> combined with the deflective objection to this assertion? We shall see. Let us turn to this deflective objection orchestrated by Plato. Listen and note the opening phrase: ***Ti de de̲***: "And here's another thing" or as the Gill Ryan translation puts it: "And what about this?".

P. *And here's another thing. Given your claim that the others* {talla; participants in a Form} *participate in* [their respective] *Forms* [**eido̲n**; i.e. these alleged Forms-as-thoughts in their referentiality to the one in question which is being referred to] , *wouldn't you also* *have to opine* [**doksei**] *that anything and everything at all (which is referred to) are composed of thoughts* [**noemato**] *with the consequence that all things are thinking* [**kai panta noein**] *or, that being thoughts* [**noemata**] *they are not thinking* [**anoeta**]*?*

Plato orchestrates a quick dismissal by our Young Socrates of this deflective side-issue:

S: ***That*** *contention, Parmenides, has no standing at all.* [[I.e., Both prongs are vehemently rejected by our Young Socrates as ***ridiculous***. As it will have turned out, he was correct with respect to the first prong but blind to the fertility of the second prong.]]

{Amalgamation of the translations contained for this passage [132b,4--132d,2] from the Loeb, from the translation in *Cooper*, and from McGinley's mind.}

This quick dismissal is given no elaboration by Plato through any of the participants in the dialogue. As we shall see below the ridiculousness of this last inference ((which, had it been accepted seriously would reinstated the conundrum of the very infinite regress which the hypothesis of Forms-as-thoughts was introduced to avoid)) is taken as not worthy of further consideration. But we shall address this matter below.

The question involved here is whether the hypothesis that Forms are in fact thoughts in the soul <mind> would lead to yet another kind of infinite regress (((i.e., things-which-are-thoughts <i.e., these referents of these Form-as-thoughts would themselves, by the argumentation, be thoughts since they share in these Forms-as-thoughts which, by the same argumentation, would be things-which-are-thoughts, thinking of their referents which in turn would then be thinking of the referents of what they are thinking about, etc., etc.>))). The series would, according to the argumentation, go on and on ad infinitum. The travesty (according to this argumentation which does not realize that the Forms-as-thoughts and their referents ***are different in kind***).

Yet these alleged Forms-as-thoughts constituted the proffered attempt in the first place by Young Socrates as a way of **avoiding** an infinite regress. Surfacely, the Forms-as-thoughts possibility is turning out, it would appear, a "solution" to this first infinite regress difficulty only by throwing the argument into an even more insidious and absurd infinite regress.

Plato orchestrates the scene such that Parmenides is presented as offering a counter to the Socratic suggestion <<a suggestion in the service of maintaining that construing Forms-as-thoughts would avoid "the third Great" infinite regress>> to the effect that the referents of these Forms-as-thoughts would render these referents themselves as thoughts with the consequence that either all things are thinking or that these referents which must be themselves thoughts <by virtue of participating in these Forms-as-thoughts> are thoughts which do not think. This clever two-pronged move in the chess tournament -- ***but only apparently and surfacely*** -- would indeed avoid the infinite regress, but only with what presents itself as a two-pronged absurdity. However, as we shall see, Plato has playfully inserted, **AS** the second prong of this alleged double absurdity, the true answer to this difficulty (and, a fortiori, the key to the central contention of *Parmenides* <and as well, the main contention of the book you are now reading>) precisely as an ONLY-apparent absurdity: ***specifically through this true-and-only-appaerntly-contradictory formulation*** **"thoughts which do not think."**

Our Young Socrates all too quickly affirms BOTH prongs of the alleged absurdity without recognizing (as we shall see below) the startling fertility of the second prong ("thoughts which do not think"). As the text continues, what we find is a Young Socrates presented as one who -- without being aware of what he is in fact doing -- avoids the major issue put before him. Without a peep of counter-argumentation, this apparent and only suggestive case against Forms-as-thoughts* is orchestrated by Plato, implicitly, to be so persuasive that our Young Socrates is then presented as scurrying away to with a new ((((new to the dialogue but old in Plato's intellectual development)))) model of how Forms are to be construed. Our Young Socrates is presented as taking refuge in a meaning of "Forms" which was operative in the pre-367 presentations of Forms: "paradigms fixed in nature." [132d,2-3]

> *. [[Let us continue to keep the alternatives proffered to Socrates by Parmenides clear in our minds: a). that the things which are referenced by these alleged Forms-as-thoughts must, because they are participating in Forms-as-thoughts themselves be thinking (thus perpetuating rather than solving the infinite regress which the hypothesis of Forms-as-thoughts had been brought in to avoid); **OR**, b). that these things which are referenced by these Forms-as-thoughts are indeed "thoughts which do not think." This second alternative would indeed preempt the need for an infinite regress, but only by leaving us with what, at first blush, appears to be an absurdity. Even so, the very phrasing of this unexamined proffered absurdity (((i.e., "thoughts which are unthinking" which seems on the face of it to be absurd from the perspective of things which obtain at all only by virtue of participating in thoughts <i.e. the original Forms-as-thoughts>))) will have turned out to be **the hidden solution not only to the alleged infinite regress difficulty** ***but also and more importantly the key for ascertaining the character of what it would even mean to speak of Forms-as-thoughts at all***. Patience.]]

In so doing -- scurrying away from his own proffered hypothesis that Forms are thoughts -- Socrates misses the opportunity to resiliate the hint given by Plato (in the persona of Parmenides) himself in his ***merely apparent*** refutation of the thesis that Forms are thoughts. Doubtlessly this only suggestive objection to the hypothesis <<i.e.,

to the effect that Forms are thoughts>> would be the occasion to resiliate just what it would mean (and, more importantly NOT mean) to maintain that Forms are thoughts. And in fact the actual resiliation of this hypothesis (to the effect that Forms are thoughts) comes to be exposed through the eight-plus-one hypotheses.

The merely apparent suggestion that there is a difficulty at all with the contention that Forms are thoughts turns out to be quite easily dismissed by our somewhat impetuous Young Socrates who has much to learn about philosophical subtlety. Plato is always coaching the reader to become a participant in the argumentation. Plato presumes that the astute reader will almost immediately understand.

So, dear cherished reader, consider:

Do thoughts EVER think? You already know the answer and certainly Plato knew the obvious retort to this suggestion and knew that you would know it: **"Of course not!"** Plato puts it on the reader to surmise that our Young Socrates was all too quick in retreating from the contention that Forms are thoughts. Consider. You think. He thinks; She thinks; They think; Gods think*; God thinks.* But do thoughts ever think? I think not. Thus there is no need to even worry about a kind of infinite regress entailing a thought for a thought for a thought ad infinitum. Further, this obvious observations that thoughts themselves do not think renders the second supposed absurdity -- thoughts which are not thinking -- as trivially-but-necessarily true. The farcicality of the two options leading to an infinite regress or to what is in fact a redundancy leaves the hypothesis that Forms are thoughts **ABSOLUTELY UNREFUTED**. The proffered suggestion <<i.e., that there would be another kind of infinite regress, or an absurdity, in maintaining that Forms are thoughts which is implicitly accepted by our young Socrates, fails (as Plato well understood)>> by not taking into consideration that Forms as thoughts ***are different in kind*** from their participants even though their very character is made to be seen for what they are by virtue of participating in these different-in-kind entities. Thus the things referenced by these Forms-as-thoughts are indeed ***different***

in kind from the Forms-as-thoughts in which they participate. They have their structure and knowability from these Forms-as-thoughts even though these things are not themselves thoughts. And, as we have just seen "thoughts" themselves do not think which means that there is no real problem in designating these Forms-as-thoughts as "Forms which do not think."

> *. [["Gods think." I take this to be the case if the "Gods" in question are portrayed as having human traits and characteristics having super-human powers. The Homeric "Gods" qualify. Whether or not there are such Gods is not clear although belief in such Gods was common in popular Greek/ Athenian circles. Plato appears -- in *Euthyphro* and elsewhere -- NOT to have believed in these kinds of divinities. It seems to me that Plato in point of fact probably only allowed, in the final analysis, in a single "God"/Divinity as seems to be indirectly indicated in Letter XIII at 363b,1-7. In any case whether Plato allowed for a plurality of divinities or allowed for only Divinity itself, such Divinity/Divinities seem(s) not to entail personality. Further, Divinity may very well obtain for Plato and have nothing to do with the principles and causes of reality. If Plato did think that Divinity was related to such principles and causes at all presumably it would be Divinity-as-Nous. But please understand: a). Nous for Plato does not entail personality; and b). Nous is indeed, for Plato, a causal factor in and of the make-up of 'the real' but obtains as a causal factor in a complex dynamic brought to its finishing touches in the very last writings of his life <<which includes the very late in life revision and expansion of the dialogue which ended up with the sub-title *Concerning the Good*>>. This second (i.e., the "b" claim) is the major subject matter of both **DSG** and of the book you are now reading.
>
> Aristotle is even more overt than Plato is maintaining that "God" and or "Gods" do NOT have human characteristics. They function as an intricate network of final causes which

by virtue of what they are as secondary prime movers and as Prime Mover. They are instantiated as NOUS and cause motion by way of attraction and NOT by any kind of efficient causality. All of this is made clear in Chapters Seven, Eight, and Nine of *Metaphysics XII.*

Paradoxically, however, Aristotle's ultimate formulation of the highest expression of Nous as divinity is really the first philosophical expression of some whisper of something like consciousness in Divinity (a notion which seems foreign to Plato). This outcome follows by virtue of his subjecting his accounting of Nous to his own conceptual and explanatory paradigm <<one quite foreign to Plato, by the way>>. I speak, of course, of his invention of the "Act/Potency" paradigm which forms the basis of his ultimate meaning of "God" as pure, SIMPLE, "entelecheia." All of this is made clear in the three Chapters of *Metaphysics-XII* to which I have just alluded. There is as well, famously, a reprisal by Aristotle of this notion of Divinity in Chapter Seven of *Nichomachean Ethics-X.*

As we shall see below, this "whisper of something like consciousness" in Divinity will be (several centuries after the death of the Stagirite) elided with the speculations of the Fathers of the Church. The net result of such cross-breeding will be notions of Divinity in which "God" is construed as overtly being conscious and overtly endowed with personality ((and, in the special case of Christianity, three personalities)). This wrong-headed development in the history of Western Philosophy still carries weight today and obscures so many issues. Of all the sorry outcomes of this Alexandrian cross-breeding the very worst is that this development functions as a mostly-unconscious-of-itself filter by which "Plato" is "understood." Certainly this sad and sorry developments radically skews the breakthrough which Plato accomplished with his notion of Forms-as-thoughts. We shall be further addressing these matters.]]

Let us return now to this breakthrough hypothesis untrammeled by this sad and sorry filter which keeps most, even today, thoroughly ignorant of Plato's teachings even when they are reading Plato's teachings. I speak of the Platonic contention that Forms are best understood as thoughts.

***** ***** *****

Yes, yes, yes. I see what you are now surmising. But do not, please, bring Kant into this equation. The very "Frame" of thinking orchestrated by our man from Konigsburg is one which -- despite its surface appearances -- is incapable of expressing what Plato is putting forth. Our man from Konigsburg is thoroughly entrenched in that Aristotelian/Alexandrian/Porphyrean Frame which I have adumbrated in this book and have analyzed in detail in **DSG**. Our man from Konigsburg offers a perspectival overturning of a Tradition which nevertheless stays well-ensconced within the Tradition. Much like the real and actual "Copernican Revolution" it accomplished what was little more than a minor change in optics. ((((e.g. Consider the conceptual naivete involved in "the fixed orbits of the stars" which characterized the overall optics of Astronomy up through the time of Kant.)))) But the post 367 Plato was neither in nor of that Aristotelian/Alexandrian/Porphyryan Tradition at all. To see his revision of Form-theory post-367 through any perspective from that Tradition falsifies what Plato was accomplishing post-367 Form-theory. This will be better unpacked below. But as a first approximation we may say that the very objectivity of things is totally dependent on Forms-as-thoughts in the soul <mind>. Ontology is ontology only on the condition that it is at once epistemology. Epistemology is epistemology only on the condition that it is ontology. There are some readings of Quantum Theory which point accurately in this direction. On the other hand there is a plethora of readings of Quantum Theory which stay within the very Frame which these readings of Quantum theory think they are overturning. Accordingly, using the language of any version of Quantum Theory is unlikely to be helpful. We shall return to these matters in the "excursus" section below. For now let us return to Plato's own turf.

*****

Are there false thoughts? But of course. And these false thoughts are not thinking either. Getting our thoughts right is the grand goal of Form theory. That happens when and as:

> *Only when all of these things -- names, accountings, and visual and other perceptions -- have been rubbed against one another and tested, pupil and teacher asking and answering questions in good will and without envy -- only then when wisdom and mind are at the very extremity of human effort, will there burst out that fire in the one who uses every effort of which mankind is capable.*

[Letter Seven, 344b,4--10. Amalgamation of the translation contained in the Loeb and in *Cooper*.]

This is Plato's crisp, accurate, and economical answer to these difficulties. For us -- living as we do after the Frame has radically blurred our ability to see and understand the post 367 Plato -- there will be much excavating which we must accomplish as a prerequisite for even beginning to see the world of Plato accurately. The nexus which started with Aristotle, includes Plotinus, and is filtered through Porphyry/Boethius keeps us in a cave. Shadows on the wall from the fire of the Frame.

At this point the astute-but-traditional reader wants to shout out that our young Socrates is immediately presented -- (i.e., right after Parmenides' apparent objection that the referentiality of Forms leads to the, as it will have turned out, equally absurd conclusions *that all things are thinking, or, that being thoughts they are not thinking?* <132c,8-12>) -- as offering the model of Forms which is so treasured in the Tradition and, truth be told, is a model which ***does*** quite accurately describe Form-theory as it comes forth in the pre-367 dialogues. For in this passage our "Socrates" is predictably presented as speaking of Forms in the "safe" manner, namely the pre-367 accounting which presents Forms as being "like paradigms set in nature" [*h̲osper paradeigmata hestanai en te̲ phusei*]. Fine.

This is the safe answer treasured by the Tradition and, indeed, as stipulated just above, such probably was Plato's meaning of Forms pre-367. In any case, you will find no endorsement in *Parmenides* itself of this "paradigms-fixed-in-nature" meaning for Forms, either directly or, indirectly ((an indirect endorsement being what was the case with the hypothesis of "Forms as thoughts")). All that follows from this retreat by the youth-called-Socrates is the immediate <albeit faulty> realization that such a meaning for Forms would appear to generate an infinite regress even more foreboding than the infinite regress which, allegedly, would follow if Forms were understood as thoughts. But please note: A Form which is a thought really is different in kind from something outside the mind which is what it is by participating in it. ((In this case, the thought adjusts to the thing but the thing does not become the thought. Superficially such sounds vaguely Aristotelian which, if you think it through means that Aristotle, in *De Anima*, sounds vaguely Platonic. But the chasm between the two obtains even here. For the treatment of the radical way in which the Platonic model of thinking and grasping differs from the model of intellection offered by Aristotle in *De Anima* one must consult pages 355-361 of **DSG**.))

{{{{{{{**Excursus on "Forms-as-Thoughts."**

Excursus A.

Plato was in fact the last of the "Pre-Socratics" even as he was the first of the "Post-Socratics." What I mean to say here is that Plato himself entered into the lists between and among the various cosmologies ((-- here from the various Ionians; there from the various Italians; and yes, even from the Pre-Socratic from Athens, Anaxagoras, who made "Nous" the Divine Cosmic Principle --)) as a contestant, so to speak, in that Pre-Socratic enterprise. Yes. Of course. *EVERYTHING* in Plato is filtered through the lens of Plato's presentation of "Socrates" as midwific "Sophist of Noble lineage" ((i.e., the destroyer of the false conceit of wisdom; cf. *Sophist* 229c,1--231e,6)) which subjects the "pre-Socratic" Plato-as-Cosmologist to the severe "Post-Socratic" discipline of Dialectic

<<<which only *starts* with that soul-cleansing of the false conceit of wisdom graduating, then, to Platonic Dialectic Proper brought about and instantiated in excruciating detail through *Sophist* and *Parmenides* and filtered through some final gentle modifications in *Philebus*>>>.

This Pre-Socratic Cosmologist coming forth as Post-Socratic Dialectician becomes (after 367), **on the one hand**, the frenzied thinker who , oscillating between the two, is in love with both the gentle Muse from Sicily and the stricter Muse from Ionia ((*Sophist* 242d,10--243e,2)). All the while, in this vein our Pre-Socratic Cosmologist coming forth as a post-Socratic Dialectician is struggling to generate a model of thinking which is neither monistic nor dualistic with regard to ultimate causal principles. Our Pre-Socratic who practices Post-Socratic Dialectic ***struggles mightily*** to find a conceptual paradigm which unifyingly instantiates *both Muses at once*. **On the other hand**, -- even has he severely castigates Anaxagoras' failure to honor Nous -- he maintains a reverence for the contention that something like Nous or Phronesis somehow or other governs the Cosmos. It was the Dramatist Aeschylus who, dramatically rather than philosophically, introduced this notion in Greek culture through his *Oresteia* <usually perceived as a trilogy but which appears to have been in fact a tetralogy>. And, in fact, it will be the Dramatist in Aristocles who will engineer the coming together of those two "hands," the one hand of which contains a dilemma to be engaged while the other hand of which engages Plato's always troubled relationship to his own piety.

In the very beginning of this book we have examined the critical attitude which Plato takes towards Anaxagoras' treatment of Nous as the Divine. But the larger issue is the internal struggle in Plato's psyche, post 367, as how to honor Nous and, more troubling, how to, so to speak, *situate* the honor to be accorded to Nous without violating the kind of thinking which struggles with that tension, in history and in Plato's mind, between the gentle Muse from Sicily and the stricter Muse of Ionia. I have addressed this last issue in **DSG** hereby beg the reader's indulgence to cite directly from that work:

c). **Timaeus** ***as the Handmaiden to the Final Project which culminates in*** **"Concerning the Good"** ***<i.e., the subtitle of*** **Symposium>**

---- *I do not give Plato a free pass. There is a struggle within Plato's own psyche which had been alive when he first started to engage questions about the character of Divinity in dialogues such as* Theages *and* Alcibiades II. *In this struggle Plato is never in denial of the factor entailing a positive, active, and intractable unruliness in the make-up of things. This is to his credit. But a certain strain of piety in his make-up seems always to have tempted him to separate Divinity itself from this unruly and intractable character in the make-up of things. Plato imported this internal struggle of his into his great planned project inaugurated after the second voyage to Syracuse. The struggle was that struggle -- alluded to above -- between his attraction here to follow the stricter Muse from Ionia and his attraction there to follow the the "easy-going" Muse from Sicily in his overall project of explaining how and in what sense the unruly obtains in reality as a whole. My contention (here and elsewhere) has been that the planned trilogy of trilogies which was to have constituted the great planned project ((the first of these,* Sophist/Statesman/Parmenides <aka "Philosopher">, *all introduced by* Theaeatetus, *being the only one completed)) sided with the stricter Muse from Ionia on this matter.*

With Timaeus *we get a glorification of what Plato counted as Divinity:* Nous. *Untrammeled. But now -- in apparent unity with the "easy-going" Muse from Sicily -- we have* Anangke *functioning as the "errant cause" which spawns unruliness in the make-up of things. The causal principles are now named* Nous/Anangke *rather than the* Philia/Eris<*aka*Neikos> *of Empedocles. Fine. But in the final analysis, this apparent bow to that "easy-going" Muse from Sicily really ends up anyway,* ***through Plato's own post-Timaeic machinations****, in the service of the stricter Muse from Ionia. Our guide for this contention is, as always,* Philebus. Nous *is the causal element obtaining in the fourth class (the class of combination) of the four ((but really* *five <cf. the remarks at 23d>)).* Anangke *is, in effect, the causal element of the fifth class (i.e., the class of separation* [diakrisin] *as referred to at 23d) of those four-but-really-five kinds/classes of* Philebus). *But it is in the* **third** *class/kind -- the class of mixture -- wherein the drama is played out. Precisely by virtue of the* ***elcitative*** *feature of the third class the drama reverts back to the stricter Muse from Ionia, with the fourth and fifth kinds playing causal-but-ancillary roles in the Drama. And who is the star of this all-important third class/kind (aka, the "between" celebrated by Diotima)? Here its Form-name is "One"; there its name is "Good." Its secret name is "truth." All of these matters will be explicated in and through percopes sixteen through twenty.*

[**DSG**; pages 220/221. Phrasing slightly amended. With reference to the planned "grand project" and how it was re-constituted by Plato after the news arrived from Syracuse in 354/353, the reader is referred to Pericope Three of **DSG**.]

Excursus B.

I shiver to mention even the possibility. But it must be done. The journey of Philosophy from Aristotle, through the Alexandrian greenhouse, and to Porphyry/Boethius, requires this effort as the condition for the possibility of understanding Platonic Form-theory. ***OUR*** journey is, at root, one of **catharsis** whereby we free ourselves from that radically misrepresentative filter so as to read and understand Platonic Form-theory for the first time.

That grandchild which emerges almost a millennium later in Philosophy requires and even greater catharsis. There is no darker region of the Cave than the unfolding of Philosophy from Descartes up through the Nazi and Sartre. The whole thing is an egregious wasteland. There are only two exceptions. The first is Schelling and he shall have his encomium later on in this book. The other is Husserl.

Husserl does not even come close to Schelling when it comes to the thinking which is no longer circumscribed by the "Frame." Even so our convert to Lutheranism has much to offer to this "khora" wherein epistemology is epistemology only on the condition that it is, at once, ontology and wherein ontology is ontology only on the condition that it is, at once, epistemology.

Read and study *Logical Investigations*. Read and study *Cartesian Meditations*. You will start to get a feel for what it would mean that Subjectivity is the condition for the possibility of Objectivity. NO! I am not speaking of Kant. Still less am I speaking of Hegel. In the final analysis I am not even speaking of Husserl himself. But he alone in the swampy morass of Modernity points the way to what Platonic Form- theory was to have been before the "Frame" ruined everything. But Husserl only points the way out of this miasmatic atmosphere of Modern Philosophy; he does not, however, take us out of the morass.

This will have to suffice.

Excursus C.

We start with the man who first gave thematic identity to the "Frame" (which would become operative in its full sense from the time of Porphyry/Boethius) and, as well that same one who made it a theme for Philosophy. He posed the issue (i.e., the *Was Heisst Denken?* issue) accurately. Please note that the issue for thinking is not exactly the "Frame" itself although the Tradition thinks of the issue for thinking through the "Frame" without, however, noticing this "Frame" as the transformative filter of the issue for thinking which sabotages the ability to think through the issue for thinking. So, "the Frame" is neither the question of the issue nor the issue itself. Heidegger's long and carefully thought through attempt to answer the question of the issue was, in effect, the original awakening to the all-permeating presence of the Frame. Aristotle's long and carefully thought-through attempt to adjudicate <<i.e., the Aristotelian attempted adjudication of the issue was in fact the creation of "the

Frame">> the question of the issue for thinking was filtered through that Alexandrian greenhouse for several centuries and, in the process, this Aristotelian Frame became decorated with the baubles of "Neo-Platonism" {whose real name was "Neo-Plotineanism"}. But the heartbeat of the now-birthed Frame was Aristotle's own heartbeat.

Let us listen then, with awe, to Aristotle's awe-full formulation of the issue keeping in mind that the formulation of the issue is not the same as the Aristotelian attempt at adjudicating the issue. The formulation of the issue is worthy of a Plato and helps us to understand just what Plato meant by a "Form." Aristotle's attempted adjudication of this awe-full formulation is but the birthing of that sad and sorry Frame which, even today, ((((((and yes, that attempted adjudication still blocks access to that remarkable Question *What E-vokes Thinking?* even though the one daring enough to have articulated that question of questions remained, in the final analysis, in the gravitational field of the Frame)))))) keeps us blind to Plato even as we read Plato and which blindness, a fortiori, stymies and stunts the *E-Voking* of what calls to be thought. Even so, Aristotle's formulation by which he posed the issue is breathtaking and stands as the greatest achievement of this man whose response to Plato ended up blocking access to Plato. Let these great words stand as his proper monument:

Indeed, the question raised long ago and which is still raised and always will be raised and remains always baffling to us [aporoumenon]:
ti to on [what is being?]
is precisely the question:
tis he̲ ousia [what is the (to-)beingness of being?]
… …
and so too for us; our chief and primary and virtually our only concern is to investigate that which is in this sense.

[*Metaphysics VII-1; 128b,3-9*. The incompatible manners by which Aristotle and Plato privileged ousia is usually not even recognized by most of those who claim to have authority with regard to the understanding of these two thinkers. This radical incompatibility of Plato and Aristotle concerning the privileging of ousia is discussed with excruciatingly painful detail on pages 234--261 of **DSG**]

Doubtlessly this passage from the Stagirite inspired Heidegger. Unfortunately, in revolutionizing the very terrain of how the question of "Being" is to be posed so to as to be worthy of Heidegger's greatest question (i.e., *Was Heisst Denken?*), Heidegger -- more unconsciously than consciously -- absorbed the Aristotelian Frame even while he, Heidegger, claimed to be undertaking an "overcoming" and "getting-over" the Frame. *Heidegger contra Heidegger*. In doing this he destined his readings of Plato -- and particularly Form-theory in Plato -- to be circumscribed by Aristotle's manner of Presenting Plato's Form theory. He never engaged Plato on Plato's terms.

Even so it was Heiedegger who, in his writings post 1927, opened up a fertile meditation on the originary ***difference*** which gives rise [["es gibt"]] to both Sein and Seinende. Likewise he was able to point to a non-Hegelian manner in which "thinking" and "being" are the same. Yet in all of this fertility he ended up bypassing the only factor which would have allowed him to have escaped the very "Frame" which he thought he was "overcoming"<*Ueberwindung*> and "getting over"<*Verwindung*>. Only an encounter of Plato's post-367 Form-theory free of the gravitational pull of the Frame would allow for such an "overcoming" and "getting over." Heidegger never set himself free.

He ended up with a remarkably naïve meaning of Form-theory post-367. Indeed Heidegger rendered Platonic Form-theory as paradigmatic of "the Frame." Yes indeed, there was that postumously-to-be-published set of lectures <circa 1923> on Plato's post-367 *Sophist*. And that is precisely the point. You, dear cherished reader, should read those lectures and you will understand the fatal flaw of Martin Heidegger. For in those lectures he, de facto and without conscious intention, uncritically and axiomatically takes Aristotle's presentations of Platonic Form theory as valid accounts of Platonic Form theory. Heidegger never got the rid of that Aristotelian prism when he, Heidegger, attempted, all too naively, to present the alleged significance for the Tradition of Platonic Form-theory. He never quite got over his reading of Brentano. The Nazi connection had its tawdriness about it and his failure after the War to own up publically to that chapter in his life turned such tawdriness into something of a moral monstrosity. But that is not the true tragedy of Heidegger. He was too much of a minor player in the obscene horror of those years when it's all said and done. The real tragedy of Heidegger is to be found in the "highest" and most rarefied dimensions of his thinking. He remained "Framed" despite himself. He never encountered Plato.

Das Sein des Seiende.

Heidegger and the to-beING of being.

Aristotle and *what is ousia?*

*****

In the final analysis, Heidegger in his dissertation, did not really thematically deal with the central issue of Duns Scotus which was *Haecceitas*. Heidegger overlooks, in that dissertation, the grand and all important centrality of Scotus' great achievement. Rather, as he rummages through the unorthodox character of this Soctian neologism (in concert with his rummaging through some of other unorthodox wordings of the "Subtle Doctor") Heidegger, in such rummaging, ends up drafting these Scotian gems <<which have a genesis and telos for Scotus quote separate from Heidegger's appropriation of those gems>> into the service of his already developing musing on what he will later designate as the "existentialia' of human subjectivity (for which he would coin a new usage of the common German word "Dasein" in his landmark production of 1927).

When it came to the essential features of Aristotle's *Metaphysics* Heidegger simply did not understand just how radically and innovatingly Scotus had understood the Stagirite. The writings of Scotus which centered around his radical notion of "the principle of individuation" constitute, so to speak, a "retrieval" of Aristotle's ontology which honors Aristotle by making explicit what actually animated Aristotle in his later years. Aristotle's shortcoming here resided precisely in his failure to explicitly emphasize and thematize sufficiently the significance of his own neo-logism, "*entelecheia*" (for which "energeia" is but a pale synonym) and the conceptual usage of that term in his later productions [[i.e., Books Seven, Eight and Nine of *Metaphysics*; all throughout *De Anima*; and his treatment of Pleasure <and Divine Pleasure> in Chapters Four and Seven of *Nichomachean Ethics*]]. The Tradition (and in this respect Heidegger again remains caught in the nets of the Tradition), by and large, does not fully appreciate Aristotle's radicality (and still less, the radicality and precision of the Scotian reading of the Stagirite).

In contrast, Heidegger came to the reading of Aristotle by way of the more traditional Brentano who himself leaned on Aquinas ((the "esse" theme thereof which Scotus had explicitly found to be of little use when it came to understanding just how radical Aristotle's ontology had become in his later writings and how this radicality was predicated on Aristotle's treatment of the primary meaning of ousia)). [[All of these matters in these three paragraphs are given their labored and detailed explication in my 1996 publication entitled *Haecceitas* and to which the astute reader is referred. There is, as already indicated just above, a shorter treatment on some of these matters on pages 231--264 of **DSG**.]]

In any case, the net result was that in the grand formulation <cited above> of what Aristotle counted as the issue for thinking ((his adjudication of which was the birthing of the "Frame")) in effect became the prism-for and prison-in which Heidegger inaugurated what he thought was the re-invention of "ontology" by thematizing the "to-beING of being." But this Herculean effort never emerged from, so to speak, that strong gravitational field (i.e., the "Frame" articulated by Aristotle) from which ((some of his great insights notwithstanding)) he never escaped. He was indeed "framed" in the final analysis despite himself. *Heidegger contra Heidegger.*

Further, the following must be emphasized. Whether we are speaking of the radical greatness of Aristotle himself and the even more radical greatness of the "Subtle Doctor"; or whether we speak of the somewhat mediocre Aquinas and Brentano; in ALL of these cases one remains in the "Frame." Heidegger showed us that there was a "Frame" but he himself was more unconsciously enmeshed in it than he ever realized. Further, the greatest tragedy of all is -- whether one speaks of Heidegger prior to OR POSTERIOR TO the so-called "kehre"> -- Heidegger ends up with a reading of Plato which is itself a product of the Frame. The post-367 Plato remains utterly unread ((even as one reads it with great and labored linguistic acuity <<which is exactly what happened in Heidegger's review of *Sophist* in those posthumously published lecture notes from the relatively early twenties>>)).

Do you begin to appreciate what has happened in all of this? Heidegger spilled his fertile sperm in and on the bathtub rather than bringing it to the fair lady. Heidegger was trapped by his reading -- a rather good one -- of Aristotle and how he, Aristotle, "framed" the problem of Metaphysics. Aristotle, in the final analysis is the quintessential thinker (along with his more subtle colleague, John Duns Scotus who was also carefully studied by Heidegger) of what I have termed the "Metaphysics of Identity," Yes. Heidegger intuitively knew the dead-end which comes with the "Metaphysics of Identity." But he never freed himself from the gravitational force ((i.e., the Metaphysics of Identity)) of those early years (starting with Brentano). Instead of spilling his fertile seed on and in the bathtub he should have sought out the fair lady. Something spectacularly wonderful would have been the result. But he never recognized her since he only read her as a proto-Aristotelian.

The sadness of it all. Martin had so assiduously understood what Aristotle was up to. But he did not know how to break from him and follow the longing and fertile siren song of "Difference." Rather he ensconces his meditation on "Difference" in what came to be the trap of the "Frame": *the to-beING of being; Das Sein des Senende*. Fertile seed, of its nature, dies when it is deposited on dry ground. He stayed bonded with Aristotle. Even when he was "called" by "the issue/matter for thinking" we was sabotaged. The only home he ever had was Aristotelian. However it was not Aristotle who was "calling" him. It was the fair lady. But he never recognized her for what she was. He, in the final analysis, understood her as a weaker and somewhat simplistic version of the "metaphysician of Identity" who was trumped by the allegedly more astute Aristotle. The "difference"-imbued lady of her post-367 writings was calling him. But he never heard the call. The result was just a disaster on so many levels. Heidegger sabotaged himself. He could not sustain his own encounter with Difference and he sputtered into superficial poetry of the worst kind. Holderlin was wronged by Heidegger's usage of him. The fair lady was there all the while but he never even noticed. Heidegger ended up solipsistic.

*****

Excursus D.

And here's another thing. Given your claim that the others {talla; participants in a Form} *participate in* [their respective] *Forms* [**ei-do̱n**; i.e. these alleged Forms-as-thoughts in their referentiality to the one in question which is being referred to] *, wouldn't you also have to opine* [**doksei**] *that anything and everything at all (which is referred to) are composed of thoughts* [**noe̱mato̱**] *with the consequence that all things are thinking* [**kai panta noein**] *or, that being thoughts* [**noe̱mata**] *they are not thinking* [**anoe̱ta**]*?*

[*Parmenides* 132c,9-12]

Do you hear what I hear? Aristotle was probably just on the cusp of taking off his philosophical training wheels when these words were written. More than likely Plato composed his final draft of *Parmenides* right before or just after that third voyage to Syracuse in

361. It is clear from the context that Plato -- a wordsmith of the first order -- was playing around with these linguistic oddities. Even more certain is the dismissal of this last wrinkle by "Parmenides" to suggest that just maybe there would be further possibilities of infinite regress. The magister ludi of the whole show (aka Aristocles) would want to pre-empt and render ridiculous any suggestion that this breakthrough hypothesis ((to the effect that Forms are thoughts in the soul/(mind))) would still somehow entail an infinite regress. Little did he understand that his playful usage of these verbal articulations of these ***noein***-oriented words and their correlative absurdities would function as a seed in the brain of the one whom Plato himself would call "the mind of the Academy" which, over time, would (to mix metaphors a bit) marinate into that Act/Potency Metaphysics which would be developed in the Lyceum.

The sad irony of all this. For most certainly -- a case I made repeatedly all throughout **DSG** -- It was Aristotle's Act/Potency paradigm which became a prism through which Aristotle and the Tradition misrepresent Platonic Form-theory. Based on this fundamental misrepresentation Aristotle and the Tradition chortlingly dismiss Platonic Form-theory as a category mistake when in fact this misrepresentation (unbeknownst to these fools) de facto represents history's greatest, sustained, and most egregious exercise of *petitio principia.*

*****

For Plato Divine Nous -- analogous in this sense to Heraclitus' Polemos; or Anaxamines' Pneuma; or Anaximander's Apeiron*; or the Water Divinity of Thales -- is a cosmic principle. In his usage of it there is no hint of "subjectivity"; or consciousness; and still less of personhood/personality.

> *.[[Please understand. Anaximander, Plato, and Aristotle all use "Apeiron," although in significantly different manners. And yes, in the case of Plato and certainly in the case of Aristotle, a certain non-Divinity meaning of "infinite" can

be validly used as a translation for "Apeiron." Fine. No problem so far.

But the following needs to be emphasized. NONE of the usages of these three thinkers -- including here the usage of "Apeiron" as Divine Cosmic principle by Anaximander -- have anything in common with that invention <<the ineffable One>> used by Plotinus in *Enneads*. Plotinus breathed the air of that Alexandrian greenhouse wherein Jewish and Christian tropes for radical Divine transcendency were a commonplace. To be sure, Plotinus was neither Jewish nor Christian. But, more by osmosis than by conscious intention, Plotinus created a philosophical notion of Divinity which froze in for the subsequent Tradition a meaning of Divinity in which God/One/Divinity is said to be ineffable and beyond human comprehension. In this manner he set in motion a radical transcendency model of God/Divinity which became axiomatic for Jewish, Christian, and, eventually, Islamic Theology and which model is still operative today in those theologies.

That too is fine. But it would be the height of ignorance and bad-faith to read the Plotinian paradigm of Divinity into Anaxagoras' usage of the same word. There is no evidence, however, that Plotinus himself did this. On the other hand there is no limit to the amount of evidence available by which Plotinus quite consciously read this meaning of Apeiron into the "One" of hypothesis # one in *Parmenides** and into Plato's treatment of the "Good" in the 'Sun Passage" by which Book Six of *Republic* comes to a close. This two-fold travesty of falsification is reviewed in excruciating detail in pericope Twelve of **DSG** to which the astute reader is now referred.

*.[This Plotinian reading of the Platonic "One" of *Parmenides* sometimes is pushed to ludicrous claims. I am thinking in particular of some Plotinianesque

readings of "apeiron" at 137d,10 of hypothesis one. Any fair reading of this word in context would indicate "un-limited" -- without any theological significance AT ALL -- as the natural plain sense of Plato's argument here.]

Finally, the following must be noted as well. The famous Qabbalistic usage of *Ayn-Sof* ((and, for that matter, Maimonides' usage of the same phrase)) is simply the Hebraicization of the Plotinian *A-peiron.* I have argued extensively and persuasively in my Jewish productions from 2005 onward that Qabbalah owes much more to Plotinus (and in several major ways including "emanation theory") than it does to Jewish sources.]]

Continuing on.

In contrast Aristotle's ruminations on Divine Nous as those ruminations are filtered through the Act/Potency paradigm [[Confer *Metaphysics XII,* Chapters Seven and Nine; and *Nichomachean Ethics X,* Chapter Seven]] inaugurates a transformation in the very meaning and character of Nous as a Cosmic principle. Compared to what will happen with the tortured formulations of the Fathers of the Church, Aristotle's indirect hints of a whisper of consciousness <and thus something like "subjectivity"> in the Divine "Nous" are modest indeed. Yet such was used ((albeit in an exponentially graduated manner)) by the Fathers of the Church as they addressed the various conundra of the claim that Jesus -- a human being after all which is graphically testified to by the sheer facticity of his brutal crucifixion -- somehow was also God. Still, the seeds of this wrong-headed model of a Subjectivity-laden First-Cause emerged in fact from "the mind of the Academy." What Aristotle would accuse Plato of ((i.e., *A small mistake in the beginning*, etc. etc.)) in his misrepresentative presentation of Form-theory is, in point of fact, just what Aristotle is guilty of. The ironies in the History of Philosophy are both immense and painful.

*****

So. First there is Aristotle's invention of something like a whisper of consciousness in Divinity. Notice how simple this "something like consciousness in Divinity" actually is. God is not thinking of the cosmos and certainly not thinking of the thoughts, emotions, shadows and what-not of the human soul. Aristotle expressly makes this clear. Rather, God thinks Itself and only Itself. Notice I did not say that God thinks of Itself. No. It is direct and immediate. It is, for Aristotle, the quintessential perfection of his Act/Potency ontology/metaphysics. Even so, the hint of what later on will be called "Subjectivity" has entered into the West's perception of Divinity.

People with a better grounding in the history of Philosophy could better map out how this hint was exponentialized into a huge cauldron whose final outcome was the Hegelian Metaphysics of Subjectivity. ((We will put aside -- for now -- the special case of Schelling in this sorry denouement.)) But I am not the one to trace that journey.

Suffice it to say that it was the Early Fathers of the Church who set in motion this exponentialization of Divine Subjectivity. As was mentioned just above, it emerged from the conundra involved with Jesus being God and yet being other than God which led the early articulators of what this novel phenomenon (i.e. second century Christianity) ((which presumed to call itself the carrier of God's revelation)) to borrow from the Stagirite two features of his thinking which, together, would set the mold for this notion of Subjectivity in Divinity. First the hint of something like consciousness in God from his (the Stagirite's) conceit of the perfection of his Act/Potency Metaphysics. Second the theoretical scaffolding for the language of "persona" which theoretical scaffolding is predicated on and emergent from the Aristotelian radicalization of the principle of individuation. Although Aristotle did not thematize the language of hypostasization, these early Fathers took hold of Aristotle's mature meditation (especially in the last Chapter of *Metaphysics-VII* and all of *Metaphysics-IX*) on the radically individuating character of “form” for Aristotle which was his primary meaning of ousia. This non-Hebraic Greek gift (i.e., hypostasis; <<“I fear the Greeks even and especially when they bring gifts”>>) is what permitted them, conceptually, to address the conundra of what was being said about that man, Yeshu. One knows the outcome: God as triune with each “person” having a real and discernable identity in and of the identity of this single God. It is the Aristotelian thinking of the “this in the this” graduated to Theology.

With this energizing conceit, the West came to “Subjectize” Divinity and it was not long after this development that Boethius could take it as a commonplace that “Forms” were really eternal thoughts in the mind of God. And this Subjectivizing of Divinity did not have to include a triune notion of God. Whether it was Avicenna or Maimonides this orgy of Divine Subjectivity was able to be sustained without the triunity of God characteristic of Christianity. ((((I am mandated to speak of this Boethian “thoughts in the Mind of God” trope so as to pre-empt from the get-go any notion whatsoever that this Boethian conceit has anything to do with the major proposition of this book to the effect that for the post-367 Plato “Forms-are-thoughts.” This theme will be pursued below.))))

*****

(((((SIDE NOTE ON “SUBJECTITAT” OF HEIDEGGER. Please do not get these “Subjectivity” matters confused with Heidegger’s “post-Kehre” meditations on “Subjectism” <”Subjectitat”>. These meditations are not without some peripheral interest especially with regard to the question of Technology as it becomes, in effect, the very character of the world. And yes; his usage of Plato’s “eidos” as a way of accounting for the origins of this world-dominating destiny -- taken, basically from Aristotle’s presentation of Form-theory (although not with the agendum of Technology becoming a world destiny) -- gets a lot of play in some circles. But as always Heidegger’s thinking suffers radically and without redemption from the true “turn” in his career. To be sure the meaning of technology as world destiny is worthy of serious attention. But to predicate such a meditation <<i.e., his musing on "Subjectism" and Technology>> on a false reading of the only thinker who truly could guide mankind away from its overt and/or implied ((and with or without a hegemonic God concept)) domesticating <and thus destructive> agendum is, in effect, a sabotaging of the whole undertaking.

Heidegger's "turn" of overweening proportions occurred far earlier in his career than most Heideggerian aficionados understand. It was rather early in his career and it predates *Sein und Zeit*. I speak again of those posthumously published lectures from the relatively early twenties on Plato's *Sophist*. From beginning to end he reads that rich and subtle dialogue through the eyeglasses of Aristotle and, in effect, treats Plato as a, so to speak, "pre-Aristotelian" who said some perceptive things but who, in Heidegger's eyes, pales in significance to Aristotle himself.)))))

*****

And then there is the question of the holy and of Divinity.

But "what is the case" is far grander and glorious than the world of Aristotle and the correlative world of Heidegger's reading of Divinity.

Divinity. I speak of the true Divinity. Divinity is all that is the case.

Divinity is that which can only be encountered through a painful ***wresting***. ((It's not that Divinity/God is unknowable and beyond our comprehension as per Plotinus and the whole so-called "mystical" tropes which he birthed. Not that at all. Rather the wresting involved is on of wresting our own thoughts from the inhibiting factor of **DENIAL**.))

Divinity is struggle. It is unity-in-duality, duality-in-unity. It is other-ING--OTHER-ing. Its energy may be called Eros or its energy may be called "the yeitser ha-ra." In both rubrics there is a recursive dynamic by which the outcome -- an outcome of the Divinity as partially-yet-essentially obtaining in and of the human situation -- leads the whole struggle-imbued ((from start through finish)) drama by which God becomes what God was to have become.

This drama is God and it is never --((neither could it be nor should it be)) -- free of struggle. **Polemos**. The drama is played out primarily in, by, and through the human situation irrespective of the immensity of the universe. Perhaps it would take that degree of permutations to allow for our kind of species to have been brought about, strutting on our mirrored stage for about a dozen thousands of years (which are now coming to a close). Are there thoughts in the mind of God? Of course. Billions upon billions. Trillions upon trillions. The mind of God is in and through mankind <see below>. It's a real circus, but a circus whose distilling and self-recursive discipline is just this:

> *Only when all of these things -- names, accountings, and visual and other perceptions -- have been rubbed against one another and tested, pupil and teacher asking and answering questions in good will and without envy -- only then when wisdom and mind are at the very extremity of human effort, will there burst out that fire in the one who uses every effort of which mankind is capable.*

[Letter Seven, 344b,4--10. Amalgamation of the translation contained in the Loeb and in *Cooper*.]

***** ***** *****

There is nothing "pantheistic" or, to use what some people think is a more subtle jargon, "panentheistic" about the Divinity of which I speak. Further it is not a Dualism of first principles nor is it anything like "Monotheism" Yes. Each of these terms can be construed as having a smidgeon of truth. But so long as these labels are understood ontotheologically they become not only trite, but also function as an interference which keeps us alienated from Divinity/

God. The Revelation of God is trashed when such conceits are used in the articulation of Divinity. As they are presently understood they are all blasphemies.

Divinity is all that is the case. The not-Divinity **OF** Divinity is itself a mode OF Divinity in its self-recursive manner of obtaining at all. The emergence of non-Divinity from Divinity is, so to speak, a major development in the history of Divinity. This is a "history" which at root has no sequential timing about it except in so far as it evolves and becomes headed towards consciousness. The timing of time which is sequential then comes into being. "Prior" to time -- sequential time being a phenomenon which requires something like experience/primitive-consciousness to be at all -- there is no temporal sequencing.

In this "pre-history" of Divinity it comes to pass that Divinity, of itself and without a plan or telos, instantiates itself as non-Divinity which "non-Divinity" remains a mode of Divinity by way of its self-recursive manner of obtaining at all. This is the raw emergence of the most primitive kind of experience which -- of itself without plan or telos -- comes eventually to be instantiated as consciousness. ((The life force -- call it Eros or call it the "yeitser ha-ra" -- does this of its own accord without plan or telos.)) Consciousness itself comes -- of itself and without plan or telos -- eventually to reach a critical mass such that Divinity instantiates itself as non-Divinity which, as we have seen, remains a mode OF Divinity. Scripturally, this is the story recorded in Chapters Two and Three of *Genesis*.

Divinity, qua Divinity, remains without consciousness. Divinity as non-Divinity (which non-Divinity never ceases to be OF (both senses of the genitive) Divinity initiates the painfully slow process of birthing consciousness. This is the passage from the pre-history of Divinity to the history of Divinity. This is, so to speak, the time of Play in the history of Divinity.

The critical moment in the early history of Divinity as non-Divinity is recorded in Chapter Six of *Genesis*. It is a two-fold moment:

And Hashem regretted that He had made man on the earth, ***and it grieved him in His heart****. And Hashem said: "I will destroy man whom I have created from the face of the earth. Both man and beast; and creeping things; and the birds of the air. For I regret that I have made them.*

[*Genesis* 6:6-7. As an aside it can be noted that what God <<i.e. the complex "the not-God OF God">> gave mankind dominion over loses its flavor if mankind <<the "not-God," which does the thinking of the complex>> is not to be around. God (the whole complex) loses the only variable which allows for the greater overall environment of the "not-God of God. Entry 8-6 ((using traditional language)) of *Genesis Rabbah* effectively muses on the key role which mankind (the essential of the "not-God" Od God) plays in there being a developed Divine economy. The reader is referred to this entry in *Genesis Rabbah.*]

and then:

Noakh found favor/grace in the eyes of Hashem.

[[*Genesis* 6:8. The syntax of this key statement is odd. Read it literally and it seems almost like a mirror-like statement between Noakh <<who, as the story unfolds, represents mankind which is the "not-God" OF God>> and Hashem. Most scholars take refuge in that domesticating answer which simply reduces the odd syntax to a domesticative idiomatic expression. But *Genesis Rabbah* <confer entry 29-4> plays around with the strangeness of this statement for the statement, in fact, seems to say that Noakh is doing the finding with the "eyes of God" being the recipient. Rather than take refuge in the avoidance of this strangeness <i.e., taking refuge in the "idiomatic expression" option> *Genesis Rabbah* teases out of the strangeness of the statement a deep intimacy between God/Hashem and Noakh, the representative of mankind <<"the not-God" portion of the complex "the not-God OF God." This intimacy is given expression by Rabbi Yochanan <who very name connects God with "favor/grace">. Listen:

Imagine a man walking on a road [life's journey] *when he saw someone to whom he "attached" himself. To what extent? Until he was knit to Him in love.*

[*Genesis Rabbah* 29-4; Soncino, page 231. Translation slightly amended; interpolation is mine.]
]]

This two-fold articulation by Divinity marks a critical change in and of Divinity. And indeed, even though we have been using the expression already, it is precisely at this point that Divinity can be called "God" and, as well, not-Divinity which is OF Divinity can now be called "the not-God OF God." Recall that the consciousness of "God" resides not in God but in the not-God OF God. *That* is intimacy indeed.

Just as Divinity comes to be differentiated from itself by instantiating itself as not-Divinity, so too the critical moment in this history of Divinity is when, by virtue of developments in the "not-Divinity" of Divinity, Divinity brings about the emergence of itself as "God." In turn the non-Divinity OF Divinity now becomes the "not-God" of God rendering God as differentiated from "not-God." It is only at this point that one can speak of lesser divinities. They are not Homeric Gods. But Thales ((and pre-historic Animism as well)) is quite correct in stating: *The world is full of Gods!*

Have you yet noticed? Whether the rubric is "Divinity" or "God" the heartbeat of all (("all that is the case")) is and always was differentiation better expressed as **diapherein**.

This huge crossroads in Divinity by which Divinity came to be "God" set in motion a process which would come to include ***tsimtsum*** <<<in the Nachmanian sense and certainly free of the Plotinian tropes which surround Nachman's radicalization of this phenomenon first articulated by Isaac Luria (whose treatment of ***tsimtsum*** was also not free of those Plotinian tropes)>>>. This crisis-like development (which will have entailed ***tsimtsum*** <as we shall see

in Heading C> set in motion two derivative-but-decisive developments in the history of the "not-God OF God": a). The emergent need to narrow the Rainbow Covenant with mankind to the Abrahamic Covenant by which Israel -- the people, the nation, the religion -- became the surrogate for mankind <<i.e., mankind being, far and away, the portion of the "not-God" OF God which is the most essential>>; and, b). The beginning of the Formal history of God and the workings of God in, through, and AS the "not-God OF God." This beginning of the Formal history of God and the workings of God is recorded in Chapter One of *Genesis* (stopping however at the end of the first sentence of verse 31 <a verse which is properly expressed in Rabbi Meir's written version of Chumash {Confer *Genesis Rabbah*, entry 9-5 and my commentary on Meir's written version of this verse on pages 8-10 of *The God with Moral Thought*}>). In other words the episodes in the history of Divinity *becoming* God in Chapters Six through Nine of *Genesis* ((((a series which is better adumbrated through the "J" document rather than through the "E" document which intersperses it but which interspersement reflects the inner differentiation (**diapherein**) in Divinity as it becomes God)))) actually constitute the ending of the "pre-history" of Divinity/God allowing the Formal History of God and the not-God OF God to be initiated in Chapter One. The sequence of things created in verses 3 through 27 is the story of how Divinity/God incrementally instantiates itself as not-Divinity/not-God in an ever expansive experientiality which culminates in the height of consciousness in verse 27. Thus what happened in the age of Noakh posteriorly is the condition for the possibility of the prior sequencing of proto-humans and humans which led to that decisive critical turning point. The child is father to the man.

All things, in the final analysis, end up in and AS the future-pluperfect. Those sayings of Schelling from his 1814/1815 posthumous *Ages of the World* and his1809 Freedom book are most germane here:

> --- *Therefore the whole thing can only be considered as having happened in a flash, since it it conceived as smething which happened without really having happened.* [page 192]

and:

In creation there is the greatest harmony, and nothing is so separate and sequent as we must represent it; but the subsequent cooperates in what precedes it and everything happens at the same time in one magic stroke. [page 65]

*****

The theology of this whole business has been covered and covered well in my book, *The Secret Diary of Ben Zoma*. The most important parts of the book -- dispersed throughout the entire book -- are my treatments of *The Forbidden Relations*; *The Work of Creation*; and *The Work of the Chariot*. Pages 277--374 are particularly intense in this regard. As far as "Eros" or "the yeitser ha-ra" is concerned -- two ways of designating the same -- they i.e., it <two names for the same> constitutes the stuff of "Divinity/God" (and, definitionally, of not-Divinity/not-God **OF GOD**). The discussion of these two names for the stuff of Divinity/God (and Divinity/God as not-Divinity/not-God **OF GOD**) is a major theme of **DSG**. Pages 466-485 of that book are particularly helpful.

It is to be noted that the true *Work of the Chariot* has little to do those famous Chapters from Ezekiel. The imagery from Ezekiel's vision on the banks of the Chebar Canal is, in the final analysis, just window dressing for the "Work of the Chariot" which keeps the uninitiated focused on Ezekiel while the highest dimensions of Revelation are reserved for the cognescendi. They are found, in ascending order, in certain portions of *Isaiah*; *Genesis*; and *Exodus*. The classical Rabbis give an indication of this when they pronounced:

Rava said: "Everything that Ezekiel saw, Isaiah saw. To what is Ezekiel comparable? To a villager who saw the kind. And to what is Isaiah comparable? To the city-dweller who saw the king.

[Bavli commentary on tractate *Hagigah* of the Mishna; Art-Scroll, 13bii. <<<Side issue: The figure in Ezekiel's vision addresses him as "Son-of-Man." To be sure, Yeshu took his inspiration for his own

self-designation from *the Book of Daniel*, especially with reference to Chapter Seven, and NOT from *Ezekiel*. Granted. But the writer of *Daniel*. Was that person trading on *Ezekiel*?>>]

*****

Finally, there will be further resiliations of these matters in the next two Headings of the book you are now reading.

*****

I must interject here with what is, in effect, the heart and soul of Islam. I speak of "yihad" (aka "jihad"). It was the Prophet himself who designated the "greater yihad" as the great spiritual principle for all individuals; for all Muslims; for all Jews especially; and ultimately, for all humans. Yes. Of course. He acknowledged as well the "lesser yihad" which was the military/political "yihad." There is often enough great confusion, bad faith, ignorance, dissembling, and a cancerous disingenuousness concerning this "lesser yihad" spoken of by the Prophet both on the part of Muslims and non-Muslims alike. I choose not to get involved in this intricacy at this time.

Rather I wish to concentrate on the "greater yihad." The great spiritual struggle both of every human being, Muslim and non-Muslim, Jew and Gentile alike, as well as the great spiritual struggle of the human race itself. Being true to the "struggle" will bring great reward for all who are true to this "greater yihad." And it is the very glory of Islam that "the greater yihad" is, I suggest, the very heart of Islamic religion. It is this teaching in particular which raises Islam -- sometimes (even often) despite the sorry and horrible crimes in its history -- to the status of co-partner with "Israel" (i.e., the People; the Nation; the Religion) in leading humanity to the status of deserving the favor ("khein") of Hashem/Allah. I must suspend this discussion at this point. I do send the interested reader to my remarks on this matter (as well as the Scriptural support for this matter in the Chumash) in my various books on Judaism, particularly

The Secret Diary of Ben Zoma. Yet even that masterpiece should be read in concert with **DSG**.

End of Excusus on "Forms as Thoughts.}}}}}}}}

Continuing on.

vav.

vav-i). Platonic Forms obtain in such a way that, as we have seen, the pairings "material/immaterial" or "physical/non-physical" are not so much true or false, but irrelevant. Plato's preferred pairings, "sensible/intelligible"; or "visible/invisible" <for which the pairing "bodied and not-bodied" is subset to and smaller than "visible/invisible"> cannot be accurately parsed out along the axis of "material/ immaterial" <or "physical/non-physical">. And even the preferred (by Plato) distinction between "visible/invisible" is not sufficient as a paradigm for distinguishing between Forms and participants. Yes, all Forms are invisible and, at once the condition for the possibility of intelligibility. But it turns out that participants in a given Form are also and often just as invisible as the invisible Form, participation in which makes the participant real. What I mean by that is that the epistemological/ontological/both-at-once structure of a participant is quite separable from its visibility or perceptibility. More than that, the very character of some classes of **participants** are such that they are not even visible or perceptible. Let us never forget that there are MANY classes of participants (a "like;" a "same;" a "different;" a "one;" a "many;" an "other;" etc., etc., etc.) which are participants in a Form and, ab initio, are not visible/perceptible as such.

For instance there are Forms, as Plato explicitly maintained (as we have seen just above) in Letter VII, for the various "pathe" of the soul. The fear obtaining in John right now about radical financial deficit is a particular fear which, in the Platonic schema, is a fear at all because it participates in "Fear itself." Yes, of course. One can engender visible image of John, the human (who is a human by virtue of participating in the invisible form "Human Itself"). Yes of course one can imagine and visualize John-being-in-fear or images of his Retirement Account statements which are correlated to John's fear. But John's fear has no image proper to itself qua fear. And one could cite innumerable examples the invisibility of states of emotion/pathe̲ which are what they are by virtue of participation in the Form of the emotion/pathe̲ in question.

Likewise the true and real "objectivity" of a Form is not in any way lessened by pointing out that it is something which, for all practical purposes, does and can exist only in a thinking mind. Characters in a novel. Flights of imagination. Santa-Claus. These too are Frms.

And what about clearly visible things in "our experience" which have a more simple relationship as "participants" in their respective Forms? I speak of, say: *hair*, *mud*, *shit*, *fire*, *water*, *a-tree*, *a-pipe*, *a-stone*, *a-fence*, *a-bed*, *a-house*, or *a-ring*???? Yes of course, to use the language of the Tradition, these things surely have "extra-mental" reality. But the Forms for these "extra-mental" realities basically obtain "in" the mind or soul. [[[Recall here the passage from *De Anima* III-4, 429a,26--28 wherein Aristotle maintains that Plato was onto something when he, Plato, maintained that the Forms were in the soul. Cf. as well, precisely on this matter, **DSG** pages 359-360*]]] Their "objectivity" <<or, for that matter, even their eternity in some fundamental sense> >is not thereby lessened in any way, except in models of Form theory generated by Porphyry and taken over by Boethius** (based, by the way, on Aristotle's misrepresentation of Forms as "universals."). The very objectivity of Forms obtains in the mind/soul.* The Forms ARE 'really real" stable nodal pints of identity in that sea of ***diapherein*** [differENcing/differencings] whose natural home is, precisely, in the mind or soul.

*. {{{Let Aristotle himself speak here:

It was a good idea to call the soul 'the place of the Forms'...

[*De Anima III-4* 429a,27-28. Aristotle often enough gives what appears to be reliable information on Plato's teachings which may not have been immediately evident from the writings of Plato. What is maddening -- and ultimately disgusting -- is that in so doing he presents <as he is definitely doing in this passage> this useful information through the prism of a conceptual framework <in this case his Act/Potency metaphysical schema> which has the effect of misrepresenting Plato's teaching even as he conveys information that Plato had a teaching such that, after 367, Forms were understood to be thoughts in their primary meaning rather than "paradigms fixed in nature," a coneit which Plato leaned upon prior to the second voyage to Syracuse.

In point of fact, the Act-Potency framework for this just-cited comment by Aristotle was generated by Aristotle in Book IX of *Metaphysics* as an alternative to Platonic Form-theory. That he uses this frame of reference in ***presenting*** Form-Theory is a breathtakingly egregious begging of the question practiced all too often in Aristotle as I have repeatedly noted and explained in **DSG**. All that having been stipulated, we nonetheless can garner from this short report the implied coalescence and unity for Plato of what the Tradition calls "epistemology" and "ontology;" an account which no longer makes the primary meaning of Forms to be "paradigms fixed in nature." Post 367, Forms are thoughts.] }}}

> **. [As soon as Boethius is referred to a whole tribe of philosophers will start speaking of "Forms-obtaining eternally-in-the-mind--of-God <as eternal exemplars>." Such a conceit -- even if Plato had generated such a notion of Divinity, ***WOULD BE*** <<<emphases indicating that such a notion of Divinity was counter-factual to Plato's notion of Divinity and for that matter Aristotle's, even as it remains true that their (i.e., Plato's and Aristotle's) respective accounts of Nous-as-Divinity are radically non-isomorphic with each other>>> *simply incidental* to Plato and as well -- had he, Aristotle, retained his even post-Academy orientation in Platonic Form-theory (except for artifacts as we have seen) -- *simply incidental* to Aristotle. Granted, the difference between Aristotle and Plato on Divinity are huge, but neither

of them indulged in the kind of God-concept which would lead to the Medieval conceit which emanates from Boethius. Platonic Form-theory was subjected to a slow-but-growing process of marination over the centuries in that Alexandrian greenhouse of currents and counter-currents ((many of which currents and counter-currents had no pedigree in Philosophy although they were grafted onto Philosophy, changing the very character of Philosophy in the process)). Such a process ends up speaking a language which then ends up having nothing to do with Platonic Form-theory. It was this process which brought about conceptual models of Divinity thoroughly different from Plato's model of Divinity. Further, during those centuries Platonic Forms were almost exclusively (and, of course, misrepresentingly) presented in terms of Aristotle's understanding of Forms as "Universals." Anyway you look at it, Plato is no longer discernible through the layers and layers of misrepresentation all set in motion by Aristotle's presentation of Platonic Form-theory and how such was marinated over centuries in that Alexandrian greenhouse.

The point, of course, is this. Any paradigm of thinking which would require that the "objectivity" of Forms can be justified only by placing them in the mind of an ontotheological God is simply not Platonic even and especially if such a God-concept is referred to as "Neo-Platonic."]

vav-ii). Now, with these clarifications on our mind, let us get back to post-367 Platonic Form-Theory free of the various caveats from the Tradition about what -- Plato's actual texts notwithstanding for these people -- Forms must be. There is entrenched in the Tradition a great deal of emotional attachment to a certain way of understanding what Plato really meant by Forms taken form the pre-367 treatment of such in Plato's corpus. This is the comfortable understanding of forms as "paradigms fixed nature" (albeit and tellingly, the how of such is never addressed). This comfortable model of understanding Form theory becomes, then, a way for many of understanding Plato's post-367 presentations of Form-theory. The price these scholars and reader pay -- usually unconsciously -- is a reading of Plato crippled with the blinders of such an emotional attachment.

So let us turn to Plato's own way of referring to Form theory in his later productions. We will start with a teasing remark of his concerning Form-theory from the Dark Middle of *Timaeus*. Then we shall turn to the ***gnonai ten diaphoroteta*** from the *Theaetetus/Sophist/Parmenides nexus*.

vav-iii.) A tease directed at the "Friends of the Forms."

Plato was well aware that Form-theory had been, by his own hand, *radically*, transformed through and by that "second voyage" to Syracuse. Some followers in the Academy clearly resented this. Emotionally they had invested themselves in that "good-old Platonic" manner of presenting the forms as they were put forth in, say, Book V of *Republic*. Plato calls them "Friends of the Forms." He rejects their contentions (which were once his own) but he offers them something of an olive branch of privilege if they are willing to come on board with the post-367 accounting of things. These Friends of the Forms are not so very different from scholars throughout the centuries (including ours) who, by virtue of such emotional investment, put on blinders when they read the way Form-theory comes forth in *Sophist* and *Parmenides*. But then as well as now, if they remain blind and recalcitrant, they must be left behind.

In the dark middle of *Timaeus* Plato generates a suggestion concerning the Forms which is, at once, both a tease to these recalcitrant member of the Academy and at once the essential germ of the revised theory of Forms. Listen:

> *Is there such a thing at all such as Fire "Itself"? Do all these things of which we always say that each of them is something "by Itself" really exist? Or are the things we see, and whatever else we perceive through the body, the only things which possess any reality, such that there is nothing else besides them at all? Is our*

time-worn claim that there is an intelligible Form for each thing nothing but a linguistic expression [logos]*?*

[*Timaeus* 51b,7--51c,7]

Yes. There then follows, as I have pointed often in **DSG**, a **conditional** argument [51c,8--51e,7; reviewed in **DSG** on pages 115-119] whereby the speaker in *Timaeus* affirms as true some version of Form-theory. If the distinction between understanding ("Nous" and its linguistic variations is used) and "true opinion" is valid then Form-theory is valid; if not, not. But its very conditionality points to the radical change *in Plato's own assessment* of Form-theory emergent from the "second voyage." This is not a Plato who rests comfortably with the "paradigms fixed in nature" accounting of Forms. Not at all. Some far more subtle is occurring.

This citation can be best understood when and as it is contextualized in Plato's excursus contained in Letter VII which addresses precisely the somewhat precarious manner by which Forms exist at all. [342a,1--344,10] This is also the passage which calls to mind the procedure practiced and delineated by Plato himself in the eight-plus-one hypotheses of our dialogue:

For in learning about all of these things one must learn, at once, ***both what is false and what is true about all of being [tes holes ousias]*** *through long and earnest labor as I said at the beginning.* [344b,1-4]

In this passage from the Seventh Letter Plato designates the Form itself as the "fifth" (using "Circle Itself" as the paradigm) and four "steps" (so to speak) which by travelling them up AND DOWN and repeatedly <<and "rubbing them one against the other" <344b,4-5>> by which we approach the Form. These four "steps" (so to speak) are: a). the name; b). the accounting of it (i.e. "logos"); c). the perceptible things which comes and goes out of being <<the tcase of a circle what is drawn or erased; or what is generated by a lathe and which may go out of being; <<earlier, at 342b,2 this third is spo-

ken of as "eidolon") d). the grouping of "knowledge" [episteme], thought/mind [nous] and true-judgment [alethes --- doksa]; all of which grouping obtains in the mind or soul and is thus to be distinguished from both the first three and from the Form itself. It is this fourth which is nearest to the fifth in kinship and likeness. [342b,4--342d,2]. For the Form is not itself Knowledge <<<except of course for the Form Knowledge>>>, but rather a thought. But again, without these four (and especially the fourth) the Form escapes us and, in effect, loses its possibility to be at all something known.

Of the four, it seems as though it is the name Itself which Plato is referring to in our cited *Timaeus* passage above (taking "logos" there as "linguistic utterance" rather than as "accounting"). To be sure, Plato, both here in the Seventh Letter as well as in *Cratylus*, reminds us of the instability of names over time. Let this be acknowledged. But in a sense Form-theory does constitute as kind of Platonically idiosyncratic "nominalism." In fact, when we actually speak of any Form we are speaking of the "name" (whatever name, even "name") plus Itself. In one sense this is exactly what a Form is and the tease in *Timaeus* is something more than a tease. The Form itself, while never completely circumscribed by any and/or all of the four, truly is for thinking only by virtue of the four and the least complicated way of referring to what any Form is by and through the name plus "Itself." That IS what a form is: A stable, nameable, nodal point of identity for thinking and speaking obtaining by and through the ever-obtaining/ever-changing sea of ***diapherein*** ("differENcings"). It is now time to explore that sea of ***diapherein***, thereby "getting to know"; "becoming familiar with" [**gnonai**] "the differENcings" [**ten diaphoroteta**].

*****

vav-iv). ***exploring the Sea of DIAPHEREIN with* DSG *as our guide.*** (We now turn to the preparatory grounding of these things accomplished in **DSG**. Some of the citings have been slightly amended.)

vav-iv-a). Comments on *Posterior Analytics II-19*, 100a,6-15.

Aristotle is speaking of a series of developmental processes by which, in animals (including the human animal), raw sensation gives rise to memory and repeated memory gives rise to "empeiria" (experience) which sets the stage for the possibility of intellection. Listen to his words:

Aristotle speaking: ---- just as, when a rout has occurred in battle, if one man halts do does another, and then another, until the original position is restored. The soul is so constituted that it is capable of the same sort of process. [100a,10-15]

So let us acknowledge that an element of "struggle" is, at least metaphorically, allowed for by Aristotle on the path of intellection. But such is still basically receptive. The intelligibility resides in things which, when and as the phantasm is presented to the intellect, is made actually intelligible through abstraction and the "light" of the "nous poietikas." Such "conceiving" is largely mechanical. In contrast, "conception" for Plato is a real birthing of intelligibility requiring many stages by which intellection is achieved. It is the process referred to as ***gnonai ten diaphoretega*** *as complex patterns of developed "differENcings" in the soul/mind resonate and resiliate with patterns of differencings in the macroscopic world and all being mediated in the micro-scopic (i.e. that "Cratylean swirl" which is delineated so carefully in* Theaetetus*) manifold of sensation all in the service of producing pre-epistemic* ***recognizability*** *made possible by such intricate networks of differencings.* ***That*** *is a struggle.*

*****

Again, let Plato be Plato, and Aristotle be Aristotle. But as usual -- and here [PA 106a,6-9] *it is done so swiftly that one could all too quickly pass over its significance -- Aristotle presents a Platonic trope in terms of a trope invented by Aristotle in* Categories.

As usual, Aristotle muddies the waters (thereby telescoping a presentation of a Platonic teaching into an implied critique of a Platonic teaching) in this passage describing ***his own*** <Aristotle's> *"universal" by using* ***Plato's*** *manner of referring to the Forms (i.e., "the one over many"). Doing such is both unfair and tremendously obfuscating. Yet even today it is often and* regularly *presumed that Aristotle was correct in understanding Platonic Forms as "universals" which misrepresentation lead to the unhappy state of affairs that Plato, under this prevailing presumption, never gets read even when he is read.* ***For even when Plato speaks of a Form as it obtains in the soul (or in the mind), it does NOT obtain as a "universal."*** *But one would never guess such from the sophisticated minions (which includes many otherwise astute translators of and commentators on Plato's writings) who are ever-so-certain- that, "really," "after all" such is what Plato* ***MUST*** *HAVE MEANT. An incredibly sad and obscenely misrepresentative story.*

[227]

*****

Only a thinker who explains knowledge of sensible substance through "abstraction" (i.e., Aristotle) would see any strict isomorphism between the pairings "material/immaterial" and/or "physical/non-physical" on the one hand and "sensible/intelligible" on the other hand. Plato is not one of them. For the post-367 Plato there always obtains -- in all perception and all intellection -- a constant and multi-faceted dialectic whereby what comes to be counted as "known" results from a huge pattern of diiferENcings unconsciously (and, to a lesser extent, consciously) perpetrated by the soul (or "mind"; call it what you will<e.g. "the living brain" if you prefer).

As we have been seeing and will be further analyzing, "knowledge" <from Plato's perspective> -- itself always a tricky and non-final proposition -- of tangible beings occurs through what the soul/mind itself ***brings*** *to the content of sensation. Such is not at* *all a Kantian-esque schema of "categories"* [a word SO revelatory of how the "Kantian Revolution" remains circumscribed by the Aristotelian frame] *automatically imposed on the sensory manifold. Not at all. Rather what occurs in the Platonic model (neither Kantian nor Aristotelian) is quite, and literally, "different."*

It is that fertile/tender part of the soul/mind which births, first, patterns of ***recognizability*** [this word being used as a translation for noun derivatives of **gn<u>o</u>nai**]. *Such is always the first step in the journey towards knowledge. Thus not, at first, "epist<u>e</u>m<u>e</u>," but rather a "learning/getting to know"* [**gn<u>o</u>nai**] *the differencings* [**t<u>e</u>n diaphorot<u>e</u>ta**] *It is from this never-finished "learning/ getting to know" which constitutes the from which and to which of anything approximating "epist<u>e</u>m<u>e</u>." What happens here is a* ***birthing*** *rather than an abstracting. It is, in effect, a birthing of intelligibility emergent from an ever-growing, ever-contracting network of differencings. It is by through and AS differentiation that "knowledge" -- and never in a once and for all sense -- is made possible. It is not so much that the soul/mind* ***receives*** *intelligibility from sensible ousia. Rather, the soul/mind births intelligibility by bringing this fertilizing process of and by the soul/mind* ***to*** *the sensory manifold.*

[page 181]

*****

A further remark. The following is not found in Plato nor could it be. But not only do I suggest that it is compatible with the Theaetetan accounting of these things. I also claim something more. Something more which seems to be implied by that accounting, even if it were not Plato's conscious intention.

Evolutionary Biology makes it clear that the organs of perception evolved in, through, and by that subtle interplay between the needs of the individual and the needs of the species (or species-in-transition) of which the individual is an instantiation. These organs of perception are not themselves organs in the service of "truth." They become the organs that they become what they become through adaptation, quite apart from any concern for "truth." And what is my purpose for bring up this truism at this time?

The -- ultimately biological -- process by which the organs of sensation become what they become over evolutionary time is itself a kind of initial (((((--in all species, although in a rather advanced manner in some particular species including the species <<species-in-transition???>> to which we belong))))) process of a **gnonai ten diaphoroteta**. *The emergent organs of perception (which organs eventually entail ever-more-subtle patterns of brain organization) function (already with unicellular organisms) as Hermes-like* **translators** *by which the raw Cratylean swirl <<so carefully delineated in "Theaetetus>>* [aka the sub-atomic world of Quantum theory] *is channeled into patterns of* ***differencings which work.*** *This means channels of* ***differencings*** *which constitute, through these microscopic and neurological patterns of adaptation by which emergent organisms -- and organisms in transition -- successfully adapt to that macroscopic world of that emergent organism.*

Thus the journey toward intelligibility already entails --- long, long, long before homo sapiens sapiens makes its appearance -- the generating of and by those emergent organs in concert with the emergent and correlative patterns of brain organization all of which allow those organs to do what they do: the generating of networks of differencings which itself is a birthing of "proto-knowledge" long before our species makes its appearance.

"Knowledge" emerges from and returns to that fertile portion of the soul/psyche (leave "mind" out of the equation for now since we are including here the workings of species other than humans over thousands upon thousands of years) which sorts through differencings and brings to them its own proto-differENcngs. DifferENcing is the heart of and soul of knowledge and it is a grand affair indeed.

In all of this there is no room for those alleged Forms which are "paradigms set in nature." Only by Plato's OWN "Copernican Revolution" which understands Forms as "thoughts" allows for the requisite condition that "thoughts" -- while always referential -- can, over time, sharpen themselves and come to serve as those ever-more reliable nodal points of stability and objectivity in that all-encompassing "sea of ***diapherein****."*

[pages 181-183]

*****

For Plato [[and always, unless otherwise specified, "Plato" in this book refers to Plato after that "second voyage" to Syracuse]] the key resides in the resonations and Resiliations of the negative. "Episteme" is the (always conditional) product of an inseminating activity which **does truly** *<as opposed to Aristotle's usage of the term in* De Anima III-5> *merit the term "poietikas" whether the thing in question has body ((Plato does not use "matter" or "material" when speaking of the corporeal character of things known)) or is bodiless. Whatever comes into the soul/mind is inseminated, by the soul/mind, with schemas of differentiation which are differENCED by the soul/mind which process varies according to the training and natural ability of those who are doing the knowing. Revelation (a way of speaking of the wresting character of truth as "a-letheia") can never be a once and for all thing and never is simplistic. The resonations and Resiliations of and between the network of* ***difference*** *in and of the thing and the* ***differENcing*** *work of the soul/mind is what constitutes the condition for the emergence of knowledge (qua "episteme") from* **gnonai**. *And through a grand cacophony of such wrestive revelations(made possible by such wrestiveness which is largely unconscious) there emerge many of these inseminative* ***differencings*** *which lead to "conceptions" worthy of being called knowledge (episteme). The return of the midwife motif which constitutes the ending of* Theaetetus [210,b-c] *reminds us that the enterprise of "knowing" is one which is never complete and final.* [358-359]

*****

In contrast to Aristotle, for Plato such intelligizing is a "making/ rendering" kind of intelligizING validly and truly worthy of the adjective "poietikas." For the very "Itself" of any Form obtains as the product of the resonations/Resiliations between the network of differences in the "thing" {{{and such is the case for any "thing" whether it be corporeal ***OR bodiless*** <<Aristotle notwithstanding "separate substances" for Plato are NOT simple at all since they are each a conglomeration of "intercoursings" involving always the play of difference. Indeed these "separate substances" -- and again contrary to Aristotle who insists that such are known through direct intellection -- would even have the possibility of every being known or even recognizable without such intricate workings of differentiation.>> *}}} and the degree of refinement of the differENcing generated by the knower. Of course there is and must be stability in both the knower and the thing. Without such there wouldn't even be the possibility of naming. But we humans go way beyond that. We humans can arrive at something which rises above "opinion/judgment" even as it always remains "opinion/judgment."*

Yes. that last sentence ***does*** *imply that the "knowledge"-status of a true "opinion/judgment" depends on the quality of the "account" addended unto such a true "opinion/judgment." But the source of validation for any such "account" emerges from the network of* ***ten diaporeoteta*** *which is furnished and made possible by the* ***gnonai*** *of our 209e passage from* Theaetetus. ***Gnonai*** *is a "learning" -- a "getting to know" - always subject to further refinement. Certainly this "getting to know" ("become familiar with") these "diaphoroteta" sometimes achieves such a remarkable degree of refinement that it would be wrong to refer to such as merely a "true opinion/judgment." So the word "episteme" is used, and used properly, for such a state. But the "getting to know" never ceases and what is validly referred to as" knowledge" at any given time is subject always to further refinement. Only in certain circumscribed endeavors,* whose foundations are themselves subject to further investigation, *<<<e.g. "Geometry" whose first principles*

<i.e., axioms/assumptions> are not established in the system of Geometry itself>>> is a relative apodicticity achieved. Not because the objects are unknowable. Not that at all. But rather by virtue of the fact the network of "difference" in the thing can be further resiliated by those inseminative differENcings on the part of advanced knowers.

This difference-grounded meaning of "Form" in Plato post-367 is not what the Tradition attributes to Plato. But the Plato who did inaugurate what the Tradition attributes to him (in the relatively early Phaedo*) did not abandon "those" Forms of* Phaedo *and* Republic-V. *Rather, he subsumed "those" Forms into a network far more fertile -- and ultimately far more credible -- than what he had started out with. What he ended up with was a conceiving of Form which effectively shows how the mere simple name of a Form [i.e., "x-Itself"] covers over a* ***dynamism*** *which is remarkably lively and not at all free of change even as it remains stable:*

For Heaven's sake!!!! Are we going to be convinced that it's true that **motion, life, soul,** and **intelligence** are not present in "that which wholly is," and that it neither lives, nor thinks, but stays motionless, solemn, and austere, and lacking mind? [248e,10--249a,2]

[360-361]

vav-iv-b.

Hypothesis five examines the consequences which will follow if "one" is supposed to "not be" [me̲ esti] *with the understanding <<taken from the generic overall schema given at 135d--136d>> of this "one-**which-is**-not" that such is to be taken by itself. "One," taken by itself in hypothesis # 1, turns out to have been basically barren. In contrast, our "one-**which-is**-not," taken by itself is totally fertile. The two faces of "one."*

*It will turn out to be the case that the "one-**which-is**-not" in its fertility can be considered as capable of achieving and losing ousia-status. It is, so to speak, the mother of "difference" (and of the "diaphorot<u>e</u>ta" of* Theaetetus 209e. *"Difference" <the off-spring of our "one-**which-is**-not"> is far and away the "one" [i.e., a "Kind/Genos"; a "Form"' a "Monad" to use the language of* Philebus at 15b*] of those five great kinds which is most critical in the ontological/linguistic edifice generated by Plato through* Sophist/Parmenides.

*When you read through hypothesis five you will notice a sustained and steady oscillating manner in which its beingness [ousia] and non-beingness [m<u>e</u>-ousia] are converted/changed one to the other. Our "one-**which-is**-not" is -- when taken in combination with that same one, taken by itself, of hypothesis # 1< <which hypothesis presumes at the beginning that it "is" only to find out at the end that, as such, **"is" CANNOT be predicated of it*** [141e,14]>> *-- that which renders the one of hypothesis # 1 **to become** fertile. It <our "one-**which-is**-not"> is the great dyadicizing differentiator which allows that same one of hypothesis # 1 to be fertilized and incarnated as the one of hypothesis two, thus allowing it -- the one taken by itself of # 1 but now fertilized (thereby open to "othering" in general and open as well, in effect, to the "others" of hypothesis three) -- to "be" ousia* [142b,6-9] *and to be as well all the ways of being and becoming enumerated in hypothesis two. From the perspective of hypothesis two, our now fertilized one displays that whole network of differentiation which constitutes what "participation" means whether the participating is of and between Form and participants or of and between Forms and other Forms.*

*Accordingly then, our "one-**which-is**-not" is not a principle separate from the one ((((whether the "one" be construed as a grammatical place-holder for ANY form and or is the "one" as some trans-Form status, albeit **NOT** of a Plotinianesque character)))). Rather, "one-**which-is**-not" is the fertilizing-qua-dyadicizing force intrinsic to just what it means to **be** a one at all. So too our "one" of hypothesis # 1 -- insofar as it obtains as one -- as it achieves* *ousia-status (displaying its ousia-status towards the beginning of hypothesis two) through such dyadicization -- effectively becomes that in terms of which all things which are one <<i.e., not only Forms but participants in Forms as well>> achieve a measure of stability allowing for the first step on the journey towards "episteme," namely: **naming**. You recall, I hope, the ending of hypothesis # 1 wherein, the one taken sheerly by itself, is not even an "itself" **and lacks even the name "one."** Listen:*

If we stay true to our argument the one **neither is "one" NOR IS** [at all]! Therefore, no name belongs to it, nor is there any accounting or any knowledge [episteme] of it nor any opinion or perception of it at all. Thus it is not named, nor spoken of, opined about, **nor is it even RECOGNIZED [gignosketai**; i.e., not only not known, *but not even recognized*]. And in the whole world it there is no sense of it at all. [142a,6-7]

*****

*This "one-**which-is**-not," as it fertilizes the other face of itself (understood as the one-without-even-a-name) brings to this other face of the one differentiation which allows our one to be named at all. It is this first primitive differentiation which brings the first whisper of stability: a **named** one. And the process grows. Our "one-**which-is**-not" of hypothesis five practically shouts out FROM ITS VERY BEGINNING **recognizability*** [**gnonai** derivatives] *and being known* ("episteme" derivatives) **AS ITS VERY CHARACTER**. *Our "one-**which-is**-not" is the, so to speak, the "is-not-ing" function at the heart of all differentiation. And it is differentiation which is the mother and nurse of all **gnonai**. This "is-not-ing" reveals itself AS the "**gnonai**-ing" function.* [[Confer, right now, 160c,--160d,10]] *And it is precisely this which our "one-**which-is**-not" brings to our impoverished one of hypothesis # 1 (thereby becoming the fertilized one of hypothesis two).*

*Again, this fertilizing "one-**which-is**-not" is the great differentiator which allows any Form term (and, for that matter, any participant* *in such a one) to be recognized and, eventually, known. Difference is the mother of episteme. Our "one-***which-is***-not" is indeed the great dyadicizer as is evidenced from the opening lines of hypothesis two. If one* **IS** *(possible only by virtue of fertilization) it obtains,* **eo ipso**, *as one and at once as* **something else**, *namely the IS which renders this one as ousia.* [142b,5-9]

*****

*Now, as it turns out, our "one/being" of hypothesis two <<i.e., what the one becomes when and as the one is taken from the perspective of just by itself and is perspectivally super-imposed by the dyadicizing "one-***which-is***-not">>, with and through the aid of the "te dianoia"* [143a,9], *turns out to have always harbored, within and as its dyadicized status, difference as, so to speak, as a silent third partner. In the passage which immediately follows this "discovery" of difference as always having been harbored, albeit silently, within our dyadicized "one/being" we find the key by which Parmenides (i.e., the character in the dialogue) is able to show the ousia-status of number and, in effect, of the "mathematical intermediates" in the passage which immediately follow upon the mention of this "te dianoia."*

This "te dianoia" is not to be understood in terms of the three levels of abstraction which is operative in Aristotle Physics *and in the earlier-written books of* Metaphysics. *To be sure, the germ of Aristotle even having the idea of analyzing being in terms of "abstraction" is this "te dianoia" which makes several important appearances in hypotheses two and seven. But still, the finished products <Plato's "te dianoia" and Aristotle's three levels of abstraction>> are products of conceptual frames of reference which are incompatible with each other.*

For one thing, these questions about what the soul/mind does in the journey towards knowledge, for Aristotle, are joined-at-the-hip with his "hule"-orientation and correlative abstraction <<except, of course, for the acquired capacity to have direct intellectual intu-

*ition of separate substances not composed of matter at all>>. In contrast, Plato does not engage the intelli***gizing** *of things (be they perceptible or not> from any thematic treatment of the materiality or non-materiality of the thing -- be it a Form or otherwise -- in question. But what even more radically differentiates Plato's "te dianoia" from Aristotle's "abstraction"-oriented <i.e., "matter"-oriented> way of dealing with intellection is the following. Aristotle's "abstraction"-orientation lacks the immense* **generative** *power of Plato's "te dianoia."*

Whether it is "in the order of being" or in the "order of knowing" <<<to use scholastic terminology for a distinction which, without label, is indeed present in Aristotle's frame of reference but not present at all in Plato's frame of reference>>> Aristotle's "nous poietikas" from De anima-III-5 *does nothing more than supply the receptive intellect with an activation of the intelligibility* **already present** *[at least according to Aristotle's schema]* **in the thing being known**. *Plato's "te dianoia" -- which opens up the role of difference in its dual epistemological and ontological significance -- brings an advanced differENcing from the soul/mind TO the content of perception itself which emerges from the thing which itself is imbued with patterns of differentiation. For Plato, the soul/mind does not simply "light up" for receptive intellect the intelligibility allegedly already contained in the thing. On the contrary, the "te dianoia" function of the soul/mind <a function which does not obtain at all in the soul/mind in the absence of nourishing and training over a long period of time> TO the content of sensory perception. To be sure, "difference" is dispersed over the whole realm of being as is made perfectly clear in* Sophist. *But difference,* ***AS difference****, does* ***NOT*** *present itself in the manifold of sensation. Difference has to be differ***ENCED** *in order to be* ***recognized*** *at all which is the first perquisite towards knowledge. In other words -- Aristotle's usage of "poietikas" notwithstanding -- knowledge is not made possible simply by "lighting up" for receptive intellect an intelligibility allegedly already present in the thing. For the very feature of things which allows them to be* *intelligible at all does not, of and by itself, even present itself in the sensory manifold.*

Yes. the whole and intricate network of difference and diffeer-encing in the thing, while there (in utero, so to speak), ***does not present itself*** *to the soul/mind. Rather, it must be* *<u>rendered/made</u>* ***recognizable*** *as what it is by and through the* ***differENCING*** *on the part of the soul/mind as it works over the network of differen-tiation in what is made available to the soul/mind. Nor is such a capacity automatic. the majority of humans merely operate on a level of* ***differENCING*** *WHICH DOES LITTLE MORE THAN IDENTIFY THINGS. We are thrown back to those pregnant words from* Timaeus 51,d-e:

If Nous and true-opinion are two kinds wholly distinguishable from each other, then these "by themselves" [akth'auta] <i.e., these Forms being objects of nousing but not of sensation> do exist. On the other hand, if it appears that Nous and true opinion do not differ at all [***diapherei*** to meden] then what is perceived through sensation must be considered to be the most stable things there are. However, we do have to speak of Nous and true-opinion as distinct [khoris] of course, because we can come to have one without the other; and the one is not like the other. It is through teaching-and-education that we come to have the one and through persua-sion that we come to have the other. The one **always involves a true accounting** [al<u>e</u>thous logou], **the other** [by itself] **lacks any accounting** [alogon]. And while the one remains unmoved by persuasion, the other gives int persuasion. And of true opinion, it must be said, all men have a share; but of Nousing, **only the Gods AND A SMALL GROUP OF PEOPLE DO.**

*****

For Aristotle, intelligibility is an accomplished state already in the thing and its intelligibility, already included in the phantasm, is ***revealed*** *through the "lighting up" accomplished by active intel-lect. With this "lighting up" on the part of active intellect the mind* *and the form-principle of the thing become identical. It was indeed presumptuous on Aristotle's part to have called a merely "activating" intellect "poietikas" for in the Aristotelian schema there is but removal from various levels of matter of an intelligibility which is then activated. In that schema there is no real "**making** intelligible" in the sense of "rendering intelligible." Aristotle's active intellect, even considered as "energeia/entelekheia," is rather mono-dimensional and simplistic. Further, we find, in Aristotle's frame, that with things with no endowment of matter at all in their composition there is simple and immediate "identity" between mind and thing (or principle) which is grasped, without abstraction, in an act of intellection which is the very quintessence of simplicity. For Plato the soul/mind's encounter with bodi-**less** entities does not, at all, just by virtue of contact, bring with it intelligibility even to one well-trained in Philosophy. On the contrary such contact is only the beginning. The to-be knower* **is just getting started** *via the work of differENcing which will allow a* **grasping** [i.e., struggle-imbued] *intellection to occur. In contrast, intellection for Aristotle flees difference. Noetic "contemplation" is an Aristotelian goal. Plato, post 367, offers something different.*

*To be sure, both thinkers allow for elaborate schemas (which are not at all isomorphic with each other) which, for Aristotle, leads towards a putative apodicticity and which, for Plato, births a non-finalizable journey which, on the level of mathematics, has a contextual apodicticity, but which passes onto a Dialectical process allowing only for a conditional claim to "knowledge." But even here the more important point is that, for Plato, initial apprehension itself of the thing is made possible through this **differENCING**, a process which has nothing to do with separating a formal principle from what is apprehended by abstracting from some level of "matter." For Aristotle, degrees of separation/abstraction from matter is what allows for intelligibility **already in the apprehended as such** to be known. In contrast, even on the level of initial apprehension, intelligibility is **made to be** by the truly "poietikas: process of differencing.*

[pages 353-358]

*****

*Of course Plato is aware of a "one-which-is-not" which is only a privation/absence of being. This is addressed in hypothesis six. The very existence of hypothesis six exhibits, by way of contrast, that the "the-**one-which-is**-not" of hypothesis five is **anything but** a mere privation of being. The real being of non-being -- in contra distinction to non-being as privation or absence of being -- was Plato's great gift to the Tradition. A gift which, starting with Aristotle, was largely ignored or denied that it was really in Plato at all. Or, perhaps worse, with Hegel, domesticated, thinned out, and rendered as something which no longer represented a **wresting**.*

[363-364]

vav-iv-c.

Dialectic IS First Philosophy for Plato. Dialectic is preparation for First Philosophy for Aristotle. For what elicits knowledge for Plato is <paradox noted>, in the final analysis, ever-shifting in its status of being ever the same, be such on the level of the Forms or on the level of the sensible. What elicits knowledge for Aristotle remains the same only in a far more simplistic sense.

vav-iv-d.

This feature of what is knowledge, on Plato's accounting, all turns on how difference obtains. There is no time, strictly speaking, when difference obtains at all. Yet it does obtain, so to speak, all of the time and throughout all time. Plato delineates this feature without which there can be no knowledge in Parmenides *at the end of 146d and the beginning of 146e wherein it is pointed out that difference can never obtain in anything at all for "any stretch of time" which, as the analysis continues, shows that sameness always obtains. But it is not until the "insert hypothesis" that we find that difference is always obtaining, even if it never obtains for any stretch of time. It obtains as the strange* ***eksaiphnes*** *which is ubiquitous, never-ceasing, but also never obtaining for any stretch of time. <<<Memories here of what might be labeled the "catastrophic theory of change/motion" as exemplified in Zeno's paradox of the "flying arrow."*

*****

*The "insert" hypothesis -- the "eksaiphnes hypothesis -- permeates all perspectival changes from one hypothesis to another, to say nothing at all of countless multitudes of transitions undergone by any one or by any other (including "the-**one-which-is**-not") from one state of affairs to another, with special attention to transitions from ousia to non-ousia and vice versa. It was put in the* **third** *position as a device to draw attention to its transcending critical function relative to all of the hypotheses. It ought not to be construed as a numbering which would affect the numbering of the remaining hypotheses. After all, the delineation by the character Parmenides of the "exercise/training" clearly indicates four "is-oriented" 'positive' and four "is-not" 'negative' hypotheses.* [[[In Platonic parlance "the third" shares position of privilege with "the fifth." These two designations indicate both special status to what is being talked about and brings with them the flavor of esotericism. It will be noted that in the numbering of the properly eight hypotheses <<<i.e., the number of hypotheses predicted by the review of the requisite "training" as presented by the character Parmenides at 136a,5--c,7>> our "is-not-ing" *one-**which-is**-not* occupies **fifth** position.]]]]

Plato's idiosyncratic useage of "eksaiphnes is in the service of supplying a word by which to reveal the all-permeating "presence-which-is-a-non-presence" as it simultaneously connects and keeps apart the terms of any transitions whatsoever, but with special attention to coming into ousia-status and going out of ousia-status. Connecting and separating at once and never actually ***being*** *as it* *does such. Does that not remind you of someone? Someone from Ephesus?*

The Secret Unity of "Parmenides": ***diapherein***

Period.

[pages 363-365 along with additional material not contained on these pages in **DSG**]

***** ***** *****

zayin
always 209e:

----- *"learning/getting to know"* [**gnonai**] *the differencings* [**ten diaphoroteta**]

***** ***** *****

zayin-a). It all reduces down to this <not cited from **DSG**>:

> Forms are stable nodal points of reference for thinking and speaking obtaining in a sea of ***diapherein*** [differENcing/differencings].

*****

And please. Does it have to be stated yet again? Hypothesis one's only positive feature is that it is used as a vehicle to introduce the set variables <<i.e., whole/parts; Same/Difference; Like/Unlike; the meaning of Contact and non-Contact; the becoming and being modalities of time; and others as well>> which will be parsed out in several of the other hypotheses with regard to Form-theory and especially in hypotheses two and three. That is the whole of its positive content. As for the "One" of this hypothesis it is the most barren and impoverished all the hypotheses excepting only hypotheses six and eight.

It is testimony to the holding power of the Alexandrian greenhouse that some people, even today, fool around with the Plotinian tropes of "beyond being"; "the Ineffable One" (etc., etc.) in their reading of this hypothesis. "Fooling around indeed." For they are fools. Please. There are none so blind as those who *will* not see.

*****

B-2-b-i. The whole/parts difficulty. (heading towards the finish) 131a,5--131e,7.

As we now begin our inauguration of the "whole/parts difficulty" (this time, from the very beginning*) we shall have to remind ourselves to leave behind most of the post-Platonic tropes characteristic of the Tradition. In particular the pairings "material/immaterial" or "physical/non-physical" have no bearing at all in allowing this passage to say what it properly is saying.

> *. [[The careful reader will recall that such -- i.e., NOT beginning from the beginning of the whole/parts difficulty -- was followed by virtue of the logic of the analysis which we were and are pursuing. Thus some important features of the first infinite regress difficulty were passed over so as to facilitate the continuation, without interruption, of a line of argumentation which had been inaugurated. This line of thinking was the lead-in to the central contention of this book. [[i.e., That for Plato Forms really are thoughts in the mind/soul.]] To have immediately started with all the features of the first infinite regress difficulty would have led to interruption and confusion. We now return to the previously passed-over features of the first infinite regress difficulty which were not sufficiently delineated in that "quickie" reprisal there of the first infinite regress difficulty. All of this transpired back in

the Heading "hey-ii" itself under the heading "131a,--131e,7 (yes again)" itself under the heading "B-2-b-i."]]

The passage involved is best approached if we make a conscious effort to emphasize what I would call the "logical/linguistic" attitude to the words and terms in question. Yes. All of the key terms in *Parmenides* are totally permeated by epistemological and ontological weight. Even so, this weight can be appreciated in its full PLATONIC significance only if we let the terms be understood, from the beginning in the simplicity of their "logical/linguistic" function <<keeping in mind throughout that we are not speaking of "logical/linguistic" function as such comes forth in Aristotle's *Organon*>>.

This difficulty is, first and foremost, a difficulty concerning the nature of "participation." Parmenides sets the agendum:

Parmenides speaking: *So, does each thing that gets a share get its share of the Form as a whole or as part of it? Or could there be some other way of getting a share apart from these two?* [131a,9-10]

The answer to that last question is critical. And it is not until we get into the details of hypothesis two that we shall find that the answer, as is the case with virtually all issues in *Parmenides*, is this: neither/nor-and-both-at-once. We shall address this later. For now it is important to note that young Socrates seems committed to the proposition that participation (sharing) in a form must be by one or the other and, further, he is presented as preferring the claim that, somehow, the whole Form is present in the participant.

Now as we enter into the manner by which Parmenides shows that *either* option entails absurdities, we should also acknowledge that Parmenides is taking the meaning of "whole" and "part" in an ordinary, common sense, manner. To be sure he is NOT driving at any distinctions predicated on the materiality or the immateriality of whole and or parts. Rather he is quite simply and quite straight-forwardly parsing out the apparently unacceptable consequences which will follow if participation is accounted for as *either* by whole *or* by part. For Plato -- who is choreographing a Form-based "retrieval" (so to speak) of the Poem of Parmenides through *his* character of Parmenides -- it is absolutely critical that the "difficulty" first be understood in all of its ramifications ***as a difficulty***. It is true that if our thinking stays at this level there can be no adjudication of the difficulty. But as we shall see, when he gets to the hypotheses proper, Plato (through the character of Parmenides) will show that the adjudications (which are anything but simple) can be expressed only through a dialectical level of discourse which instantiates the complex, but thoroughly tight and self-consistent , logic of the "neither/nor-and-both-at-once."

He begins by questioning our young Socrates if the whole of any given "one" is in its many participants as the whole Form. Socrates indicates that maintaining that does not entail a difficulty. He is countered immediately by Parmenides who draws out the implications of maintaining such. For if the Form as a whole is in each one, which are many and separate (khoris), then the Form itself would be separated from itself.

Socrates, famously, counters with a metaphor:

Socrates speaking: *What's to prevent its being one, Parmenides? Not if it's like one and the same day. That* [the day] *is in many places at the same time and is nonetheless not separate from itself. If it is like that, each of the Forms might be, at the same time, one and the same in all.*

Parmenides speaking (with condescension): *Oh how pleasant you make it sound.* [131b,4-8]

Metaphor delivers us unto metaphor and there is no end to allusion. Parmenides counters with the metaphor of a sail hovering over each of the participants. With this metaphor it is immediately clear that only a part of the sail is over any one of the participants and, according to the internal logic of the metaphor only a part of the whole (sail) is over (i.e., participated in) any one of the many participants.

The point is clear. Plato is eliminating from the discussion any cutesy short-cuts on this matter of participation. Aristotle was only partially correct when he reports that Plato had left the exact dynamic of "participation" as an "open question" [*Metaphysics I-6*,987b,11-13] which, in effect, left it as a kind of metaphor. Nice poetry but shallow Philosophy. But Plato post-367 will not settle for such and answer which is really an avoidance of the issue. Post-367 he radically notches up just what it means to be a form and/or to participate in a Form through the grandest dialectical exercise ever accomplished. And in so doing he generated what is, in effect and as well, the greatest poem ever written.

Prior to 367 (e.g., Book-V of *Republic*) there was no serious accounting of "participation." Post-367 Plato becomes meticulous in spelling out the Logic of participation. [[A Physicist doing First Philosophy <and within a frame of reference wherein Dialectic is necessary preparation for Philosophy but not, of itself, Philosophy> would never be satisfied with Plato's de facto practice of a non-finalizable Dialectic as the functional equivalent of First Philosophy. The Dialectical logic of participation given in hypothesis two would be, for Aristotle, just a higher order of "metaphor." The simple truth is that a Physicist-at-heart doing First Philosophy will never understand First Philosophy AS Dialectic.]] This interchange from the whole/parts difficulty is simply a pre-emptive move on the part of Plato/Parmenides to, say, to the "Friends of the Forms," that metaphor is no longer suitable as an accounting of participation or of anything else in Form-theory. {{{{Oh please? Are you now going to put forth that truism to the effect that words in in any language (Greek, English, whatever) are but "ossified metaphors"? Well of course they are. But what is being spoken of here is an ordinary meaning of metaphor as a conscious manner of portraying-beyond the actual word something or some state of affairs.}}}}

Before we leave this "day"/sail" trade-off of metaphors we must make it clear that this commentary does not repeat nor endorse what is often found at this point of commentary on the text in the history of commentary on *Parmenides*. Some amateurs of Platonic irony have tried to make the case that by putting the metaphor of "sail" in the mouth of Parmenides Plato is inaugurating the view that in this listing of difficulties [131a,5--135c,8] he, Plato, is "artistically" showing that this character Parmenides does not have a nuanced view of form theory since he uses a "materialistic" metaphor (i.e. "sail") for Form-theory while his Socrates uses a metaphor ("day") which does not have to be construed. And this observation is then said by these aficionados of shallow nuance, with some glee, that Plato is presenting Socrates in this passage as really getting to something substantial and significant. How pleasant!!!! But it is not the character Socrates who is the true protagonist of this dialogue. The true protagonist is the character Parmenides and any fair reading of this section reveals that the true protagonist, while appreciating the force and energy of this young mind, is being dismissive of this gambit by our young Socrates.

*****

Oh Lord! How long will it take before Plato begins to be understood on his own terms? In the first Place Plato, post 367, does not engage Form-theory through the prism of "material/immaterial" or of "physical/non-physical." In the second place the Parmenides who is delineating these critical difficulties makes it clear at the end of those difficulties that he maintains, ***and insists upon***, Form-theory. More than that. Philosophy would be impossible without Form-theory. [135e,10--135b,3]. He is the one who is presented as the true defender of Form-theory on contrast to this young Socrates who tends to hesitate and equivocate concerning the validity of Form-theory.

What the character Parmenides is doing is setting out the real problems which must be encountered and dealt with if Form-theory is to remain credible and, for that matter, if Philosophy itself can be maintained as a serious discipline. In this clarifying endeavor he is using the logic of ordinary language to make the difficulties of and challenges to Form-theory clear. It is not until the inauguration of the eight-plus-one hypotheses that he will switch gears and present Form-theory in the only language and syntax appropriate to Form-Theory: Dialectic. Dialectic which instantiates the "neither/nor-and-both-at-once."

Continuing on.

At this point Socrates is presented as now persuaded that participation cannot mean that the participant shares in the whole Form. So now a number of situations will be brought up which entertain that participation in a Form means participation in part of a Form. There are several of these, and with one exception at the end, they are not difficult to follow. And as could have been predicted, so long as we remain on an ordinary language meaning of "whole" and "part" it is even more ludicrous to maintain that participation is participation in part of a Form than the now discredited notion that participation is participation in the whole of the Form.

So as Plato turns to the alternate possibility -- to the effect that participation is a function of having "part" of a Form -- Plato has his character Parmenides bring up three (but really two, as we shall see) exemplifications which demonstrate that this alternative is at least, if not more, filled with untenable conclusions as the first possibility (i.e., that participation is, somehow, participation in the whole of a Form). His exemplifications are "the Great <Big> **Itself**;" "the Small **Itself**:" and that default [i.e., "the Equal Itself"] which sometimes comes into play as these two, somehow or other, bring "Great" and "Small" to and into things which participate in "Great" and/or "Small."

What we have he is something which is something which of its very nature is intrinsically perplexing. For Plato is maintaining that there are "**kath auto**" <auten, etc.> **which are INTRISICALLY relational**. Beginning with Aristotle and largely due to Aristotle's influence on the Tradition we find, more often than not, in ourselves something of an initial resistance to the notion that something ***intrinsically relational*** could have anything like a "**kath auto**" status.

Fine. One can, with integrity, deny that such is possible and, in effect follow Aristotle on this. For while Aristotle came, over time, to reject Form-theory, he still maintained that some beings (i.e., individual substances) have a "kath-auto" status. But never in a million years would Aristotle, once he had left Form-theory behind, maintain that anything ***intrinsically*** relational could have "kath auto" status. It is true, as I have demonstrated all throughout **DSG**, that Aristotle, in his presentations of Form-theory, radically misrepresents Platonic Forms as "universals" thereby assuring ((with or without conscious intent being a separable issue)) that his critique of Form-theory comes forth as already validated. An egregious begging of the question. That having been stipulated yet again, it should be noted that Aristotle at least has the integrity of not denying that Plato maintained that there are "kath auto" Forms for terms which are ***intrinsically*** relational. In contrast, the Tradition often (and often enough in the twentieth century and on into the twenty-first century) dishonors Plato on this matter even further by simply ignoring the central and decisive role which ***intrinsically relational*** Forms have in Plato's core Philosophy.

There are many Forms which are contrary to each other. But it is precisely the Forms "Great" and "Small" which puts flesh, so to speak, on that key oscillating/dyadicizing "one-**which-is**-not" of hypothesis five. To be sure, Aristotle presents (i.e., misrepresents) "the Dyad of the Great and the Small" as a Platonic first principle paired off with "one" as though it were a free-standing principle in its own right. In fact this is a misrepresentation since the oscillating/dyadicizing <fleshed out as the dynamic of and between "The Great and the Small"> is not a free-standing principle but rather the other face of the "one" itself. ((This particular misrepresentation is addressed in some detail all throughout pericopes fourteen and fifteen of **DSG** <and particularly on pages 369-373.)) But, nonetheless, Aristotle recognized the overweening significance for Plato's post-367 ontol-

ogy of these ***intrinsically relational, and dynamically interactive*** Forms. This last will be addressed when we go through the eight-plus-one hypotheses. For now we will just follow along by delineating the unacceptable consequences, delineated in this second part of the "whole/parts" difficulty, under the supposition that "participation" can occur by sharing in a part of the Form.

These unacceptable consequences are made clear in our dialogue from 131c-15 through 131e-2. The exposition in the case of the "Great" and of that default [i.e., "the Equal Itself "] which sometimes comes into play for Plato as these two, somehow or other, bring "Great" and "Small" to and into things which participate in "Great" and/or "Small." However it is not until the exposition of the "Small" (131d,9--131e,2) that we come to realize (even as it is maintained that participation does not occur by way of sharing in a part) that the "Great" and the "Small" bring to things this character of being Great and or Small while the character of the Equal is brought by default into this or that thing by virtue of reaching, relative to another, an equilibrium entailing neither Great nor Small. Although in the writing of the difficulty Plato is only showing that participation in the Small is not achieved by participating in part of the Small, this passage already points ahead to a dynamic by which, in this case, the Small is brought to the thing along with the paradoxical consequence of such a dynamic . Only in hypothesis two will we be given the dialectical accounting of this paradox. For now, listen to the paradox itself:

> *And that TO which* [i.e., the thing which, of itself is neither Great nor Small] *the part subtracted* [i.e., an alleged part of "The Small Itself"] *is added will turn out to be smaller, not larger, than before* [even though this alleged part of the Small is **added** to whatever the thing in question <e.g., a chair> since such a thing is not of itself great or small ***but WOULD*** *<<i.e., conditional to the terms of the immediate argumentation>>* ***become such***, somehow, by participating in the Small Itself <<but not by a part of the Small Itself>> and thus becomes smaller and not larger than it was before]. 131d,12--132e,1.

And please keep the following in mind. The full and complex **dyadicizing dynamic** obtaining as "the Great" and "the Small" is not at all hinted at in the delineation of this difficulty. This **dyadicizing dynamic** (which will always come to express itself in terms of whole and parts) involves **a causal dimension which brings about whole/parts structure to participation but which causal dimension is not constituted by whole/parts structure**. While this is true in all cases, it is precisely the **dyadicizing dynamic** characteristic of the "Great/Small" nexus which displays the causal element in participation. This **dyadicizing dynamic trope**, when presented through "the Great and the Small" is a specification geared to the visible dimension ((which designation, as we have seen time and time again, is NOT at all congruent with the materiality/physicality tropes generated by Aristotle and then entranced in the Tradition)) of the overall dyadicizing dynamic operative, in Plato's thinking, all throughout the visible and the invisible. This dyadicizng dynamic is caught in Plato's usage of ***DIAPHEREIN*** (and its multiple linguistic forms and derivatives) for which, both all throughout **DSG** and in this book as well, I have supplied the neo-logism "DifferENcing" (and its multiple linguistic forms and derivatives). It must be noted that this dyadicizing dynamic by way of the "Great and the Small" as it pertains to the visible realm turns out to be grounded in and derivative from the "ur-dyadicizer," namely "the one-**which-is**-not" of hypothesis five.

It is precisely this all-consuming principle which animates the **swirling perspectivism** endemic to these eight-plus-one hypotheses. It is a **swirling perspectivism** whose epistemic value is completely predicated upon and derivative from its dialectically ontological structure which itself cannot occur without knowledge. These matters will become clearer as we examine key passages on these matters in our review of the eight-plus-one hypotheses.

*****

It is my contention that the dialogue *Theaetetus* is peppered all throughout with passages which are explicit vectors which, in effect, are intended to delineate the contours of matters both raised as "difficulties" in our present section of *Parmenides* AND which are adjudicated in the eight-plus-one hypotheses. Two of these passages which deal with our present subject-matter are integrated into lively and more colorful treatments of Theaetetan themes which thereby have the advantage of accessibility but which fall short of adjudicating the matters being raised. In contrast, these same matters as treated in the eight-plus-one hypotheses of our dialogue are starkly presented without a colorful context but DO achieve adjudication in our dialogue. One of these passages from *Theaetetus* [201c,4--210b,3] deals, quite explicitly, with this whole theme of "wholes and parts." The other of these passages [154c,1--155c,10] deals the set of puzzlements and wonderments associated with "the Great and the Small."

*****

It is likewise my contention that Plato's accounting of Form-Theory in *Phaedo* is itself a relatively late-in-life amendment of the contours of Form-Theory inserted into this earlier produced dialogue. It occurs in that passage [99c,7--105b,5] which constitutes a segue into accounting of how the Soul, while remaining Soul, withdraws from the living body when death comes near. It is a passage which from beginning to end entails the paradoxes of how "the Great and the Small" operate in the ever-changing ((and *diaphoreinin***g**, although the word is not used in this passage)) dynamic of how things become bigger and smaller and vice versa. Even if you do not accept the hypothesis that this passage is a late-in-life addendum on Plato's part, the passage remains valuable in as much as it also, in a more colorful and concrete manner, introduces the reader into the puzzlements and wonders associated with "the Great and the Small." Let us begin with the *Phaedo* passage.

*****

Phaedo 99c,7--103c,8 **ton deuteron ploun**

Yes. I realize that his discussion of the Forms continues on past 103c,8. But the discussion which begins at 103c,9 is really his segue into his justification for the immortality of the soul. Even as a discussion of Form-theory it holds one's interest and there is subtlety about it. But it is what precedes that segue which is most germane to the section of *Parmenides* which we are discussing.

"The Second Voyage?" "The Second Sailing?" "Second Best?" I say, "The Second Voyage." I won't be coy. I believe that Plato here is making an indirect reference to his second voyage to Sicily which, it appears, was an experience which came to catalyze a radical revision of Form-theory. This claim, if credible, gives support to my contention that this passage before us was a relatively late-in-life modification. Even if that contention were disputed, the passage has value with regard to the dynamic of "the Great and the Small." Further, there are some other features in this passage which suggest something composed after that second voyage to Syracuse.

First of all, the tropes of the radical distinction between "Being" and "Becoming," which often (and even in *Timaeus*) surround Plato's *Republic-V* oriented treatment of Form-Theory are in fact absent from this *Phaedo* discussion of the Forms just as is the case in the post-367 accounting of the Forms in *Sophist*, *Parmenides*, and *Philebus*. Indeed, the most important passages of *Sophist* (wherein it is said directly) and *Parmenides* (thematically and at length in and through the eight-plus-one hypotheses albeit in a more technical and less obvious way) it is made very clear ***that there is real genesis, change, and motion in and of the Forms and as well that there is Being (ousia-status) in the so-called realm of "Becoming."*** [[In Sophist the Eleatic Stranger forcefully insists on all of this AND that there is LIFE in the realm of Forms. A hint, if you can catch it, as to WHERE one would find the Forms.]] This last point is taken as axiomatic by the time we arrive at *Philebus*. {{{The whys and wherefores of an anomalous reappearance of the these Being/Becoming tropes in *Timaeus* <<and, as important as the "dark middle" of that dialogue is for understanding certain features of the later dialogues, it is noteworthy that *Timaeus* does NOT gain entry into the first three

tetralogies and, like all other dialogues not in those first three tetralogies, it takes its place in the merely chronological ordering of all the other dialogues which Plato choose to save for posterity>> is are addressed on pages 211--215 of **DSG**.}}}

Then there is also the feature that the language of "hypothesis/supposition" permeates this entire discussion of Form-theory in *Phaedo*. To be sure, the language of "hypothesis/supposition" permeates, in differing manners, the third and fourth levels of the Divided Line passage with which Book VI of *Republic*. Readers of **DSG** will of course recall that this divided line passage immediately succeeds the "sun" <i.e., tokos/offspring/interest> passage which for sure was a very late insert by which the imperious and autonomous presentation of the good was cleverly modified to bring that already disseminated passage in line with the final teaching on the good brought about through *Philebus*-introducing-the-late/in/life-revision of the dialogue (the third dialogue of the third tetralogy) subtitled "Concerning the Good."

And, finally, there is the rather daring gambit on the part of the Phaedean Socrates to have the extended exemplification of this "second voyage" NOT with the safe, tried, and true examples of "The Beautiful Itself," "The Good Itself," and "The Just Itself" or even with the less safe but tried and true examples of, say, "Fire Itself," "Horse Itself" or "Bed Itself." Rather, Plato has the Phaedean Socrates exemplify the "second voyage" version of Form-theory through the most challenging exemplifications: two Forms, "the Great and the Small," each of which have "kath auto" status even while they remain ***intrinsically relational***.

The treatment of these interesting Forms in our Phaedean text is parallel to the initial manner which the Parmenidean Socrates first describes Form-theory at 128e,7--130a,3 of *Parmenides*. Contraries ("opposites," if you prefer) can never share in each other although the participants which are made what they are at a given time (i.e., large <aka 'great'> and/or small by virtue of sharing in the Large <aka "Great"> Itself and/or the Small itself) can be generated one from another and, indeed can, from different perspectives <<<<recalling here that ultimately "perspectives" in the Platonic schema have epistemic weight only by virtue of their ontological weight>>>> be sharing in both contrary Forms at once. But the contraries themselves are presented in our *Phaedo* passage and in our *Parmenides* passage just cited [i.e., 128e,7--130a,3] as never allowing to intermingle with each other. In both of these passages the following is passed over: that an individual participant CAN and DOES instantiate both contraries at the same time, being large relative to such and such and, at the same time, being small relative to such and such. So in fact the "Large" and the "Small" THEMSELVES do, somehow <<confer the pei of *Sophist* at 256b,6-11 whereby the contraries Rest and Motion end up being presented as intermingling>>. Of course, this "pei" comes to be exhaustingly addressed, in its ONTOLOGICAL status and function, in and through the eight-plus-one hypotheses of our dialogue wherein in fact contraries are presented as intermingling and intercoursing with each other through the all-pervasive Five GREAT KINDS although this is not brought out in either our present *Phaedo* [wherein Socrates is at death's door] text nor in the original adumbration of Form-theory by young Socrates at 128e,7--130a,3 of *Parmenides*. To be returned to, of course. of course when and as we come to understand the all-pervasive significance of the "one-**which-IS**-not" of hypothesis # 5

*****

As referred to above, *Theaetetus* is peppered all throughout with "failed" accountings of themes which will not get their full adjudication until they are treated in that long and arduous "training" of those eight-plus-one hypotheses of *Parmenides*. But these "failed" accountings introduced the variables in question. Indeed in both cases there is a sketching which indicates what the true accounting would be although in both cases Plato has "Socrates" notice a flaw in the sketch which does not allow either of these proffered accountings to be validated. Let us now mine these two Theaetetan passages in the service of better understanding them as vectors to key passages in *Parmenides*.

Theaetetus, 154c,1--155c,10.

*****

Theaetetus, 201c,4--210b,3.

*****

To my dear cherished reader. Those two passages *cry out* for analysis and commentary.

The first passage raises the perplexing view ((but does not analyze or adjudicate that view)) that something ("x"; or, "six dice") can **become and be** something greater, or smaller, or equal while remaining the same (i.e., the six dice which certainly remain six dice) **precisely by virtue of somehow coming into the range and suasion of things ("the Great Itself"; "the Small Itself") which are intrinsically relational.** Please keep in mind here that we are not dealing with an Aristotelian analysis which adjudicates these things only on the epistemological plane in terms of competing perspectives. No. This is Plato. This passage in *Theaetetus* is already a vector to hypothesis # 2 [149d,10--151e,3]

The second passage allows us to surmise what will become overtly stated (by way of the "neither-nor-and-both-at-once" Logic which permeates the Great Dialectical "training" of *Parmenides*) in hypothesis two. We come to see that the whole is, at once, greater than the sum [pan] of parts **and at the same time** nothing but the sum of parts. The passages are rife with the key words of Form-theory. And, in particular it is the second of these passages [201c,4--210b,3], through elaborate parsing on Plato's part, which brings us to that "most beautiful" accounting of knowledge which has about it a curious circularity which allows Plato to bring *Theaetetus* to a close according to Plato's plan to make *Theaetetus*, technically, an aporetic dialogue by treating the pregnant circularity of the passage [209e--210b] as though it were a mere redundant circularity and not worthy to be called a definition or an accounting of knowledge. But

Plato consciously has tipped us off to the immense substantial and positive meaning of this third accounting by referring to it as "most beautiful." I am speaking of the very climax -- and major point of the entire dialogue:

gnonai ----- ten diaphoroteta

[209e]

But wait.

This commentary has, without planning, started limping as it now de facto transforms itself into something different from a commentary. The called-for detailed analysis of the two passages -- especially that key second-listed passage <let alone any detailed analysis of the eight-plus-one hypotheses> -- is simply not going to happen in this lifetime. And, really, doing such (what I am about to do) is far superior to those efforts which by mere brutal force <absent understanding> slog through those eight-plus-one hypotheses shouting "Eureka!" but not really encountering Plato's achievement. Yet, with what has been given already in conjunction with this transformation which this book is now undergoing, Plato is enabled to get to play his essential role in what was always was to have been said. A fond farewell to this "second comnmentary"! Bring on the interruption! Something different is to emerge.

C. *Coitus Interrptus and Beyond.*

Caesura.

You made me so very happy
You made me so very very happy
I'm so glad you came into my life

Blood, Sweat, and Tears

*****

Coitus has been going on for some time. But now she is saying -- with eyes, face, and that frightening sternness of voice -- that she wants to take NO CHANCE AT ALL OF BECOMING PREGNANT. So this is where the *coitus interruptus* begins. But there are more conceptions, Horatio, than are contained in your Biology.

*****

Encomium for Aristocles

Son of Ariston! Aristocles! Through
How many masks are you to be revealed?
Stranger who speaks through the mouths of Strangers!
What are you hiding and why?

*****

I am tempted to say something like:

Dear to me is Plato; dearer still to me is truth.

Such is a true statement. And the economy of the statement is tempting. But it is not equal to the reality of Plato. Yet by even entertaining that mode of introduction I am acknowledging that Plato does not circumscribe the *What E-Vokes Thinking?* question. To be sure, the issue for thought will always intersect, in a major way, with Plato's writings (when understood accurately). But *What E-vokes Thinking?* is a question which will never be dealt with successfully if one is limited to the writings of our friend Aristocles.

Plato's achievement has about it something which is shared by only two other philosophers. I will refer to them momentarily. The guts of his achievement is contained in the first three tetralogies. To them should be addended his revision of the Sun passage towards the end of *Republic-VI* and the "dark middle" of *Timaeus* from 48e,3 up through 55c,4. This "dark middle" of *Timaeus* is SO philosophically fertile that it cannot be skipped. But it was for excellent reasons that Plato did not make room for the dialogue in which that "dark middle" is ensconced in the first three tetralogies.

You will note here that in the final tetralogical arrangement of his progeny, these two dialogues, *Republic* and *Timaeus* were NOT included in the first three tetralogies. They each contain material which must be mined if one is to fully understand that final compromise forged by Plato when he fully understood that he would not be able to complete that grand and planned project entailing three trilogies. [[Again, cf. pericope Three of **DSG.**]] But neither *Republic* nor *Timaeus* merited -- at least not as complete works -- inclusion in the substitute compromise.

This tetralogical compromise was, in effect, the very last "work" of Plato's ((i.e., the artistic and thematic crafting of the first three tetralogies with the remaining nine tetralogies being a simple chronological listing of the remaining works)). The exhaustion was entrenched. One final gasp for the ages. The arrangement of the first three tetralogies was his last-gasp piece of poetry. Perhaps someone, sometime, somewhere would understand. The hope when all hope is gone.

*****

The writing and execution of this “dark middle” renders the text of the whole *Timaeus* itself to be a reflection of the apogee of the raw *tsuris* in Plato’s soul as he writes this section soon after the horrible news from Syracuse reached him. This dialogue, more than any other, instantiates the ***Plato-contra-Plato*** motif which was a guiding and major theme of **DSG**. And *tsuris* was his companion from childhood up to and beyond his collapse at the wedding celebration. But this dark middle redeems, in its own troubled manner, Plato’s fumble as he inaugurated the second trilogy of the planned grandiose trilogy of trilogies which had been planned as his final grand production only to be upended and destroyed when the news arrived from Syracuse.* Later, as he recovered somewhat from the trauma, he substituted a make-do replacement for what would have been these second and third trilogies. This make-do replacement is made possible by the very late composition, *Philebus*, which constitutes the introduction to and grid for the interpretation of his remarkable re-write of *Symposium* which, in its re-written instantiation, came to merit the grand subtitle: ***Concerning the Good***. Further, the subtitle was earned. The final mechanics of how all of this was then gathered together and integrated into and as the first three tetralogies is accounted for in **DSG** on pages 37-48.

> *. [[Such is the most likely account of the evolving generation of what would become *Timaeus*. But periodically in **DSG** and, already, several times in *this* book I have -- based on some evidence from *Timaeus* itself and the role it was to have played in this second planned trilogy (of three planned trilogies <the first of these trilogies only having been executed>) -- offered alternate accounts of what is going on in *Timaeus*. In the final analysis, whatever Plato was doing or intending, the heartache and correlative melancholia exhausted him. One can easily imagine this tired and depressed old man uttering, circa 353/552, John Lennon’s cry:
>
> ***I just had to let it go!***

]]

*****

Concerning the end product of Timaeus. Both the positive value and atrocious deficiencies of this dialogue have been discussed at length and detail in **DSG** especially on pages 114-124; 132-133; 213-216; 220-223; 335-352; and 400-403.

*****

The final, special, and glorious reality of "Plato" is that in a good number of his post-367 productions [[[[*Cratylus???--Theaetetus--Sophist--Statesman--Parmenides*--[the "dark middle of *Timaeus* despite itself]--*Philebus*--and the glorious--*late-in-life-revision-of-Symposium*]]]] Plato generates an AWE-FULL frame of reference concerning the tight belonging together of what would come to be called "epistemology" and "ontology" along with and at the same time ((once it is understood in its complexity <i.e. a reading of the revised version of *Symposium* **as introduced by *Philebus* which furnishing the grid for the interpretation of the re-caste DRA-MA**>)) a final accounting of "the good" (i.e., as elicitative calling which brings into being that which allows it to be at all). Even with the interruptive murder which blew asunder the original plan, what resulted was nonetheless breathtaking in its conceptual audacity. These writings have Divinity written all over then. And indeed [[--- and here I consciously and vehemently skip-over his explicit remarks on Divinity, especially when he waxes adolescently poetic in his celebration of Nous ---]] it is my contention that these writings (again, especially when he is NOT talking explicitly about Divinity) constitute what is in effect a grid revelatory of the inner life of Divinity. To use language totally foreign to Plato himself, what he achieves (without conscious intention) in these writings (especially in the last three dialogues in the second tetralogy followed by the first three dialogues in the third tetralogy) is a stupendous accomplishment which allows the Self-Revelation of Hashem through and as (Jewish-of-course) Scripture to be appreciated for its grandeur.

Without the sometimes contortionistic achievements of these particular writings there most likely would no ability to ascertain and appreciate the very inner dynamic of the Divinity exposed through Jewish Scripture. In this sense, much of Plato's post-367 achievement, certainly unbeknownst to himself, stands outside the Frame of mere Philosophy and becomes (without intention and unbeknownst to himself) the tool by which the Self-Revelation of Hashem through and as Scripture is awakened to its glorious plenitude. This is Plato's greatest achievement.

But Plato remains always ***Plato-contra-Plato***. In his own writings his own overt meaning of Divinity is a rather simplistic "Nous" which has minimal or no inner dynamic. Plato's peculiar brand of Piety leads him to always associate Divinity with the purest kind of being which not only has no touch of evil about it but which also is not causal of evil in any sense. This meaning of Divinity is not worthy of those above-mentioned works of true Divinity even if Plato shies away from overtly ascribing Divinity to that complex nexus.

Encomium for Heraclitus.

This is a lot easier. Divinity as **polemos/struggle**. Yes. Our "skeinos" thinker was a shade too haughty and thereby did not integrate that elicitative calling, the ultimate center-piece of Plato's late in life achievement, into his meaning of **polemos**. Even so our man from Ephesus has probed extraordinarily well into the inner workings **and fundamental tension** characteristic of true Divinity whose own task is Self-Revelation through and as Jewish Scripture. And this Self-Revelation would be crippled without the dissemination of our Ephesian's wisdom as a kind of eye-opener to the God described as ***Ha-Godol, Ha-Gibor, v- HA-NORA*** of Nehemiah 9-32. Heraclitus catches much of this wisdom through his exposition on and of one of the great words in all of history:

diapherein

Encomium for Schelling.

Please be advised. When I speak of Schelling I speak **ONLY** of two of his productions. First is his Freedom book of 1809. Second is his posthumously published production (with editing by a son of Schelling) **Ages of the World**. It is in this book that the most important theological proposition EVER was articulated. Listen:

--- Everything depends upon comprehending that unity in God which is at once duality, or conversely, the duality which is at the same time unity.

[*Ages of the World,* page 157. Please understand that Schelling most definitely is NOT trading here on any kind of Hegelianesque identity of identity and difference. There is a chasm between Hegel and Schelling of which the great preponderance of professional philosophes have no clue despite the fact that Schelling himself had made his rejection of Hegel (both the man and his Philosophy) this explicitly clear.]

Yes, yes, yes. Let's get some things out of the way. Firstly let it be stipulated that Schelling's works often instantiate the tropes, themes, philosophemes, and theolophemes of Christianity. Indeed, there is even, in his writings, a smidgen of endemic European/Christian Anti-Semitism. So stipulated. But it remains that this articulation concerning God is an exact exposition of just what God is.

But be aware. Such a view of God is not "binitarian" the way Christian theology is "trinitarian." What I am saying is that there is no hypostasizing AT ALL of the two which is one and/or the one which is two. The Church Fathers brought in this notion of hypostasizing (ultimately emergent from Book Nine of *Metaphysics* in concert with certain key passages from *De Anima* which conceptually allow for Aristotle's not un-fertile meditation on "this in the this"). [[[It is not without irony that Aristotle himself never used his invented conceptual paradigm in any of *his* theological writings.]]] All of that's fine. A very interesting chapter in the emergence of Chirstianity. But Schelling's dictum is not forged as a function of this paradigm of hypostatic thinking and, at fortiori, cannot correctly be understood within such a paradigm.

Again, Schelling has articulated just what God is. I would claim -- although there is no overt and quotable extant evidence of this -- that virtually the same phrasing was used by that greatest of all the Rabbis at the dawn of the Rabbinic Movement some time after the destruction of the Temple. His name is Elisha ben Abbuyah who came to be referred to as Ishmael ben Elisha. His theological teachings came to be radically suppressed and expunged from Rabbinic thinking and he himself did, in fact, apostasize from the Rabbinic Movement. {{In contrast, his halakhic achievements were recorded and saved, albeit attributed to the moniker "Ishmael ben Elisha."}} His theological position came to be referred to as "The Two Powers/Authorities in Heaven." Memory of this teaching in Tractate Khagigah of the Babylonian Talmud is found in a section of the Talmudic commentary on that Mishna Tractate which includes a discussion of what came to be called "The Work of the Chariot." Further, as the Bavli commentary on that Tractate continues we find that, by and large, this apostate was largely and honorifically rehabilitated if one can read, so to speak, between the lines. [[Confer the Bavli commentary on Tractate Khaggigah from 14b-ii through 15b-v; ArtScroll pagination]]

In Jewish letters there is a long history of presuming that Elisha had endorsed something like a Persianesque Dualism. This is a radically wrong-headed contention as Elisha's best student, Rabbi Meir, understood. Indeed such a contention is **egregiously** wrong-headed. Nonetheless the contention has gained tremendous traction in Jewish letters and Elisha is falsely saddled with this teaching even today in mainstream Jewish Letters. More recently authors such as Daniel Boyarin have taken up this "Two Powers/Authorities in Heaven" motif and have tried to explain it in terms of that "binitarian" model predicated on the language and conceptualization involving hypostases. While this is a more subtle interpretation of ben Abbuyah's teaching, it too radically misrepresents Elisha's teaching as I have made clear in my book, ***The Secret Diary of ben Zoma***.

*****

--- Everything depends upon comprehending that unity in God which is at once duality, or conversely, the duality which is at the same time unity.

Again. This formulation by Schelling is just what God is. Ubeknownst to Schelling he was speaking Jewish. I myself have taken a shot in my writings at a parallel articulation as to what God is:

otherING-OTHERing

If it takes a Christian-oriented philosopher with a smidgeon of endemic Christian/Eurpean Anti-Semitism in its make-up to allow Judaism to re-gain its most fundamental teaching, then so be it. Who, after all, would want insist on burning *The Merchant of Venice*? I suspect that Schelling and Edward deVere, had they been alive at the time, would not have made Heidegger's horrible mistake.

*****

There is also another citation by Schelling in *Ages of the World* which can function as a bridge to the next subject of this book. I speak of the Qabbalistic teaching of ***tsimtsum***. The citation -- especially its last sentence -- evidences that there was some Qabbalistic influence on Schelling when he wrote *Ages of the World*. His phrasing is not at all the best or most accurate. But it is an indication of this influence. And indeed it turns out that Schelling was very familiar with the writings of Jacob Boehme, a Christian, who allowed for significant Quabbalistic influence on his writings.

The reader should be advised that in my several books on Jewish philosophy and theology I have radically besmirched most of the history of Qabbalah as conceptually shallow and not truly representative of Judaism. And I most certainly sand by and insist upon that overall assessment. Yet even those Jewish-oriented writings of mine which condemn virtually the whole of Qabbalah for its extreme deleterious effect on Juduaism, I have excepted some versions of the Lurianic/Qabbalistic teaching of *tsimtsum*. Those same books also make it perfectly clear however that the only conceptual model of *tsimtsum* which I count as authentic Jewish teaching and as revelatory of God's workings is the radicalization of Luria's teaching on *tsimtsum* achieved by Rabbi Nachman of Bratslav and Uman.

Fine. Those books on Jewish Philosophy and theology ought to be consulted. Let us now turn to Schelling's citation which also gives us a way of understanding one feature characteristic of *tsimtsum*.

The systems which wish to explain the origin of things by descent from above almost necessarily come to the thought that the emanations of its highest primal power at some point or other attain a limit below which there is nothing, and which, itself only a shadow of reality, a minimal degree of reality, can only to a certain extent be said to be, but really is not. This is the meaning of non-being among the Neo-Platonists, ***WHO NO LONGER UNDERSTAND THE TRUE MEANING OF PLATO****. We, following the opposite course, also discern a limit below which there is nothing, but with us it is a first,* ***FROM WHICH EVERYTHING BEGINS, AN ETERNAL BEGINNING****, and it is not merely a deficiency or lack of reality,* ***BUT ACTIVE NEGATION****.*

[*Ages of the World*; page 133. It is to be noted that Schelling also uses the term "original negation" as synonymous with "active negation."]

When it's all said and done Schelling is remarkably free -- in those two writings -- of overt (or, for that matter implied) Christo-centism. Yes. One will find, if one is looking for such, a fair amount of Christian tropes in these two writings. Yet even with these silly -- and sometimes distasteful -- accoutrements this man speaks Jewish.

*****

Please understand, as we enter into these *post coitum-interruptus* waters, that it is **only** these three thinkers from that wasteland which calls itself "philosophy" who are worthy of bringing to the heart of Jewish thinking the conceptual apparatus which allows the Self-Revelation of Hashem in and as Jewish Scripture to display itself in the manner which it needs and in the manner which it should be. ((((I shudder when I realize that I have earned my VERY modest living teaching Philosophy. I shudder because I could have earned far greater income in almost any other profession and, as well, it is a waste of talent to spend SO much time in what -- except for these three figures -- is, in effect, a wasteland. Yet without such immersion in that wasteland would I have been able to encounter these three great figures which have transfomed my life???? Paradox delivers us unto paradox and there is no end to confusion. Ainsi soit-il.))))

*****

Note on "*tsimtsumING*" and 'the good.'

*****

I will arrange for all my good [kol tovi] to pass before you

[Exodus 33:19]

*****

For purposes of this note, 'the good' refers to my treatment of 'the good' in **DSG** and any enhancement of that Platonic teaching contained in *The Second Commentary on "Parmenides"* <aka: "The Seventh Chamber">.

For purposes of this note, "*tsimtsumING*" (the verbal form of this word being intentional) I am referring ONLY to this teaching as found in the writings of Rabbi Nachman of Bratslav/Uman and to no other teaching of "tsimtsum." I include the teaching of Luria on this matter in making this broad exclusion even though Nachman himself, even as he modified the Master, admired Luria.

In my previous writings I have made it clear that Rabbi Nachman has indeed radicalized the Lurianic teaching of "tsimtsum." It is ONLY that radicalized meaning of "tsimtsum" -- involving THE RADICAL BEFEFTMENT OF GOD in that utterly empty space generated by the "contraction/withdrawal" of the Divine Economy -- which is at issue. In my previous writings I have made it utterly clear that I, idiosyncratically, abstract this Nachmanian teaching from all the other Qabbalistic tropes ((emanation-theory; "the breaking of the vessels;" "the *siferot*;" etc., etc. ad nauseum)) which, in the writings of Nachman himself, surround his radicalization of the Lurianic teaching of "tsimtsum." Arguably my "modification" of Nachman is so radically idiosyncratic that perhaps I should not really call it a teaching of Nachman's at all. Such is fine with me. But it would be intellectually dishonest not to mention the source and inspiration for this idiosyncratic teaching.

*****

'The good," then, IS elicitation. That is its intrinsic character. It is elicitation for itself to be. It produces -- calls into being -- the causal factors which produce it. Thus, other than this elicitation (which is a species of need), **'the good' has no autonomy of its own**. It calls into being the causal factors which produce and allow it to be at all. It calls into being the causal factors which sustain it in its being. 'The good' of its very nature is always precarious in its mode of being. Even so the elicitation (even when it, so to speak falls short as it must), once established never goes away.

What Plato did not address in those final key writings ((((*Parmenides* as the keystone which culminates the trilogy *Sophist/Statesman/ Parmenides* even and AS it inaugurates the trilogy *Parmenides/ Philebus/"Concerning-the-Good."*)))) is the mechanism, so to speak, which allows for for the space for the coming to pass of elicitation OF <in the sense of "by" {i.e., in the sense of calling-for at

all} and for 'the good'> in the first place. I am speaking, of course, of *tsimtsum* (at least when that teaching is understood from the paradigm furnished by Rabbi Nachman). Without withdrawal (which, of its nature entails compression/contraction) there is no good. And let me be clear. Plato is silent on this key mechanism exercised by Divinity without which the good does not become operative.

*****

The Pre-History of God.

To paraphrase Wittgenstein in a way never intended by Wittgenstein, one might say:

The Divine Economy is all that is the case.

There is nothing at all which is other than the Divine Economy. Everything, sooner or later so to speak, is nothing but instantiations and specifications of the Divine Economy. Notice that I did not say that everything is nothing but instantiations and specifications of God. No. Not at all. "God" is itself an instantiation/specification of the Divine Economy.

"Before" 'there-was' [es gibt] God there was Play. Play energized by and ***AS*** the energy of what the Rabbis would refer to as "the yeitser ha-ra." [[[[In my other writings I believe I have sufficiently made the case that the "yeitser-tov" is itself but an instantiation/specification of the "yeitser ha-ra." Thus the "yeitser-tov" is not a principle or reality correlative to the "yeitser-ha-ra." On the contrary, it was only through the Great Upheaval of the Divine Economy that the "yeitser-tov" came to be at all AND, even at that, as a derivative and special, recursive, instantiation OF the "yeitser ha-ra." In all respects, the "yeitser-tov" is derivative from the "yeitser ha-ra." I do not claim that this view of the relationship between the "yeister ha ra" and the "yeitser-tov" is the mainstream Rabbinic view of this relationship. Quite to the contrary. But I do maintain that there is an overt Rabbinic whisper, so to speak, which agrees with me. I have addressed this in my other writings.]]]]

Play animated by the "yeitser ha ra" becomes a comi-tragic Drama as the Divine Economy, so to speak, plays with itself. The story of this development is told in Chapters Two [from the "baiyom" in the middle of verse four] up through the end of Chapter Three of Genesis. This development in the Divine Economy makes for something of an alienation of and between the human specification of the Divine Economy and the rest of the Divine Economy. This human specification/instantiation of the Divine Economy evolves into something which is something of great embarrassment and shame for the rest of the Divine Economy. The other-than-human portion of Divine Economy -- "thinking" so to speak through and as the not-Divinity OF Divinity ("later" to be called the "not-God OF God") effects a plan to obliterate the human specification of the Divine Economy:

And Hashem regretted having made humankind on earth and it grieved Him in his heart.

[*Genesis* 6:6]

Then something amazing happened.

Noakh found favor/grace in the eyes of Hashem.

[[[*Genesis* 6:8. A change of heart. But why and in what sense? That is the secret knowledge of which explains the symbiotic bonding of Humankind, Hashem, and creation. Read carefully. It was Noah̲ who found grace/favor in the eyes of Hashem. Hashem discovered something in Himself by virtue of what Noah̲ found in Hashem but of which Hashem had no clue. That humankind -- or at least one of them -- could bring this about was enough to change God's heart.]]]

And thus was set in motion the story of the pact ("the Rainbow Covenant"), a process [a process having priority and posteriority on the side of the what was now "God", but a priority/posteriority which did and does not entail the "before/after" sequential timing of time characteristic of the human-in-creation portion of the Divine Economy] by which humankind and creation as a whole more radically differentiated and separated from what now was "God" whose proper name is Hashem. This process was to be one whereby the embarrassment/shame portion of the Divine Economy (i.e., humankind) was to be transformed into a connubial partner for what was, now, "God" whose name is Hashem. And further, following another hint from Rabbi Nachman ((as teased out of his writings by Wiskind-Elper, 1998 pages 103-114 ***and correlative endnotes thereof***)), This connubial partnership became such that each partner in the YIKHUD could and would, androgynously, become the other partner all in the service of the greatest pleasure possible.

The process, the plan, as it would turn out, ended up requiring a major adjustment since the process, the plan, was found not to be working. So with mankind falling back into the condition of an unworthy partner for what had, now, become "God" whose name is Hashem (i.e. chapter Eleven of Genesis), a restrictive-but-more-focused version of the plan/process was effectuated <<by, through, and AS the thinking and consciousness of the "not-God Of God">> through the calling of Abram by God whose name is Hashem. In other words, this great pact ((the articulation of which occurs by, through, and AS the thinking and consciousness of the "not-God OF God")) with humankind would have to be engineered through a particular people which would function as the surrogate of all mankind in the engineering of the Great and Glorious androgynous YIKHUD.

The pact with the particular people was itself a troubled proposition. God, whose name is Hashem, came very close to abrogating the pact after Moses killed more than three-thousand of his followers when he descended Mount Sinai. But God, whose name is Hashem, settled for the premature death for Moses on Sinai. The pact ((the thinking and consciousness thereof effectuated by through, and AS the "not-God OF God")) with this stiff-necked people was sealed in -- for better or for worse -- for eternity on Sinai.

*****

The beginning of "*tsimtsumING*" is set in motion when the Divine Economy, now on the brink of becoming God whose name is Hashem, with these words:

Noakh found favor/grace in the eyes of Hashem.

The completing of "*tsimtsumING*" comes to a close with verse twenty-eight of Chapter thirty-four of *Exodus*. God, whose name is Hashem, and mankind through its surrogate the Jews, become the dyadicizing couple. Sinai allows for the formal creation memorialized by Chapter One of Genesis (free of the Priestly overlay which continues up until the 'b-yom' of 2:4 of Genesis). A timeless creation becomes the character of this interaction by which the Divine Economy ceased to be only the Divine Economy and became God-whose-name-is-Hashem in consort with his partner, humankind-by-way-of-the-People-Israel.

*****

"TsimtsumING" is that great contraction/withdrawal which allows for all of this to happen. The utterly empty and uncanny space made possible by the great contraction/withdrawal is, of itself, UTTERLY BEREFT OF GOD. The home of creation is this: of itself, horrible emptiness and raw need. But it is this opening which allows for and which becomes the elicitation for the good.

The Drama of God, whose name is Hashem, and humankind plays itself out under the suasion of this elicitation for the good, which, of itself, has no autonomy of its own. Only through the work, generation-unto-generation does this elicitation for the good produce the causal factors which allow for the good to obtain.

[[[The surrogagte <Moishe> for the surrogate of mankind <<the People Israel>> is the human witness for the power of the good (even though the good has no autonomy of its own other than elicitation):

I will arrange for all my good [kal tovi] to pass before your face ---

<*Exodus* 33:19>

]]]

It through and by this process, that something stupendously grand and holy comes to pass. By virtue of "tsimtsumING" **the other-than-God-WITHIN-God** -- I speak of **kavod** -- incrementally comes (((if things work out between God whose name is Hashem and the people Israel))) to fill creation with **kavod** and render the whole as holy. Of course, if in the course of human history the people Israel fail and/or if they are hounded into disappearance, then the fate of humanity is negatively sealed in forever.

How precarious.!!!!! Is there sufficient critical mass in and through the people Israel to effectuate a defense against such a horror???? But wait. There is evidence from Scripture. Listen to these words of Hashem to Rebeqa realizing that "Esau" in the final analysis, is not to be identified either with Rome and or Christianity, but with Islam. Paradox delivers us unto paradox and there is no end to allusion. Islam, the first born and older < paradoxically enough given the de facto sequencing of history > is to become the ally of Israel, the younger, but stronger by virtue of the aid of mighty Islam in bringing humankind to holiness:

Two nations are in your womb
and two separate people shall issue forth from your womb.
One people will be stronger than the other
and the older is to serve the younger.

[Genesis, 25:23-25]

[[Please understand. Of course I am aware that the Rabbis of the classical period made Esau emblematic of Rome/Christianity. But Islam was not on the radar of the classical Rabbis. It did not come into being until 622ce. It came into being by and through military force. This means that it is the weaker of the two parties. It, Esau, is older than Jacob/Israel even as it is younger in the sequential timing of time characteristic of our human experience. But it is this older in the story (who is younger in history) who is to serve the younger (in the story but older in history) and in so doing the people Israel will be aided most significantly in its surrogative task.

It is true that the greatest present threat to the survival of the nation Israel is from the militancy of Islam. Israel must keep its powder dry in our time and do whatever is necessary in this regard. But in the long stretch of human history it will turn out to have been the case that Islam will ultimately come to the aid of Israel and sustain it.

*****

All is precarious. The life of humankind; the life of God whose name is Hashem, is sustained by that all important, difficult, sustained producing of the causal factors which allow for the good <and holiness> to obtain. Amen.

Baruch sheim KAVOD malkuto l'olam vaed.

Praised be the name KAVOD; ITS majesty always and forever.

***** ***** *****

***** *****

***** ***** *****

Commentary Endnotes to this COITUS INTERRUPTUS.

1.
So. Yes. Knowledge and Wisdom are the same indeed. But both words, separately and in their sameness cover over the very dynamic which allows for them to obtain at all. My contention is that, with *Theaetetus* acting as a very pregnant sign-post, Plato wrests that dynamic in and through *Sophist* (in broad outline form) and more exhaustively in the eight-plus-one hypotheses of *Parmenides*. And the very heart of both dialogues is ***diapherein***.

2.
I emphasize that the "differencING" [[a translation for the "diapheronton" of Fragment Eight]] is an ever-obtaining condition which allows for "things" (which then recede as "things"), and **NOT** as an oppositional pattern of priorly existing things, or unities, or neat oppositions. Again, "differencING" is primordially and originally (and, so to speak, the ever-"there" *behind the scenes* operation <<the harmony which does NOT show itself>>), the never-ceasing/never-beginning heartbeat producing, ***derivatively***, identifiable oppositions which, precisely in their neatness of oppositions, bring about a "coming together" <i.e. the harmony which DOES show itself>. Let it be repeated. Once more, as we follow the primordial "logic/logos," we find that *the harmony which does not show itself is stronger than* [i.e, continuously and ceaselessly undergirds and sustains] *the harmony which does show itself*. In other words, *opposition itself*, is continually, ceaselessly, and without beginning, derivative from this heartbeat of "the real" obtaining always as ***diapherein*** which ***births*** opposition.

3.
The two infinite regress aporiae. [[First, 132a,1--132c,13 which evolves to entail the highly suggestive, and implicitly affirmed, contention to the effect that Forms are thoughts [noe̱mato̱n/noe̱ma]>. Then followed by the Second infinite regress difficulty at 132d,6--132e,7]].

The first of these conundra [[132a,1--132c,13]] starts out <<having disposed simplistic accountings of participation reviewed from 131a,5-- 131a,9>> what the tradition refers to as "The Third Man" following Aristotle by maintaining that once a Form (in this case, the Big/Great Itself) for all of its participants) is postulated for the the many greats it would then be necessary to postulate another for the new set which is constituted as "the Great Itself and all the other greats which are participants in the first Form. Such an accounting, then, will indeed, by the logic of the situation, become a senseless infinite regress. the "Form" for the Form and the participants followed by another Form for that set containing the Form for the Form and the participants, followed by another form for that Form for that set of the Form for the Form and the participants, etc., etc. This farcical situation emerges precisely because one thinks that the Form and its participants have status in themselves rather than understanding that both Forms and participants emerge (eternally, in a manner of speaking, here; with temporal before and after there) as nodal points of intelligibility emergent from differENcing/ *diapherein* in general and the more important differENcing as and when the Form and participant are come to be known. <<<<The allusive side issue concerning Forms as thoughts results, at first blush, in a double *reductio ad absurdum* predicated on the presumption {{**ultimately NOT Plato's own**}} that Forms and participants have an intrinsic identity of their own rather than coming to have identity via emergence from differENcing when and as Forms come to be known. This last matter is critical. Only through a synoptic reading of hypotheses two and five (six if the insert hypothesis is counted as third) can this key matter be adjudicated on PLATO'S ground rather than on the tradition's generally unconscious presumptions about Platonic Forms based on Aristotle's various presentations of what a Platonic Form is.>>>>

As I have argued in the portion of the book which is a commentary on *Parmenides* it is precisely this only apparent side-issue dealing with the suggestion that Forms ***are indeed*** thoughts ***which in fact is being adopted by Plato***, at least for the post-367 Plato. The superficiality of the infinite regress involved which we have just reviewed in the previous paragraph becomes even more forcefully evident once it is realized that since thoughts are, **of and by themselves**, of a different order of being than alleged extra-mental realities (be they visible or invisible), the proffered infinite regress to this hypothesis (i.e., the hypothesis offered by our young Socrates to the effect that Forms are in fact thoughts in the soul <every bit as objective in that status as extra extra-mental realities>) there is then not even the possibility of an infinite regress involving extra-mental participants (even when invisible) and extra-mental Forms since Forms, **as thoughts**, obtain on a plane different in kind from things-which-are-not-thoughts be they visible or invisible. The reader is referred back to the section "hey-ii" itself a sub-division of "B-2-b-i."

The second infinite-regress aporia is an infinite regress with reference to the participatory relationship ITSELF between Form and participant. It becomes an infinite regress only by the mistaken idea that the relationship obtaining between Form and participant <<or, for that matter the intercoursing/participation of Forms with each other>> itself shares in the character of the Form and participant. Again, the critical work brought about by Plato through a joint reading of hypotheses two and five (or, as some say, six if the insert hypothesis is counted as the third hyhpothesis) which demonstrates the root of participation to be grounded in diapherein/differENcing, resulting, then, in the realization that the "likeness" ((which is what is used in the presentation of the alleged infinite regress in this case>> of and between the participant and Form is but a generated and derivative feature of participation but not at all the primary meaning of participation.

In addition -- and ultimately more germane -- this second infinite regress [132d,7--132e,7] emerges, you will recall, from Socrates alternate contention (i.e. to his hypothesis that Forms are thoughts) hypothesis that Forms are "paradigms fixed in nature" [132d,2-3] which, it must be noted, is NOT used as a refutation against the "Forms-as-thoughts" hypothesis but only as a refutation of Forms as "paradigms fixed in nature" hypothesis. Again, in the portion of the book which is a commentary on *Parmenides*, **this** offering [i.e., the "paradigms fixed in nature" hypothesis" which is the last proffered offering of how participation can be by whole-and-parts] by the young Socrates ((((**in contrast** to the "Forms as thoughts" hypothesis <<which, as we have seen is never **declared** to be refuted by the superficial arguments proffered against this hypothesis*>>)))) is shown NOT to have been sustained. The reader is referred back to the text in the part of this book which is a commentary on *Parmenides* which is a direct continuation of the above-cited "hey-ii" text.

> *. [[And thus IS the true nature of Forms for the post-367 Plato since of all but one of the ways in which participation can be explained as involving whole and parts are **declared** to be refuted while the only proffered-but-not-**declared**-as-refutative arguments against the hypothesis that Forms are thoughts turn out to be self-consciously superficial. That having been stipulated it must be kept in mind that Plato's "Forms-as-thoughts" maintain their possibility of "objectivity" **only** by doing what Plato accomplishes through that grand dialectic journey of the eight-plus-one hypotheses wherein these Forms <as thoughts {be they called "ones" or, from another perspective, "others" or, as in *Philebus*, "monads"}> are presented as nodal points of stability, in the mind, emergent from the sea of **diapherein**.]]

4.
esse est percipi;

The Irish Bishop points the way.

Let us use Descartes and Husserl as book-ends. *That* was a mighty struggle. In vain to be sure. But filled with vectors which point the way back so as to go ahead. In every single case there was turmoil. It was never overtly phased in this manner, but it was in fact the Tradition's ((unbeknownst to itself)) great attempt to get back to the Poem of Parmenides. Throughout the whole and mighty struggle there was, with the one disgusting exception who died in 1831, was there was the noble animus to get it right with "knowing." The participants would not have phrased it this way, but at its best this "uprising" in Philosophy was struggling to shake off that perverse Aristotelian "Frame" which had -- more unconsciously than consciously as it was passsed on through the lens of Porphery -- governed the Tradition.

Yes. Surfacely, one might perceive a Kant as instantiating, consciously, an "alternative" to the "Realism" of Aristotle. So too with Husserl. But the corrosive power of that "Frame" -- so subtly entrenched in the whole Tradition -- was a signed, sealed and delivered death warrant for this mighty struggle. Yes, even Schelling -- especially the young Schelling up through his publications of 1804 -- was still governed by the corrosive power of that "Frame." In those two great and might publications of his to which I have drawn your attention, he largely (but never completely) broke free from the "Frame" and accomplished something absolutely amazing although even here the "Frame" tended to govern the ex-post-facto understanding of these two great works. And he himself was drawn back to it in that late in life flourish of his, the lectures of which produced that side-show called "Kirkegaard."

Please understand, dear cherished reader. I am telling you what DID happen; NOT how the participants would have described what they thought was happening. And the disgusting exception? The one who did not resist the Frame at all. The one who self-congratulatingly took what was best in the noble <albeit failing> struggle to stand outside the "Frame" by framing this struggle to stand outside the "Frame" WITH AND AS THE FRAME. His name rhymes with "Bagel."

If we were to go right to the epicenter of that grant-but-failed struggle (i.e., *The Critique of Pure Reason* (revised or unrevised, it doesn't matter for this purpose) we can extract from that epi-center the terminology <<while leaving the overall Kantian frame behind>> which can elucidate what was trying to get said as that grand struggle attempted (whether it was conscious or not of what it was in fact attempting) to get back to the genius of the Poem of Parmenides. Try this on for size.

The "noumenal" can only ***BE*** *at all on the condition that it is so as the "phenomenal."*

But from beginning to end, Kant sabotages his great endeavor by hanging onto that Chimera of the "Frame" which in Kantian language calls itself the "in itself." There simply is not "in itself." Nor is something like "the in itself" required as the condition of "objectivity." "Objectivity" is achieved as the mind sharpens the meaning of any given Form-as-thought.

*****

Let me try another tactic, so stubborn and entrenched is the thinking governed by the "Frame."

Something like what Hawking and others have referred to as "The Anthropic Principle." I insist on the phrase "**something like**" with the clear understanding that "like" can obtain only as "different-from" what it is like. Without this "**something like**" the Anthropic Principle becomes nothing more than a jazzed up Hegelianism decked out in the language of Quantum Theory. What is required is a Quantum based Anthropic Theory ***rendered critical***. This has not yet been accomplished by Hawking or, to the best of my knowledge, anyone else.

The contention of this book is that the pearl which slipped through the crack of that Aristotelian/Porpheryan mindset and Frame was Plato's post 367 radical recasting of Form-theory. The most relevant dialogues of this recasting <i.e., *Theaetetus, Sophist, PARMENIDES, Philebus*> EVEN TODAY have an average tendency (largely unconscious of itself) to subject this grand attempt to *choreograph* the Poem of Parmenides to the Frame. <<<<This in opposition to the choreographing of the Poem of Parmenides by and through *Parmenides.*>>>> And <<disturbing paradox noted>> the situation is not especially helped by the fact that Plato himself -- in some of his VERY late productions such as *Laws* and *Epinomos* <the joint endeavor of the Master and Philip of Opus> seem to instantiate what sounds like an eerie vacuum relative to Form-theory. Then again Form theory seems to be taken as axiomatic in circa 351 in Letter VI* There was confusion in the very late productions of Plato, at least in the ones which did NOT make it into the first three tetralogies.

*. [[322d,6-8. Cf. also footnote # two on pages 456-457 <Loeb Classical Library, 1929/2005>.]]

In previous writings I took the phrase "the beautiful wisdom of the Forms" <*te̱ to̱n eido̱n Sophia te̱ kale̱* line six> out of context and mistakenly took it as a wistful fond farewell to his dearest conception. I apologize.]]

***** ***** *****

Form-theory post 367. Diaphereining; differENcing; such is the basis of participation. It happens in souls/minds and derivatively in reality. There is no "in itself" and yet objectivity obtains. "Only the Gods and a small group of humans understand." [*Timaeus* 51e,7-]

5.

Plato and writing. So much has been said about so little. The reader is referred to pages 382-393 of **DSG** for the main treatment of this matter. But Plato had a conditional boilerplate comment on these kinds of things in Letter Seven which I failed to include in those pages although I have referred to the passage in question often-enough in other writings of mine. This Dion oriented production by Plato offers "bloody wounds" [*brotoi*, 344d,2] which here functions for Plato <the greatest wordsmith of them all> as a species of metonymy for "mortals" [[*brotoi* {indistinguishable in Plato's own hand from *brotoi* as "bloody wounds"} scripted with this meaning by the ex post facto redactors of Plato's writings]]. Plato's strife-driven life was one which well understood that human interaction often entails "bloody wounds" (actual in the case of Dion) even when no actual blood is spilled.

So listen. Listen so as the HEAR Plato's cleverly crafted case for why he **did in fact** commit his most serious matters to writing as per 344c,3-8. This passage which precedes our present citation is well explained on pages 392-393 of **DSG**. But the contextual poignancy of this boilerplate follow-up ought to have been given expression on those pages. Herewith:

But if in fact he did commit such serious matters to writing then it is not "the gods," but rather bloody-wounds/mortals "which in truth have utterly destroyed his wits."

*****   *****   *****

*****   *****

*****   *****   *****

Critias 121c:

And when he had gathered them together he said

● ● ●

D. Postscript.

A. Somewhere in and around the seventh chamber:

The Holy One, blessed be He, has a place [*maqom*] and its name is "Secret" [*b-mistarim*].

(in conjunction with explanatory context on pages 347--352 of *The Secret Diary of Ben Zoma*)

The Holy One, blessed be He, has a place [maqom] ***and its name is "mysteries,"***

[5b-i--5b-ii of the Bavli commentary on Tractate *Khaggigah* <ArtScroll pagination>]

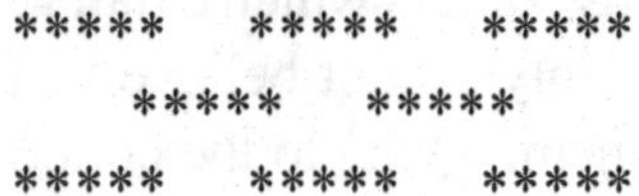

B.

For two and a half years Beit Shammai and Beit Hillel were in debate. These [Beit Shammai] *would maintain that it would have been better* [nun-vav-het; noah] *for humankind not to have been created than to have been created whereas those* [Beit Hillel] *would maintain that it is better for humankind to have been created than had humankind not been created. They took a vote on the matter and concluded: It would have been better for humankind not tohave been created than that humankind had been created. Now that man has been created, let him examine his* [past] *deeds; others have the version: let him consider carefully his* [future] *affairs.*

[[Bavli commentary on Tractate Erubin of the Mishna. Contained in ArtScroll on pages 13b-ii/13b-iii and cited, with minor changes, from page 312 of *The Secret Diary of Ben Zoma.* The translation, however, is an amalgamation of both the Soncino and ArtScroll translations.

The translation of that most key word **noah** as “better” --<<in contrast to ArtScroll’s “more pleasant” which, intentionally, deflects away from the natural meaning of “noah in this context and, in that deflective process, loses the all-important reference in our passage to “Noah” who found grace/favor in the eyes of Hashem>>-- has been extensively explained in my other books on Judaism.]]

C. Notes to Duane and a Note to Neal.

C-1. Notes to Duane.

Duane: History may end up recording the ArmYtage/McGinley entity heroically sustained a friendship in the face of antithetical views on intellectual/religious matters which entail great emotional energy. So, to be blunt, I certainly do not believe that Christianity has any sanction at all by Hashem. Quite to the contrary. And yes, Islam is to be -- but not really in its present instantiation and this will change -- the vehicle by which the world will come to acknowledge the Jews as the chosen people and Islam as its guardian. There is strong Scriptural support for this. Give me time and space and I could say this better.////Your second missive virtually substantiates my case. Take those features away from Christianity and Christianity simply is not Christianity. I agree on all the points you made in the second missive. We are, in the final analysis, closer than you may think. Be well. Through all of this I will be especially happy if things go well between you and Marisa and if things go well between Michele and me. Be well.

*****

So I guess that means you got her a fifty dollar ring. Think she'll settle for that? I got Michele a ring more than a year ago and told her to wear it when she's ready. She still does not wear it. She is wound pretty tight. She finds it hard to let herself go, especially with me. She's not always available for various reasons. At my age that's mostly OK. Tick-tock, tick-tock. Soon I'll be dead it and won't matter. I really do love her and she really does love me. That's good enough for tonight.

*****

Are you out of your fucking mind or perhaps you never had one? I hope she's worth it, both in and out of bed. What I bought for Michele was 1k although it was very much nicer and valuable than the sale price would indicate. It was from an estate sale and thus was severely discounted. The fact of the matter is that Michele is worth much more and in fact ((and I know we are both on the same page here, your page being Marisa's mine being Michele)) she is worth infinitely more than that. Where does Marisa live now and does she work? Be good.

It, obviously, will take time for the status of Islam to be appreciated. At this stage of its development it does not merit the status that it will come to have./////Once more we have to agree to disagree on your contention about Judaism and Christianity. But I will grant you that, from both sides, silly and irrelevant things have been said. One such is properly cited in your last sentence./////I think we agree on the two other points. You are tempting me to seek out Sallis and to give him a second chance. hmmmm: "The Verge." Be well.

And even more so we disagree on Justice in the Divine economy. Without proportionate retributive justice even distributive justice disappears. NORA is the key for understanding the Divine Economy. So pontificates narcissistic John

*****

Thanks for the clarification. I will make it my business to check it out. He probably said better and earlier what I've been saying.///NORA is a Hebrew adjective. There is a phrase repeated in the liturgy which comes from, I believe, Nehemiah 9:32.

And now our God, a God **Ha Godol, Ha Gibor, and Ha Nora**
Who maintains the Covenant with Loving Kindness.

It's root is "terror." I have seen "AWE-full" as a translation. "Terrible" is a valid translation. "Dreadful" is a valid translation. In my view the "AWE-full" translation is a domesticating deflection; an attempt to make Hashem be squared with things which can be construed to have a positive connotation. Terror is its root meaning. I believe "Dreadful" is the most appropriate translation. There really is something fearful about Hashem quite independent of any sin or fault we may have committed. The sheer facticity of God is first and foremost ***dreadful***. And recall that oft-cited nugget from Psalms. 'Fear of the Hashem is the beginning of wisdom.' I am not saying that there is no Love and Mercy in and about Hashem. Of course there is. But that's just the beauty of Judaism. Justice and Mercy. The second depends on the first. And, of course, the primary meaning of Justice is proportionate retribution. Everything else -- including Love -- falls apart without it. /////Again, thanks for the Sallis lead.

*****

The sloppiness of my writing doesn't merit your careful attention. In any case you did pose a question. My notion of Divinity abusively borrows from many sources without being fair to them. It also consciously FLEES certain theological tropes. As far as I can tell the distinction you refer to is enmeshed, one way or another, in Plotinus: the ineffable: i.e., that worn-out trope of finite/ human verses infinite God. Virtually all of Sufi and Christian mysticism instantiates this. By and large Qabbalah, in the final analysis, trades on this. (((Within that all so shallow Qabbalistic tent I allow that three have something to offer despite the smelly tent which they live in and I borrow from them despite what they are enmeshed in: Rabbi Nachman of Bratslov; Luria; and to a lesser extent Moses de Leon))) Maimonides too trades on this ineffability shit as well. Perhaps I have misunderstood your distinction. In any case I certainly do not take any of my insights from that "ineffable" tradition. Indeed "God" is not a mystery to the intellect although the sheer facticity of God is not only mysterious but rather shattering ((I trade on the most offensive translations of the Hebrew "NORA" when speaking of God)). In any case there is nothing ineffable about God nor is there anything about God which cannot be deciphered by the human intellect if one is honest and free of denial. In some sense God IS the human intellect. The impediment which keeps humans alienated from God -- and perhaps they live a more comfortable life whether they be atheists, agnostics, or zealous believers -- is emotion and DENIAL. Just open your eyes and you will see. God is very pedestrian and common yet NORA!!!!!! (I do not accept the cute translations of "AWE-FULL" for that word. "Dreadful" says it better.) In any case we are in and of the Divine Economy and my bet is that we are not called to comfort but rather to be in tune with the Dreadful. For without the Dreadful there would be no life at all. And it seems to me that it is better for life to be ((in all of its INTRINSIC dreadfulness quite independent of sin although sin is indeed part of the equation)). I probably have misunderstood you. If so I regret that.

We instantiate the divine more fully through intense sexual behavior with a loved one than we do through prayer, although prayer remains essential in having a relationship with God. God is not personal but prayer is one of the more essential ways by which we stay in tune with God, and such is good. In effect, prayer is simply submission/ surrender <aka "Islam"> to "God."/////As to Hosea, the Prophets, the Sh'ma, etc. I have heard too many Reform and/or Conservative and/or Reconstructionist Rabbis cite those sorts of things in trying to explain that Judaism too has all the love things that Christianity claims to have. Judaism is in deep-shit trouble if it feels it must ape Christianity so as to be "relevant."////My major inspiration(s) are from Jewish sources even though what I say about God does NOT represent any mainstream Jewish sects (Orthodox or non) to the best of my knowledge. I do not throw love --- I speak of Eros primarily and to a lesser extent Philia (and do not allow agape to have a seat at the table) -- out of the equation. On the contrary it is the energy of all that is the case Divine and human. My sense of it is that those citations and sources are better understood from their source and context rather than in a covert or overt attempt to mimic Christianity without having to genuflect to Jesus. But I really do speak for myself. I do not claim, in this God concept, to be representing any Jewish sect. I do however enter into the lists of the meaning and validity (i.e., lack thereof) of the Oral Torah and I make normative claims FOR and about Judaism there. Especially in the *Ben Zoma* book. Do tell me the meaning of Rahner's statement.//////I hope you are well. You are certainly intellectually alive. Does it go well with Marisa? There are good days and bad days between me and Michele. I get REAL bummed out when there are bad days. And aside from a deep proclivity towards workaholism, Michele has huge financial responsibilities. A seventy hour work-week leaves little time for romance. Romance is both the greatest danger/threat and, at once, the greatest boon to what little I have left of my fragile sanity. Be well.

*****

You're a tough customer, Duane. Why don't you just throw in the towel and say that I'm right on everything?/////Yes. The "love" thing, while not exclusively Hebraic, is majorly strong in classical Judaism. It becomes stronger -- for ill or good being another issue -- in Yeshu and James. But James and Yeshu ((that is a Yeshu stripped of all those Pauline <and, to a lesser extent, even Johanine> tropes WHICH ARE NOT HEBRAIC AT ALL)) are genuinely Hebraic. But they are at the extreme fringe. The Jewish celebration of love/mercy is NEVER at the expense of Justice. This is true of the Prophets; and of Hillel. (I leave Aqiba whom you also cited out of the equation. He is, in the final analysis, a monstrous figure; for another sitting.) James was still Justice-oriented; Yeshu -- who himself was not free of mania -- was close to being idiosyncratic rather than Hebraic. Even so, he falls within the fold./////I do not see a clelebration of Eros in Judaism. Comfort with sexuality is not the same as Platonic Eros. But please understand. This absence in classical Judaism is a DEFICIT. In the final analysis it is good for God's Revelation that there be the right kind of marriage between A+J. So far the only person who has achieved such is a former phil prof from Scranton who now teaches for peanuts at two community colleges, separated by an hour commute.///// enough. Michele. You can tell that there is a pathological streak in Michele. She took up with me; that alone says SO much. And she never got married or even had a live-in relationship for all of the more than two decades after she left me. And she still loves me. Pathology. But there is a fundamental goodness about her; so she is in conflict. ((She is also incredibly intelligent and a joy to be with; except when she uses her refined intelligence to demonstrate time after time just how wrong I am. And more often than not she is right.))

My romances in the intervening time were live-in ones. But that aside, all that I just said about Michele is true of me as well (except that I can only seldomly make the case that she is in the wrong; she would have made a first-class lawyer)). This time she is the husband, so to speak, and I am the wife. All the power -- basically age and money -- is on her side. She has gotten used to NOT sharing her life with anyone in a serious way. She has boundaries all over the place. I am not talking about obvious boundaries which are beneficial and necessary for a relationship. It's much more than that. Her defenses are up. Her time with me left her traumatized. She leans on the side of "My way or the Highway." For my part I am very conscious of the age difference and also of the huge money difference between us. I tend to act subservient towards her and that is not good for either of us. Can we grow into something good and genuine? I don't know. I do know that I'm a mess when we are radically alienated from each other./////I look forward to your admissions that my theological and philosophical contentions are correct. John

*****

{{{{{{{{{{{{

I am Hashem and there is none else;

I form the light and *create darkness*;
I make peace, and *I create evil*.

I, Hashem, do all these things.

[Isaiah 45:7. Emphases are mine.]

*****

You must remember this:

The "not-God" OF God is more God than God.

The "not-God" OF God is God differentiated from God. We are the "not God" OF God. It is by, through, and in the instantiation of God as "not-God" that there is consciousness at all. The drama of God is played through the "not-God" of God. In that sense God is and suffers all which obtains by, through, and in the "not-God" OF God. Where humans fail, God fails. Where humans triumphs, God triumphs.

*****

So yeah. I was pretty good at traumatizing. My name was RAGE. The recipients of my rage were, generally, weaker than I. That is, in some cases, until they proved stronger than I. I have mentioned Michele. The mother of six of my children. Some of my children. And a couple of dogs along the way. My Karma-debt is huge.

The telos of all is to be Love. But there is no possibility for Love without Justice and the primary meaning of Justice is retributive Justice.

*****

Do you want to see the Face of God? Read Hoshea; over and over. Wrath, Hatred, Confusion, Jealousy, Vindictive. And a shameless head-over-heels Lover.

*****

Honesty is the midwife of truth and truth is the Seal of Hashem. The "not-God" OF God is an instantiation of God. We are made in the image and likeness of God which means we are made in the image and likeness of God which is instantiated in the "not-God" OF God. God -- Hashem -- is just as much responsible for the horror which obtains here as are you and me. That does not lesson our own responsibility and karma debt. But God is some sense IS us. Thus God does not get a free pass on this. Yet without all this -- the very dreadfulness of "reality" resulting from the inevitable differentiaiton of the "not-God" OF God from Dvinity/God -- there would be no life. And my "faith" -- my emnuah; **A-M-N**; my trust -- is that is better for there to be life than not.

That guy Yeshu was not the Messiah and a fortiori he was no more divine than you or I. Which means he was divine. He was a confused and hurting Jew. He was the enemy of hypocrisy which is always a good trait. Hailing from Nazareth, he had great compassion for the poor and disenfranchised. He also had illusions of grandeur and, if my interpretation of these things in the Dunghill book is correct, he brought about hurt and harm to others (and ultimately to himself) through the Lazarus charade.

Certainly I understand that the New Testament put many words in his mouth which he never uttered. But there is one statement attributed to him which, if he didn't actually say it, he should have.

You shall know the truth
and the truth will set you free.

*****

V-YADAAT HASHEM

The blessing and the curse, at once. But the curse comes regardless. The blessing we must earn. Love is to be the telos and it don't come easy. Love requires travelling through all the necessary corridors of Justice to arrive.

*****

Torah scholars have no rest --
neither here nor in olam ha-ba.

[Bavli Gemara on tractate *Berahot* of the Mishna. 64a-iii<Art-Scroll translation>.]

}}}}}}}}}}}}}

*****

This is where your friend Marty comes into play. Despite himself he opened to door, so to speak, allowing one to recognize what he baptized as onto-theo-ology and how this development in Philosophy came to be hegemonic (e.g. Kant and Aristotle are brothers). It was a liberating move on his part and was a great insight on his part. But he brought to this liberation his Achilles heel, namely, the fatal error of treating Plato as a pre-Aristotelian. Derrida -- who was more nuanced in general and more nuanced in the reading of Plato -- was crippled by the same Achilles heel. Yes. As a first approximation Plato himself invented ontotheology (but not, of course, the label) through his accounting of Forms pre-367. But the revolution -- a break really -- he orchestrated by deconstructing, so to speak, the theory of Forms after 367 went unnoticed by both of them. So indeed, the marriage between A and J is -- given overwhelmingly entrenched presuppositions about the origin and outcome of Greek Phil (i.e., even shared my H and D) and the received way of collapsing Judaism and Christianity into Judeo-Christianity as though they compatible with each other (which they are not)-------- so on both counts ---------- the received way of appropriating A and J is a fraud. Not a fraud which is conscious of itself, but a fraud nonetheless. What is called for is the proper kind of *yikhud* of and between A and J.///////God's primary Revelation is in and AS the people Israel. Absent the people Israel Revelation ceases. Torah/Tanakh <<i.e., not the Oral Torah which is a matter too complex to discuss here; but this is NOT Karaism>> but the Chumash in particular -- is how God speaks to the people Israel; ((i.e., not to mankind as a whole)). And should the people Israel disappear, Revelation ceases. But there are more things in Heaven and Earth than are contained in Torah-Tanakh. Discerning the extra-Tanakh features of Revelation is tricky business. I have already alluded to the miasma introduced into Judaism by virtue of the Oral-Torah becoming normative in Judaism about a quarter century after the destruction of the Temple. I have addressed this whole multi-faceted and subtle matter at length in my Ben Zoma book. Just as huge and having a subtlety of its own is the coming to pass of "ontotheology." Anything ensconced in ontotheology most certainly is not God's Revelation. Finally I have a way of reading the story of Ishmael and Essau ((-- and the meaning of Essau is not, I claim, emblematic of what the classical (Talmudic) Rabbis maintained --)) <as I believe you will discover if you keep on reading> as God's indication that Islam is the secondary vehicle of God's Revelation. Islam has far to go before it will be able to understand that it is the brother of Israel. But I believe that such will come to pass. Hashem's other name is Allah. Read the story of Rebecca.

*****

Lo and behold! I just finsished my last bit of pontification and find that you are throwing my way another opportunity. *Of course* Justice is Retributive. That is its primary -- but not sole -- function. I suspect you do not understand the NORA of Hashem.

*****

It, obviously, will take time for the status of Islam to be appreciated. At this stage of its development it does not yet merit the status that it will come to have./////Once more we have to agree to disagree on your contention about Judaism and Christianity. But I will grant you that, from both sides, silly and irrelevant things have been said. One such is properly cited in your last sentence./////I think we agree on the two other points. You are tempting me to seek out Sallis and to give him a second chance. hmmmm: "The Verge." be well.

*****

And even more so we disagree on Justice in the Divine economy. Without proportionate retributive justice -- even distributive justice -- disappears. NORA is the key for understanding the Divine Economy. So pontificates narcissistic John

*****

You scare the living shit out of my when you compare me to Heidegger. I am familiar with those sections from his later musings wherein he speaks of a non-comforting Divinity. "The Last God." Of course he is unto something important. And yet he is not speaking Jewish. Justice and Mercy/Compassion ((Rakhamim from Rekhem: literally the womb.* There simply is no Mercy/Compassion or Hesed without Justice and yet Mercy/Compassion is the final expression OF justice.

> *.[[[Rekhem. It is not only that which is behind the cervix. It is, as well, that which is forward of the cervix. The whole nexus is, going in, the "maqom" of conception and as well the "maqom" from which of birthing. Unbeknowst to Judaism it is the quintessential Platonic word <<albeit not an actual word which Plato could have or would have used; but compare to his usage of **khora**>>

What is before the cervix. Anatomically one might say: clitoris and vagina. In so doing once bypasses what this "place" is in fact. It is the nodal point of primary anxiety for both males and females (albeit experienced in differing manners). This "place"/maqom is the uncanny par excellence.

"Clitoris" is a fine word. Check out its etymology. "Vagina" (of Roman/Latin vintage) skews the phenomenon to which it points. "Sheath." Sheath, of course, for the "sword." It is not a worthy name; it is far too circumscribed. Further, the whole phenomenon of what is before the cervix cries out for a single name by which to designate that whole nexus including smell.

"Cunt." Yes of course. A word which more often than not is used misogynistically by both males and females (albeit in differing ways). But it really is the best word for the raw sacredness for this wondrous and fearful nexus. Say it aloud but softly, slowly, and, so to speak, stretched out. Then you will begin to understand the wonder of this nexus. Misogyny withdraws in favor of celebration:

kkkkhhhuuuuuuuuuuuuuuunnnnnnnntt

]]]

(((I have read the account of Marty -- youngish and ambitious stud -- and his affair with the ridiculously young, artistic, and intellectually gifted Hannah (((Grace/Favor))) Arendt with the long flowing locks. It's an old story which is ever renewed each generation. Marty really did have some Anti-Semitic dimensions in his personality and he was conflicted all throughout that relationship. When she took up with that other intellectual (I forget his name) he pretended not to be affected; indeed -- thinking he was always in control -- he pretended to bless and approve of this new situation. But he was in fact SHAATTERED although he could not admit this consciously to himself. He never fully recovered. Basically he exiled anything

Jewish from his mindset. He walked away with an unacknowledged and searing bitterness.)))

To be sure there is no Divine Love without God's NORA. To think otherwise is naive and most Christians are naive. But love is to be the telos of all of this although it can never be the case that NORA can disappear. Indeed Love dies in the Divine economy if NORA disappears. A fortiori, love disappears from human habitation when NORA ceases in the Divine economy. The tension endemic to Judaism is enough to make one crazy. Plato's celebration of Divine mania pales in comparison to the razor's edge which IS Jewish theology when Jewish theology ((except when Jewish theology exhausts ***and demeans*** itself and destroys itself by ape-ing the Love teaching of Christianity)) is true to itself and its Scripture. Marty never really *experienced* the "two-fold" of which he spoke. Like everything else in Marty, what was fertile in him soured by virtue of his narcissistic solipsism. He couldn't even see that about himself. <<<To be sure all creative writers are waist-deep in narcissism. It goes with the territory and in point of fact it usually does not bring that much harm in its wake. <<<Yet one thinks of the atrocious harm perpetrated by the supreme narcissist who wrote *Mein Kampf*>>> The trait usually does not become destructive except when one is in denial of one's own narcissism.>>>

His case was sad indeed. He had exiled whatever Jewish inspiration he had had back in those years, not only from Hannah but from colleagues, teachers and other students. What German Christian back in those days didn't carry with himself/herself a degree of endemic European Anti-Semitism? But Heidegger was immersed in circles wherein much of this could have been lifted. But not after the Arendt debacle. His is a sad and sorry case who ends up grousing and entering into solipsistic meandering. As I said earlier, Heidegger dishonors Holderlin -- a great and mighty poet despite his Christian tropes -- when he appropriates Holdrlin's verses for his own solipsistic meanderings./////I read Otto back in the day (senior year of college? first year of graduate school?) -- parts thereof -- and found it to be insightful although he too domesticates things. Very few people can stay on the razor's edge. Even most Jews are de facto not able to do it even though it is their heritage. What I said about Otto, I suspect, will be true about that chapter in the Sallis book. Don't forget. I gave him a shot a long time ago and found him domesticating as well. Domestication keeps one in the house of ontotheology even when a person claims to understand such and to be free of such. Domestication is better reserved to men who are so in love with their partners that they merit that great encomium "uxorious." But domestication has no place in the life of thinking. Domestication in thinking is like heroine. It leads to numbness, sloppiness, and a shutting down of consciousness.

*****

I may be glum by nature and disposition. Certainly when I speak of Michele there is an element of "glumness." Always worried about whether it's going to turn out all right. Paradoxical for a guy who insists that the best translation for "Emunah" [A-M-N] should be "trust." My "trust" capacity for anything/anyone including God is no better than the thyroid function of someone who has lost the thyroid function.

With regard to that interpretation of Judaism: I don't see it. To emphasize the element of NORA in Jewish theology is simply to be faithful to the text of Scripture. To point out that in Judaism the "Love" pole obtains in conjunction with the Justice pole is simply to follow the mainstream teaching of Judaism through the centuries. Likewise a very strong Scriptural argument can be made that the primary meaning of Justice for Judaism is PROPORTIONAL retribution. There is nothing glum about that. Hermeneutic key? There are many. The truth is that whatever one dresses up as in presenting oneself before the court of academic respectability, everybody filters things through themselves ranging from their academic masteries (masterys? spelling is not one of my masterys) up through a whole range of conscious and unconscious emotions and ideation. Everyone does this whether they acknowledge such or not. It is true that I no longer give primacy to what will be acceptable to whatever academic norm is influential. I am something of a lone ranger. I'm ok with that.

*****

There are some isolated phrases in Hoshea which, taken out of the context of his whole work, seem to indicate that. But read that man again. He is a fire and brimstone man at heart and I love him for it. That having been said, his *yikhud* statement about Hashem and Israel is beautiful. It is used in the liturgy.

Hoshea was in fact the greatest of all the Prophets in his Generation, a Generation which included Isaiah. But what a clever fellow! For surely he wrote after what he experienced: the fall of the Northern Kingdom. No? This allows him to predict what he had experienced. This allows him to celebrate the only part of the commonwealth which still remained: Judah/Judea. He is disingenuous in spades. (((Also he is the prophet, if my memory serves me right, spoken of in an article which Freud cited in "Moses and Monotheism," to the effect the Moses died -- was killed -- much earlier than what Deuteronomy indicates. In my writings I have made the case that Moses did not come down from the SECOND forty-day sojourn on the Mountain of God. Whatever the mortal agency which occurred, it was Hashem who orchestrated this. "No-one can see my Face and Live." Check it out: ***Hashem would speak to Moses face to face, as one man would speak to another.*** Exodus 33:11. All of this outside of the entrance to the Tent of the Meeting pitched far outside the campsite. Moses would visit there but did not stay there. Joshua remained inside and did not leave the Tent of the Meeting. The changing of the Guard. But I digress. Check it out in my other books.))

Back to our man who was the greatest prophet in the generation which included Isaiah. The Wrath of God is his calling card. But it is the Wrath of a brutally injured God whose trust in His people has been violated. But the love remains. Wrath and Love. The razor's edge.

In that day (declares Hashem

You will call [Me] Ishi,

and no more will you call M Baalim

and then there's this" the song of the Tefillin:

And I will betroth you to Me forever

I will betroth you to Me in uprightness and justice

I will betroth you to Me in Kindness and Compassion

And I will betroth you in trust

AND YOU WILL KNOW [V-YADAAT] HASHEM

That last line, Duane. There is no greater intimacy. And yet there is no greater curse. We are on the razor's edge. But to flee the curse is insanity for the curse cannot be avoided in any case. The intimacy makes the curse worthwhile,

Ha Gadol; Ha Gibor; **HA NORA**

*****

Thanks for the vote of confidence. Coming from a guy who challenges so much of what I say makes the encomium more credible. Duane: I know you are a deeply spiritual person on a journey which has taken you far from where you were at one time. That is fine. Your only obligation is to be true to your Mazzal. If I were speaking Greek I would say Daimon.

*****

That was heavy-duty and honest. I will try my best to avoid being glib, which is one of my many character defects. We both drink from the same fountain and this is not easy for me for I love that fountain. The clearest statement that I can make is that Resentment is the worst possible outcome. When the WORK of Justice harbors resentment it is sabotaging itself. I suggest that the ONLY cure for resentment is indeed PROPORTIONATE retributive justice free of hatred and resentment. In this regard it is noteworthy that in Israel the death penalty is applied ONLY to those who perpetrate Genocide. Not even murder is punished by the death penalty. My take on forgiveness which is willed is that usually it is cheap and makes people feel good about themselves. And without retributive justice (again free of resentment and hatred) the hatred and resentment creeps back in anyway. In the final analysis reconciliation and forgiveness just happens and comes upon a person. Forgiveness which is willed is simply not forgiveness. time takes time. **This I Must Earn**. Forgiveness cannot be forced even by the person who is the injured party. If it is forced or willed it is simply not forgiveness. I am inspired on these matters by the chapter in *The Spirituality of Imperfection*. The special case wherein lovers hurt each other via infidelity (the perpetrator overtly; the other in a way which is subtle, much less obvious, perpetrating hurt through passive-aggression and/or neglect) it's a draw. A life lesson to be learned from. There is, really, nothing to forgive. When that is realized lovers become reconciled. I talk a good talk. I do not always walk the walk.

*****

Those are weighty questions, Duane; and they are not just theoretical. I can tell by the way you express them. For answers to those kinds of questions I usually charge a hundred and fifty per hour. For you I'll give the discount. Just send me seventy-five.//// To be straight forward, the "beyond" world simply does not exist. What is holy is shot through what we jerkily call the "phenomenal" world. Except for the Goddess of Truth -- who honors the so-called phenomenal world -- the Tradition tends, at best, to give it secondary status or, at worst, just plain trashes it. The reality is that the noumenal obtains only as the phenomenal. Plato came to see all of this in his last two decades of writing. But more than anyone else he was responsible for that "beyond"-oriented world-view which he had invented for the first two decades of his serious phil. Christianity almost wholesale (along with Islam) has bought into that META-physical schema. Most versions of Judaism do as well. But there are strains of Judaism which do not. The world really is full of Gods. That is not necessarily comforting, but it's true. Mystery does not belong with the "beyond" for the simple reason that there is no "beyond. The holy (which includes the daimonic) is all around us all of the time. So too is mystery. Mystery is for the most part not comforting. There are diabolical dimensions to it; it is more dark than light. Divinity/God is not incomprehensible. We are in and of it and it is dark. Comprehensible but not comforting. troubling. even dreadful ---- but evident for those who do not live in DENIAL. I have maintained that only such a concatenation of such things allows there to be life. And, in the final analysis, I aver, it is better that "there be" life than not. That is my AMuNah. My trust. I would say that if you look for the holy and God in the beyond you will never find it. Perhaps one must search within.

*****

Anna Holmes seems to have stolen the playbook from that Emperor who thought he was showing off his new clothes. To engage the question of misogyny with an Enlightenment sensibility is just plain silly.

Misogyny -- instantiated by a spectrum of female and male versions of such -- is nothing less than the defining characteristic of our species. We do not really engage what it means to be human unless and until we get honest, then comfortable, with the inevitability of misogyny as that defining characteristic of who and what we are. The patterns of denial on this matter are fueled precisely by the kind of Enlightenment-spawned sensibility which infuses Ms Holmes' article.

Sigmund Freud suffered as well from the Enlightenment sensibility combined with a genteel Victorian (i.e. condescending) attitude toward the female of our species. Even so, he was able to honor truth with regard to the twin pillars of misogyny: penis-envy and fear of castration. The layers of denial on this topic are phenomenal, particularly with those Feminist appropriations of Freudian Psychoanalytic Theory governed by the received norms of Political Correctness.

Those two pillars are not going away. We, male and female alike, must make our peace with them if we are ever to channel the energy of misogyny into less destructive paths. This defining characteristic of our species is here to stay and all the bromides in the world will not get rid of it. Honesty is the midwife of truth and truth is the condition for the possibility of genuine freedom. I suspect that it will be the next generation of Feminism which will garner the courage to speak truthfully about these things.

Duane:

Finally:

With this book I now complete what I will now refer to as:

The God Trilogy

The Secret Diary of Ben Zoma
The Dreadful Symmetry of the Good
The Seventh Chamber

*****

C-2. A Note to Neal.

Plato does address music both in the Republic and elsewhere. His reflections are more soul (i.e., psuch<u>e</u>; psyche)-oriented than religious oriented although some references to the Homeric Gods are made. I regret not having spent some time on the Homeric Gods in our course and I hope to remedy that in my next rendition of the course. At the present time I do not have the Platonic references and I am not certain that what I say here does full justice to what Plato says.

On the wider front it is indeed the case that music accompanies virtually all liturgical activity in all -- or at least virtually all -- religions. In my own Catholic background (pre-Vatican-II) music (both instrumental and vocal and both at once) permeated most services, particularly the one which used to be called "Benediction." One was transported to heaven on the spot.

Freud -- and I am not saying he was not right -- would probably point to the fact that such music, whatever its conscious intent might have been, is in the service of re-enforcing the "wish-fulfillment"/ comfort function of religion.

Even during my long period of atheism some popular rock renditions would put me into something like a mystical state even when I was not drinking and rugging'. "Music" comes from the Greek word for "Muses." There were, I believe, nine of them only one of which was specifically for "music. Also the Pythagoreans would speak of the music of the heavenly spheres.

When I ceased being atheistic ((and became a converted Jew who was only atheistic, say, about two days a week)) some LYRICS (and some with new found meaning) sent me into religious/spiritual ecstasy. I think of "Ride Captain Ride upon your Mystery Ship" <Moody Blues?>; "Ruby Tuesday" by the Stones <Ruby Tuesday as Hashem; "who could hang a name on you?">. and, of course "Hey Jude." The first time I heard it I way lying with my to-be-first wife (with whom I had six of my seven children). As you know she was/is Jewish. It was a hot Summer afternoon. and when the radio played it I heard "Hey Jew!" I was shocked and scandalized, thinking that there was some kind of slur going on. But over the years that became the song of songs which could always -- with or without drinking and druggin' -- put me in a manic condition of joy-and-melancholy-at-once with tears streaming down my face. Finally, the greatest spiritual song of all is from the Stones with the deepest teaching of all: You can't always get what you a\want; but if you try, sometimes, you can get what you need.

I'll stop there. In any case it is clear that music has for many a powerful affect which not only can accompany religious ceremony but, much more, IS religious ceremony. And, Freud notwithstanding, the music which has the deepest spiritual/religious force is not really properly called "comforting."

Clearly you struck a chord deep within me. I suspect we are more or less on the same page. I will not insult you by raising the tawdry subject of final grades. Suffice it to say that since your first exam I have always understood that you have a fine and creative intellect. Put it to good use. Yes. Making (even a shitload of) money is important. But I also hope you will tap into your creative side. Be well. Feel free to share your thoughts when you want. JWM

*****

D.

Baru<u>h</u> Shem Kavod malkuto l'olam vaed

Praised be the name Glory in majesty forever and for all time

E. OUTLINE.

A. Introductory Remarks.

B. More or Less Commentary on *Parmenides*.

A. Introductory Setting. 126a,1--127d,5.

Cephalus: When we came from our home at Clazomenae to Athens, ...
----- He himself, however, had heard Zeno read them before.

A-1. The first three names mentioned in *Parmenides* are Cephalus, Adeimantus, and Glaucon.

A-2.

When we came from our home at Clazomenae to Athens --- [126a,1-2]

A-2-a, Clazomenae.

A-2-b.

Virtually all commentaries on *Parmenides* make reference to the fact that Anaxagoras hails from Clazomenae.

A-2-b-i. Nous and Anaxagoras. Nous and Plato. Nous and Aristotle.

A-2-b-ii.

In all of this a pre-emptive observation must be made. It is only through the prism of Aristotle's system that Platonic Forms would be presented as (naively) ontologized "universals.

A-3. The Nous teaching of Plato.

A-4. The Gathering: Zeno and Socrates (and the others) then joined by Pythodorus, Parmenides, and Aristotle.
127a-1--127d-5.

Antiphon, then, said that Pythodorus told him that …
He himself, however, had heard Zeno read them before.

B. Plato's Retrieval of Parmenides: *peri ideon* as the Condition for the Possibility of Allowing the Poem of Parmenides to Say what It was always Meant to have Said.
127d,6-135c,8

Socrates listened to the end ---
--- "I don't think I have anything clearly in view, at least not at the present time."

B-1. Socrates Engages Zeno and Introduces the Subject-Matter of *Parmenides*: (**peri ideon**).
127d,6-130a,3.

B-1-a. **Excursus** on the Intertwining of Discourse/Predication and the Theory of the Forms.

B-1-b
127d,6-130a,3. (again)

Ton oun So̲krate̲ akousanta palin ---
lambanomenois epideiksei

B-1-c.
127d,6-130a,3. (yes, again)

B-2. Parmenides wrests Form-Theory from Socrates.
130a,4--135c,

B-2-a.

130a,4--131a,4

B-2-a-i. The Wresting Begins.
130a,10--131a,4

B-2-b. Journeying through the Difficulties.
131a,5--135c,8

A. Difficulties dealing with the nature of "participation."
The Whole/Parts Difficulty (131a,5--131e,7).
The First Infinite Regress Difficulty <and the rejection of a proffered solution> (131e,8--132c-12).
Forms as "paradeigmata" and the correlative Second Infinite Regress Difficulty (132c,13--133a,11)

B. Difficulties dealing with the Possibility of Knowledge.
The Knowledge Difficulty on Its own Terms. (133a,12--134a,4)
The Knowledge Difficulty as an Indicator that Mortals are alienated from the God and Gods. (134c,5--135e,9)

B-2-b-i. Difficulties dealing with the Possibility of "participation."

The whole/parts difficulty.
131a,5--131e,7.

So does each thing that gets a share get as its hare the form as a whole or a part of it? ---

--- "I don't think I have anything clearly in view, at least not at the present time."

B-2-b-i. The whole/parts difficulty. (again).
131a,5--131e,7.

B-2-b-i. The whole/parts difficulty. The actual launching of the "Dance-Writing."
131a,5--131e,7. (yes, again)

alef
beit
gimmel
dahlet
    dahlet-i
    dahlet-ii
    dahlet-iii
hey
    hey-i
    hey-ii
    hey-iii

{{{{{{{{{**Excursus on "Forms as Thoughts."**
Excursus A.
Excursus B.
Excursus C.
Excursus D.
Excursus on "Forms as Thoughts."}}}}}}}}

vav
    vav-i
    vav-ii
    vav-iii
    vav-iv
        vav-iv-a
        vav-iv-b
        vav-iv-c

vav-iv-d

zayin

zayin-a

B-2-b-i. The whole/parts difficulty. (heading towards the finish) 131a,5--131e,7.

*****

Theaetetus, 154c,1--155c,10.

*****

Theaetetus, 201c,4--210b,3.

*****

***** ***** *****

***** *****

***** ***** *****

*****

C. *Coitus Interruptus.*

Caesura.

*****

Encomium for Heraclitus.

*****

Encomium for Schelling.

*****

Note on "*tsimtsumING*" and 'the good.'

*****

I will arrange for all my good [kol tovi] to pass before you

[Exodus 33:19]

*****

The Pre-History of God.

To paraphrase Wittgenstein in a way never intended by Wittgenstein, one might say:

The Divine Economy is all that is the case.

*****

[*Genesis* 6:6]

Then something amazing happened.

Noakh found favor/grace in the eyes of Hashem.

[[[*Genesis* 6:8. A change of heart. But why and in what sense? That is the secret knowledge of which explains the symbiotic bonding of Humankind, Hashem, and creation. Read carefully. It was Noah̲ who found grace/favor in the eyes of Hashem. Hashem discovered something in Himself by virtue of what Noah̲ found in Hashem but of which Hashem had no clue. that humankind -- or at least one of them -- could bring this about was enough to change God's heart.]]]

Baruch sheim KAVOD malkuto l'olam vaed.

Praised be the name KAVOD; ITS majesty always and forever.

***** ***** *****
***** *****
***** ***** *****

Commentary Endnotes to this COITUS INTERRUPTUS.

***** ***** *****
***** *****
***** ***** *****

D. Postscript.

A. Somewhere in and around the Seventh Chamber.

B.

C. Notes to Duane and a Note to Neal.

C-1. Notes to Duane.
C-2. A Note to Neal.

D.

E.Outline.

*****

Acknowledgement

Most of the proofing of this text was done by me which fact explains the pervasive shortcomings in the final product which were a function of non-assiduous proofing.

My daughter Meghan McMahon Helms did much of the proofing for about the first quarter or third of the book. The result a far more readable text. I acknowledge that, in addition to her proofing, she often bemoaned my proclivity for long unwieldy sentences. Generally I declined to take her advice on this on this unless there was a clear lapse in syntax by virtue of such unwieldiness.

It should be mentioned that Meghan is a "seventh" as well; in several senses.

***** ***** *****

MAYA

TAT TVAM ASI (*with a twist*)

1. Prolegommena to the the 'is-ing' of appearing; the dyadicizing otherING which allows for Revelation at all.

What truly is difficult is discerning what status obtains **for Parmenides himself** as the intended meaning of "The Way of Seeming/ Appearing." There is, no doubt, a stern rebuke by the Goddess of Truth for those who follow this path. On the other hand the Goddess --((and here we have the problem concerning the fragmentary character of some of these statements and, as well, the sequencing of these collections of fragments))-- is adamant that the truth of the whole ***requires*** that this ((two-headed)) way **must** be pursued. Listen to Her cacophony of statements on this tension. It is a tension which is NOT -- (at least not with complete excision of ambiguity) -- resolved in the extant fragments of the Poem itself.

*****

It is the Goddess who announces that it right and fitting that our "Youth" come this way [hodon], a way which is portrayed as:

Far indeed does it lead from the beaten path of humans.

[267 <Kirk and Raven unless otherwise specified>]

Immediately upon designating the journey which our Youth is to be on, the Goddess tells him that it is just [dike] that he learn all things, BOTH:

the unshaken heart of well-rounded truth in conjunction with the seemings/opinions [doksas] of mortals in which there is no true trust.

[267; slight amendment of the translation].

*****

My claim (which, a fortiori, is my claim about Plato's *choreographing* of the Poem) is that THIS COMBINATION [*the unshaken heart of well-rounded truth* ***in conjunction with and ultimately not excisable from*** *the seemings/opinions [doksas] of mortals in which there is no true trust*] is that which "lies from the beaten path of humans." To be sure, "the beaten path of mortals" is ubiquitous. But what is not ubiquitous -- indeed, quite, quite to the contrary -- is the sealing together of BOTH of these accountings as the "way"/path which must be followed by the Youth for the sake of truth.

[267. Emphasis is mine.]

*****

The Goddess states the deepest mystery of the entire Poem:

Yet nonetheless, you shall have to learn these things as well: how things-which-appear, as they be through [peronta] ***in every way***

through everything, of necessity MUST genuinely achieve the appearance of being.

Or:

Even so it behooves you to learn* {you are to learn} *such things as well, to wit: that appearing things MUST BE in an appearing manner, as they <u>be through</u> everything in every way.

[267; translations somewhat amended from Kirk and Raven in conjunction with the McKirahan translation and its footnote # 5. Emphases were mine, of course.]

This extraordinary and agendizing statement which presents us with The Goddess' précis of just what is to follow sets the parameters of what the careful reader is to find in the rest of the Poem. Any accounting which is not in tune with this agendizing statement is one which is out of tune with the Poem. Since the shards left of the Poem <<and it seems clear that Plato only had access to shards and likely fewer shards than are available to us>> tend to emphasize but one pole of this dyadisizing program <<<a "dyadisizing program" which is the whole, this very whole then containing within itself a sub-dyadisizing program in one of its parts, i.e. "the Way of seeming/appearing">>>*. And that is the point which even many scholars of the Poem have not appreciated. There are **TWO** non-symmetrical dyadisizing axes which animate this Poem. If this key insight is not recognized, it becomes most difficult for readers to catch the spirit of the whole of the Poem. Further, to merely make commentary or analysis on the Poem in its sharded form is to misrepresent the Poem of Parmenides. Only a ***choreographing*** of the Poem ((provided that such ***choreographing*** is produced prior to the distorting "Frame" brought to these matters from the time of Aristotle onwards)) remains as the best possible hope of understanding the Poem as a whole. Plato produced the gold-standard on this matter with his *Parmenides*.

*. {{{{{ [[[This complex ***unitive*** paradigm introduced by the Goddess of Truth can -- ***but only <u>analogically</u>*** -- can be

drafted, as a first approximation, as an x-ray, so to speak of that **unitive** "***duality in unity and unity in duality***" motif of all of my Jewish writings. It has been given an articulation by Schelling, an articulation which I have cited often in my writings:

Everything depends upon comprehending that unity in God which is at the same time duality, or conversely, the duality which is at the same time unity.

{{*Ages of the World*; page 197. Because those superficial readings of Schelling are so often misconstrued by a reading of Schelling in which Schelling functions as something of a "connecting link" between Fichte and Hegel, it must be ***forcefully*** averred that Schelling here -- and indeed is **NEVER** -- neither in the published Freedom book of 1809 nor in this unpubished (in his lifetime) manuscript of 1814/1815 -- is NOT referring to an Hegelianesque 'identity of identity and difference.'}}

The God of Israel IS this 'unity in duality/duality in unity'. Such is a dyadicizing unity which, in one of the terms which comes to be by and through such dyadicizing, includes within itself a kind of self-dyadicizing dyad.

As a first approximation let us call "Hashem/Elohim" the initial <no temporal sequentiality is implied in this formulation; nonetheless there is real, substantial, and genuine sequentiality involved> "product" of the dyadicizing unity which is, of its very nature dyadicizING. By virtue of "creation" <<in that hard sense involving ***tsimtsumING***>> Hashem is separated off from Elohim and comes to obtain """"""in"""""" that uncanny ((and of itself **UTTERLY BEREFT OF GOD**)) empty space [**maqom**] generated (and sustained) by ***tsimtsumING***. Hashem in creation obtains as a kind of dyad -- **kavod** and **maqom** -- in, through, and by which the "world" (i.e., creation) comes to be filled with **kavod**

> all-obtaining in the uncanny "no-place" <**maqom**> which is the very place of the world. God-in-creation obtains in the medium of **kavod** sustained in the "place" <a "no-place"> which is ***UTTERLY BEFEFT OF GOD***. God in creation can obtain only as "the Not-God **OF** God."]]] }}}}}

*****

The boilerplate. In the concluding passage of *Parmenides* Plato gives his parallel wording to how the Goddess of Truth insisted that BOTH parts of the Poem -- the true and the false; the real and the unreal; being and seeming -- MUST go together if truth is the goal. Listen.

Plato's astounding boilerplate ending of *Parmenides* climaxes with this pregnant comment: ***ALETESTATA!*** For Plato, this double entwining summary -- which would be paradoxical (indeed senseless) only to someone who consciously or unconsciously has a mind bounded by the "Frame" of the Tradition which was set in motion by Aristotle and ensconced through the centuries of the Alexandrian greenhouse -- is literally true for Plato and, at once, is Plato's final choreograph for how the two parts of the Poem inter-penetrate each other. Listen:

Parmenides speaking: *If we were to summarize with one expression, "the one; if it is not, then nothing is," we would be speaking correctly, no?*

Aristotle speaking: *Without any doubt.*

Parmenides speaking: ***Let us, then, also say: "As it appears, the one, whether it is or is not, the one and the others both with respect to themselves and with respect to each other in every possible way both are and are not and both appear and do not appear,***
Aristotle speaking: ALETESTATA!
[166c,1-7]

*****

The journey into and of truth MUST INCLUDE the journey into appearing; appearing which MUST achieve the genuine appearing-of-being and indeed "is," in this sense, as well. The deceitful character of appearing -- and travelling through all its vicissitudes -- is part and parcel of the journey into and of truth. And as we shall later on [in the Goddess' transition to the Way of mortal Appearing/Opinion <278-279>] this journey into and of truth, which entails BOTH ways as **intrinsic** to itself, will keep our Youth from being outstripped by those who ONLY taste the fruit of Appearing/ Opinion and, by implication, all those who, foolishly, ONLY taste the fruit of the Way of truth:

The ordering of all these appearings which I convey to you will insure that the [limited scope] of merely mortal learning [gnome] will not outstrip you.

[279. I have amended the spirit of the translation contained in K&R.]

2.

MAYA: *The dyadicizing otherING which allows for Revelation at all.*

call it a word; call it a concept; call it illusion; call it illusion which, somehow, IS anyway; call it a 'reality' *tout court*. Any and all and none of these designations are true in some sense.

*****

In the developmental histories of Hinduism and Buddhism there are, in each tradition, various "spins" on the meaning of "maya." Generally speaking, and by virtue of the fact that in the developmental history of Hinduism there are only seldomly any un-subtle meanings of "maya," the developmental history of Hinduism on the meaning of this "word" are less paradoxical than the developmental history of Buddhism on the meaning of this "word."

In any case I neither wish -- nor can I with sufficient authority -- to trace either of the developmental histories of this word in these two great religions. I believe that my own treatment of "maya" -- inspired by the words from the Goddess of truth -- is in tune with many, but not all, meanings of "maya" in Hinduism's developmental history relative to this word and, further, said treatment is largely in tune with "later" (i.e., after the onset of the Common Era) meanings of "maya" in Buddhism's developmental history relative to this word.

So, it seems, it appears.

> <<<<<In this aside I do not wish to make any grand statement about Buddhism. In the developmental histories of Buddhism and, for that matter, Hinduism, one will find that any attempted universal characterization of either of these religions is belied by each of their intertwining developmental histories.
>
> That having been stipulated, there came to be a development in Budhhism -- long, long after Siddhartha was buried -- which resonates with these matter. I speak of a development in which what was always implied by the Buddha became quite overt. I speak of the "true-self" **AS** "no-self." Correlative with this is the fascinating teaching that "nirvana" is, precisely, NOT to escape from samsaraesque phenomenality aka, "maya." Quite to the contrary, the blessed state of "nirvana" is to sustain the true "no-self" in the phenomenality and "maya" of all. In this role such a "no-self" is generating "compassion" and aid for those seeking wrong-headedly a life which can only entail greater degrees of suffering. There is never any escaping of the "world." Suicide most especially is the guarantee of throwing ourselves ((ultimately our "no-selves" which, in this particular scenario, involves lack of comprehension of himself/herself as a "no-self")) back into the world. There are simply manners by which the "no-self" can obtain in the world. "Maya" wears two-faces: One

is the face of illusion delivering us from sorrow to sorrow. The other is the face of, so to speak, ever-surprising "phenomenality."

you can check-out at any time you want; but you can never leave

[*Hotel California*]
>>>>>>

3.

This short text of mine functions as a codicil, so to speak, to my recently "published" <i.e., at my own expense> **The Seventh Chamber**. Sometimes a codicil recasts the whole character of one's "Last Will and Testament." Sometimes a codicil only makes a minor adjustment to such a document. And sometimes the adjustment is significant without changing the character of that to which it is a codicil. I believe that this third description describes the relationship of this codicil to **The Seventh Chamber**.

The Seventh Chamber was itself presented as the third and final entry of what I referred to as:

GOD TRILOGY

So **MAYA** appears to also function as a codicil to

GOD TRILOGY

So it seems.

*****

I hereby dedicate, with admiration and gratitude, this codicil to

GOD TRILOGY

to:

DUANE ARMITAGE

Duane has both a fine mind and a fine character. I have known him for about eight years. We share similar "intellectual" ((but for each of us highly emotional)) interests in Philosophy <Plato and Heidegger come immediately into mind)) and in Theology <Judaism and Christianity come immediately into mind>.

I sense that we both participate, so to speak, in what the Hebrew language calls "Emunah" **<A-M-N>**. I tend to seek to "trust" whereas Duane already lives in the ambience of "trust."
Over the years we have sparred with each other. Sometimes, one might say, to the point of being hurt or angered by what the other has said. ((The truth is that more often than not I am hurt or angered. Poor character formation.)) For me the sparring has always been the occasion for stretching my mind and heart. Indeed, a fair amount of the material in **The Seventh Chamber** emerged from my sparring with Duane. With that in mind, let us now launch ourselves into some of the incompletely treated issues raised by our sparring which ended up in that book. It is not my right nor business to replicate Duane's words. But I feel free to more or less replicate my own words of such sparring. This codicil addresses the unfinished business of one of the matters which appeared in that book as a direct function of our sparring:

Those are weighty questions, Duane; and they are not just theoretical. I can tell by the way you express them. For answers to those kinds of questions I usually charge a hundred and fifty per hour. For you I'll give the discount. Just send me seventy-five.//// To be straight forward, the "beyond" world simply does not exist. What is holy is shot through with what we jerkily call the "phenomenal" world. Except for the Goddess of Truth -- who honors the so-called phenomenal world -- the Tradition tends, at best, to give it secondary status or, at worst, just plain trashes it. The reality is that the noumenal obtains only AS the phenomenal. Plato came to see all of this in his last two decades of writing. But more than anyone else he was responsible for that "beyond"-oriented world-

view which he had invented for the first two decades of his serious philosophy. Christianity almost wholesale (along with Islam) has bought into that META-physical schema. Most versions of Judaism do as well <including, most especially, Qabbalah>. But there are very significant strains of Judaism which do not.//// The world really is full of Gods. That is not necessarily comforting, but it's true. Mystery does not belong with the "beyond" for the simple reason that there is no "beyond." The holy (which includes the daimonic) is all around us all of the time. So too is mystery. Mystery is for the most part not comforting. There are diabolical dimensions to it; it is more dark than light. Divinity/God is not incomprehensible. We are in and of it and it is dark. Comprehensible but not comforting. troubling. even dreadful ---- but evident for those who do not live in DENIAL. I have maintained that only such an overall concatenation of such things allows there to be life. And, in the final analysis, I aver, it is better that "there be" life than not. That is my AmuNah. My trust. I would say that if you look for the holy and God in the beyond you will never find it.

4.

Perhaps, then, we should look within rather than beyond. This is true but it needs qualification. Let us first see its essential truth.

Divinity is indeed within. The pedigree for this kind of thinking is ancient and, really, trans-cultural.

*****

5.

Eliyahu. ((aka "God<is>Hashem"))

v-heenei! *Hashem passed by. A great and mighty wind ripped through the mountain, breaking rocks before the face of Hashem. But Hashem was not in the wind. And after the wind, an earthquake; but Hashem was not in the earthquake. And after the earthquake a fire; but Hashem was not in the fire. And after the fire* ***a still, whispering, voice****.*

*****

6.

Then, famously, we have Plato’s report about Socrates in *Apology* (and, less famously, elsewhere in the Platonic corpus). We are speaking here of a ***daimon***. Not the soul of Socrates, but more like a guiding spirit for his “psyche” which tells him what not to do but does not tell him what to do. Nor is Plato alone in this. Sometime later Epictetus will speak of an inner ***daimon*** distinguishable from the soul.

The word spawns our English words “daemon” and “demonic.” It is also translated as “genius,” along with the cognate “genie” with the possible connotation of an “evil genius” within. The word also is used in both *Alcibiades I* [105d-e and 124c] and in *Theages* [128d and 130e]. In these cases as well the word <<<and once explicitly referenced as “Daimon” it is then referred to as “the god”>>> does get associated with an inner voice which advises against doing this or that, (but in fact, in these two dialogues, in encounters which implicitly have an amorous aura about them). Since the charge against Socrates involved the charge of not believing in the Gods of the City (thereby corrupting those who were often considerably younger than he), it is credible that Plato, by referencing it [the Daimon of Socrates] again in *Apology*, is seeding the reader with the possibility that some members of the jury would have been, at the least, skeptical about someone whose connection to Divinity <<leaving aside the “Gods of the city”> was through this kind of inner voice.

In any case, these possible associations notwithstanding, it is minimally clear that Socrates claimed to be guided by some inner “daimonic” voice which performed something like the task of spiritual guidance.

*****

Plato’s written corpus offers much more information on his usage of Daimon than what he reports-about and/or attributes-to Socrates in those three dialogues referred to above. I am speaking of his own treatment of Daimon in the Story of Er by which *Republic* comes to a close.

Yes, of course. This story is presented through the character Socrates. It is at least clear to me that often enough Plato is primarily using the character "Socrates" mostly as a straight-forward mouthpiece in many dialogues for his own thoughts as opposed to actively developing features of the character in the service of developing all sorts of back-drops (e.g., dramatic irony) apropos to this or that scene and/or this or than interchange with certain interlocutors. Let that be stipulated in general and let it be stipulated as well that both at the opening scene of *Republic* as well as with some portions of his interchanges -- with Thrasymachus earlier on and with Glaucon later on -- the character "Socrates" in this dialogue is developed beyond the role of being a mouthpiece for Plato's own exposition of certain themes. So stipulated. Even so, the story of Er is a passage involving minimal interlocutory features. Further, the accounting of Daimon in the story of Er has a flavor about it quite separable from any of the portrayals of Socrates relative to what was probably Socrates somewhat idiosyncratic understanding of his own "voice."
Plato's account clearly and unambiguously distinguishes between Soul (Psuche) and Daimon. The soul is to choose both a Daimon [617e] and a "life paradigm", there being more "life paradigms" than souls [617e-618a]. The order of choosing these "life-paradigms" is randomly determined by lots. And the character-formation involved with the "incarnation" one has just left tends to have a huge effect on the choice of a life-paradigm. [620a]. In any case even the one who chooses last will be able to choose a decent and fulfilling "life paradigm. " (((Odysseus is cast in this role of having to choose last whereby he chooses a fulfilling but modest life-paradigm in contrast to the high-profile-but-radically-troubled life-paradigm in his soul's previous incarnation. And Odysseus, it is pointed out, having learned well the lessons of the life just completed, would have chosen such a modest life-paradigm even if he had been the first to choose. [620c])))

It is interesting ((perhaps of paramount interest)) that the process of choosing a Daimon is left somewhat vague in the accounting of this story, especially with regard to why a soul would be attracted to this Daimon rather than another. In contrast, the process of choosing a life-paradigm (((again, there being many more life-paradigms than souls-choosing and there will always be -- even for those choosing last -- fulfilling life-paradigms, enough, even when they involve negativity; they are presented as having the potential for fulfillment depending on how one deals with the vicissitudes of the life-paradigm which is chosen [619b]))) is well delineated and exemplified. The Daimon -- having been mentioned only at the beginning of this process (617d) -- returns to the scene only when the soul is getting prepped for its return to earth. [620d-e] It is here that we learn that the chosen Daimon is "the guardian and fulfiller of its <the soul's> choice <i.e., of the chosen life-paradigm at the least; but is there not something else as well?>." To be sure, it is at least that. But there is more to it. Much more as we shall see.

*****

So. Just where are we at this point? "Life-paradigms" are clear and Plato furnishes a fair amount of combinations and permutations of variables in one's life paradigm. However, one major variable is NOT contained in the chosen life-paradigm. **Arete**:

> *Virtue* <however> *knows no master* [i.e., ITS contours -- unlike other life-variables in the chosen paradigm -- are not determined by the choice of life-paradigms]; *each* <soul> *will possess it to a greater or lesser degree, depending on whether it values or disdains it.* [617e]

Virtue (or Vice) then will be earned by the soul in question in and through the actual course of living. With this last statement we are on the cusp of appreciating what Plato is accomplishing here. But it is up to the soul (i.e., the individual) to navigate his way through the virtues and vices in such a manner that the individual will actually achieve what the Daimon ultimately stands for: the chosen destiny of that individual. Plato does not say this in so many words but the phrasing, "the guardian and fulfiller of his choice," points to the awe-full choice so indicated in such a way that it cannot be construed to be limited only to the variables of this or that life-paradigm. The stakes are much much higher. **We choose what we are called to become** but making that choice just by itself does not mean we automatically become what we are called to become. Choice is a many-splendored affair.

Let us make some observations on these matters occasioned by the factors involved in this weighty story.

a). I, personally, do not maintain that this story MUST involve a conceptual commitment to re-birth and re-incarnation in its merely sequential way of being understood. Remember always, it is a story.

Human freedom obtains both in the timing of time which entails no sequential before and after as well as (and in concert with) the timing of time which does entail sequential before and after. Here I stand in the company of Schelling. Listen:

---- *Therefore the whole thing can only be considered as having happened in a flash, since it is conceived as something which happened without having really happened.*

[**Ages of the World.** Translated by F. Bolman, Jr.; AMS Press, New York; 1967. page, 192.]
and:

---- *In creation there is the greatest harmony, and nothing is so separate and sequent as we must represent it; but the subsequent cooperates in what precedes it and everything happens at the same time in one magic stroke.*

[**Of Human Freedom.** Translated by James Gutman; Open Court, Chicago; 1936. Page 65.]

Also, in these matters, listen to the Poet:

Like the flash of heat lightning that tells you all that is, is now.

[**I Lock the Door Upon Myself.** Ecco Press, New York, 1990. Page 92.]

Thus the dynamic of rebirth (i.e., in this case, radically forming and re-forming ((a forming and re-forming which can become -- for ill or good -- a substantial changing of character formation over time)) one's character) can actually be instantiated in a single incarnation. I myself tend to believe that even for Plato himself this "super-structure" of actual reincarnation is a convenience by which to get the moral teaching presented. But I won't bet the mortgage on this last contention.

b). We now -- with or without the reincarnational motif -- turn to a most-pregnant phrase of "the Dark Philosopher." It is most apropos to Plato's teaching.

ETHOS ANTHROPO DAIMON

a human's character is his destiny

Let Heraclitus' short version of The Story of Er sink in. To have chosen a Daimon is, in effect, to have chosen one's destiny. Daimon -- as our called-for-but-not-yet-achieved destiny -- obtains in each one of us as a voice -- often just a whispering but sometimes with a dramatically intrusive and thundering ***NO!!!!!*** -- urging the human to get back on track relative to achieving and becoming his or her own proper Daimon.

c). My claim is that The Story of Er is the teaching of ***CHOSEN*** **DESTINY**.

The claim, at first glance, seems oxymoronic. But it is not. In the course of a lifetime* -- in and through the vicissitudes of our life-paradigm -- we are forging our destiny in accordance with the cooperation of and between the time-bound-but-***not***-sequential choice of our whole lives with the infinite series of mini and/or major choices which we forge through sequential timing. The success or failure of that decisive non-sequential choice which sets the desired model --

which will succeed or fail contingent on the individuals conduct in the course of its lifetime -- rides on our viscissitudinous sequencing of mini and major choices in a course of that lifetime.

> *. [[*He said some other things about the stillborn and those who had lived only a short time, but there not worth recounting.* (615b-c)
>
> "In the course of a lifetime." It's only a story. Plato is neither called upon to explain every life situation and how it would fit into the story. It is not literal. Nor is Plato being insensitive. Those whose life-spans are too short for the contours of this story (or for that matter those who are so severely incapacitated that they could never make a choice irrespective of how old they become) are simply not at play for purposes of this story]]

[[In addition to the words of Schelling and Oates on this matter I addend my own two treatments of human freedom. The first is my treatment of choice in my 1980 article, *Aristotle's Notion of the Voluntary* [**Apeiron**; vol.xiv, no. 2. Pages 125-133] in conjunction with my treatment of these things in *Some Notes on Justice and Choice as Treated by Plato in Book IX of* **LAWS**. This article is contained as an Appendix [pages 143-153] to my publication of 2000: *The Walking, Talking, Wounded.* [ISBN: 0-967936-0-6]]]

*****

CHOSEN **DESTINY:** *The Story of Er.*

Conceptually the phrase is problematical. Its meaning as I adduce it is as follows.

There in in every human being an intersection between the timeless timing of time (involving ***real change*** but not involving sequential before and after) and the timing of time as we experience it in our human condition entailing temporal before and after versions of sequencing. The intersection stretches throughout a human's life time. Each and every "instant" of a human's sequential experience is permeated by his or her timeless timing and its content.

Choice is the character of this timeless timing. It is the choice of one's destiny. There is a timeless choosing of one's destiny. However, this choice for one's destiny **does not at all imply that one will achieve AND BECOME one's destiny.** In the course of a lifetime one is making trillions of major and minor; conscious, preconscious, and unconscious "choices" <<<<Yes! I am conscious of the conundrum of speaking of choices which are preconscious or unconscious. That's all right. They are choices as well by way of energy which is not yet conscious of itself even as it chooses.>>>> whereby we advance or impede our task of achieving and becoming our chosen destiny. Please understand. The "life paradigm" <<constituted by its many variables>> is only the raw material {{{the medium, so to speak}}}*through and by* which we achieve and become -- or fail to achieve and become -- our timelessly chosen destiny, That is correct. **ONE MAY FAIL IN THIS PROJECT**. There is no punishment ((life takes care of that for all, both the just and unjust)) for this failure except the deepest experience of a raw and wounding melancholia shortly before we die. There is nothing more sad. For everything about us, if we fail, utterly disappears as if we were never born. If, on the other hand, we do achieve and become our chosen Destiny we <<<<But NOT as John or Fred, or Mary or Abraham; just the daimon; just the chosen destiny emergent from John or Fred, or Mary or Abraham>>>> are guaranteed that timeless happy condition. The Seventh Chamber has been reserved for that special population. The Seventh Chamber is the Future-Pluperfect. What we will HAVE achieved and will have become is already obtaining there. What we will have failed to achieve and become simply disappears.

The major point is to realize that at every instant of our lives we are making decisions which will have determined whether we succeed or fail to achieve and become our chosen destiny.

7.

Mazzal.

In the Bavli there are many and diverse meanings of *mazzal*. Two are relevant here. The first tangentially; the second substantially.

One of the meanings of *mazzal* refers to constellational/planetary influence on human behavior and human destiny. Rabbi Yochanon asserts the following caveat with regard to Jews:

ayn mazzal l'yisrael

From this I have adduced, in an earlier publication, the following: *Accordingly -- Maimonides among others notwithstanding -- planetary/constellational influence does not affect those who are Jews in so far as they are Jews.*

This meaning of *mazzal* -- as opposed to most of the meanings of *mazzal* catalogued in this section of the Gemara -- is the one which I referred to as "tangential" relevant to this discussion of finding Divinity within. *Mazzal*, I am claiming, in its most substantial meaning does carry the force of a person's destiny.

The boilerplate given by Rabbi Yochanon on this matter allows that planetary/constellational factors normally do affect humans and their diverse destinies. Affects; not totally determines. In contrast the *mazzal* of a Jew in so far as one is a Jew is mostly free of such influence.

What has been said in the above is something of a segue into the greater (at least in this book) and more important substantial meaning of *mazzal*. There is, indeed, something almost "animistic" about the multitudinous meanings of this word. The word is alive with connotations both biological and spiritual at once. But the primary meaning of *mazzal* <<from which the other multitudinous meanings are derived in differing manners>> is, so to speak: "Jewish Daimon." "*Jewish* Daimon" means being virtually free of planetary/constellational influence. "*Jewish* Daimon" entails choosing one's destiny by virtue of a choosing which itself is largely free from extraneous factors. The Chosen People are "Chosen" by virtue of the almost exclusive character of the "choice-ing" made by Jews in choosing one's destiny. "Mazzal tov!" is the public recognition of what is presumed to be choice/accomplishment in the service of *choosing* <<and, one hopes, *becoming*>> one's destiny. God's ***own CHOSEN destiny*** is in through and AS the Jewish People, a choice engineered in, through, and BY the people of God working as the "Not-God **OF** God."

[[[The Bavli Gemara to tractate Shabbat of the Mishna <at 149a-i> effectively gives validation to this notion of *mazzal*. A question is raised about future-born proselytes relative to the firm consent-to and affirmation-by the gathered People Israel at Sinai with regard to the Law given to them by Hashem. The contention of the Gemara at this point was that the *mazzalot* of future-born proselytes were present to give surrogative consent at Sinai for those future-born proselytes. Art Scroll's footnote # 4 to 149a-i sends the reader to 39a with regard to question relative to future-born *Jews* <<i.e., not proselytes> relative to consent to the Law given at Sinai. This question is adjudicated by various understandings of certain relative Scriptural passages. That is fine. In any case it seems to me that an *a fortiori* argument could also make the point for future-born Jews. If the mazzalot of future-born proselytes to the People Israel were there at Sinai, *a fortiori* the *mazzalot* of future-born Jews were present at Sinai as well.]]]

*****

8.

Whether it is Daimon or "Jewish Daimon" one thing is for sure. Daimon/Mazzal is some instantiation of God differentiated from God. We are in the realm of the "Not-God **OF** God." What is occurring here is an incredibly HUGE incarnational project. It includes, of course, Yeshu from the Galilee. Without doubt. One of billions upon billions (perhaps more than trillions) instantiations of God as human. The whole world is **indeed** filled with His Glory. Indeed, His Glory [**kavod**] IS the Not-God-**OF**-God. **A-M-N**; Amen and Selah! [[[**kavod** IN the world can be construed as weight; the weight of the world. **kavod** at the outer limits of phenomenality is the "shining" <*Zohar*>. MAYA, enables this for **kavod** just as

kavod is the enduring condition for the possibility of MAYA.]]] We are God's honor/Glory. We are God's shame. We have come to be -- over a wild and ever-increasing intensity -- God's consciousness (and conscience). Most of all we are God's thinking; a thinking made possible only by God's self-differentiation/instantiation AS the "Not-God **OF** God." We are, in effect, God's voice. But of the many and multifarious voices of God, which is the *called for* voice which is to be pulsed through what we are (i.e., the Not-God **OF** God)? Eliyahu heard it.

*****

9.

tat tvam asi
that art thou
that is you!
you are it!

The great teaching of Upanishadic Wisdom. But there is, it may appear, a fly in the ointment.

Yes. Of course I know. The language of "metaphysics" and of "ontotheology" was not on the minds of the Great Upanishadic Gurus. Yet, in any culture at any time, a mindset and its linguistic instantiation can easily be permeated by such without the rubric The articulators of such a statement may or may not be imbued with such a mentality quite irrespective of any conscious awareness of the significance of such a mindset.

I smell here the great buga-a-boo of the "metaphysics of identity," that ultimately disappointing first-born of "ontotheology." That it came to pass in a land not then affected by the tropes of Ancient Greek Philosophy only makes it more insidious since our guard is down. And yet there is grandeur in these three words provided that they are weaned from the poisonous venom of the "metaphysics of identiy."

This great revelation -- and it is indeed a grand and glorious revelation when it is understood in its true fertility -- is the fabulous transmission of that ultimate core truth of the Divine Economy: "Brahman" <<<The Great Cosmic Principle of all; aka "God">>> **IS** you!!!!!; **IS** me!!!!! For the "Atman" in you IS Brahman!!!!! The "Atman" in me IS Brahman!!!!! But can this be true?

It is sometimes alleged in "World Religions" textbooks that the notion that my very being (Atman) is different from the Great Cosmic Principle "Brahman" is exactly what is meant by "maya," it being understood that in this usage of "maya" one is speaking of illusion. But, in effect, this reading <<<<<leaving it as an open question whether or not the great Gurus of the classical period of Hinduism themselves understood differently and to the effect that maya-as-illusion occurs precisely when one passes over the essential **difference** between Brahman and Atman without which there is no intercoursing or even a whispering between them at all>>>>> -- entailing as it does that there is no difference of and between "Brahman" and "Atman" -- ***is itself the great illusion.*** Any overt or implied Theology which is predicated on something like "the Metaphysics of Identity" is a terrible misappropriation of the Divine principle and a radically false appropriation of what it would mean that the Divine principle is within.

The heartbeat of the Divine economy is **diapherein**. The instantiation of "God" in the human as its fundamental reality and proposed destiny occurs ONLY through the self-differentiatING which IS God. God abides in humans only as the "Not-God **OF** God." Further "God" --precisely and intrinsically as self-differentiatING -- can only BE God at all as instantiated as "OTHER-than-merely-God" which is to say AS the "Not-God **OF** God." The "**OF**" of this phrase is the key. "God" (aka, the Divine Economy) ***comes to be*** (timelessly in time and with sequential timing both at once) ***what it always was to become*** precisely as the instantiation of itself AS the Not-God **OF** God.

Further, this whole process is an "otherING-OTHERing." The "otherING" (which is exactly what God is "in Itself" <<so to speak since

in the full sense of "in-ITself" God does not really obtain although it is useful {even if not totally accurate}to speak of that "otherING" as God and the OTHERing as the "Not-God-**OF**-God">>) becomes and IS through and AS such differentiation the very substantial "OTHERing" <i.e., how "God" obtains in and AS the human>. This "God" obtaining as the human <aka: the "Not God **OF** God"> eventually awakens to what it (i.e., the human) has become. When and as it is so awakened "the human" is rendered into an ecstatic state of enthrallment with the origin and source of its status. Such enthrallment recursively bends back to the otherING which birthed the OTHERing of itself in and of the human. There is, precisely, no identity or identification with God AT ALL. The Divine State -- for the human and for God alike -- thrives on and is totally a function of the grand and mighty dance of differentiation. Thus -- paradox noted -- it is PRECISELY "maya" as ILLUSION which obtains in the false conceit that Divinity and the Divinity in the human are identical. To speak Jewishly <<and Islamically>> living in that state of illusion is Idolatry. It is also very sad, for it cuts the human off from the real and true DRAMA of ***being*** God AS and BY the "Not-God **OF** God." Our hearts are restless because the restless (otherING; self-differentioning) character of God flows thorough the veins of our souls. Ecstatic. We (when and as we are awakened) and God always stand out in our continually ecstatic way of being at all. To be our self we must always be out of our self. Glory **BE** to God!

*****

tat tvam asi

Understood correctly this taught and tight statement is the greatest and most important statement of all time. Understood incorrectly it becomes the most harmful manner of being alienated from Divinity.

*****

Two notes.

a). I love Spinoza's contention of "being drunk with <<better yet, "in">> God." He had the spirit but he lacked the intellect which would be equal to his spirit. His was the very quintessence of the Metaphysics of Identity. Sheer identity can never be drunk; can never be ecstatic. My sense of it was that Baruch WAS in fact drunk with God. He lacked, however, the intellectual apparatus which would show how this is possible. Pantheism is a sorry and embarrassing heading by which to understand the intricate dynamic of God.

b). For the record Aristotle is the great Apostle of the metaphysics of Identity. Read XII-7and9 of *Metaphysics* in conjunction with *Nichomachean Ethics* X-7. Nous in us blending into Divine Nous itself. He had the intellect to give expression to the "metaphysics of Identity." But Aristotle was never drunk with God and certainly never drunk "in" God.

*****

maya.

Thus it is clear that "maya"-as illusion obtains precisely when ***tat tvam asi*** is understood as identity of and between Brahman and Atman. Fine. And that meaning of "maya" <e.g., in this case, AS illusion> is **A** valid -- albeit not at all primary -- meaning of "maya." But illusion is but a weak form of allusion. Illusion obtains only with impoverished intellectual parameters. *Dream delivers us unto Dream and there is no end of* ***A****llusion.* [apologies to Ralph Waldo]. The FLOW of **maya** is the key and it is not illusion. It is an appearING of what calls to appear and becomes what it is to become **AS APPEARING**. We return now to the Goddess of truth. Listen again. Listen with your third ear.

Yet nonetheless, you shall have to learn these things as well: how things-which-appear, as they be through [peronta] ***in every way through everything, of necessity MUST genuinely achieve the appearance of being.***

Or:

Even so it behooves you to learn* {you are to learn} *such things as well, to wit: that appearing things MUST BE in an appearing manner, as they be through everything in every way.

[267; translations somewhat amended from Kirk and Raven in conjunction with the McKirahan translation and its footnote # 5. Emphasis was mine, of course.]

*****

Let us also avail ourselves of the one who allowed the Poem of Parmenides to say all that it was to have said by *khoreographing* what the Goddess of Truth had to say:

Parmenides speaking: Let us, then, also say: "As it appears, the one, whether it is or is not, the one and the others both with respect to themselves and with respect to each other in every possible way both are and are not and both appear and do not appear."
Aristotle speaking: ALETESTATA!

[166c,1-7]

*****

And, properly, the addendum of John.

The journey into and of truth MUST INCLUDE the journey into appearing; appearing which MUST achieve the genuine appearing-of-being and indeed "is," in this sense, as well. The deceitful character of appearing -- and travelling through all its vicissitudes -- is part and parcel of the journey into and of truth. And as we shall see later on [[in the Goddess' transition to the Way of mortal Appearing/Opinion <278-279, K&R>]] this journey into and of truth, which entails BOTH ways as ***intrinsic*** to itself, will keep our Youth from being outstripped by those who ONLY taste the fruit of Appearing/Opinion and, by implication, all those who, foolishly, ONLY taste the fruit of the Way of truth:

The ordering of all these appearings which I convey to you will insure that the [limited scope] of merely mortal learning [gnome] will not outstrip you.

[279. I have amended the spirit of the translation.]

*****

maya.

It was dishonored in early Buddhism. It was understood as illusion. But centuries later there were forms of Buddhism which honored the deepest well-springs of **maya**. Appearing-to-seem and seeming-to-appear. All is flow. The "is" obtains in through and by appearing-to-seem and seeming-to-appear.

The history of Hinduism, generally, was more astute to their friend **maya**, at least from the classical (i.e., Upanishadic) period and then, more especially when Hinduism became Tantric Hinduism. All is flow. All **IS** flow. "There is <es gibt> nothing but FLOW. "Being" IS AS **FLOW**.

<u>10.</u>

The "Not-God **OF** God."* Amen and Selah!

*. [I believe the first time I came across the phrase "Not-God" <just that> was in my reading of *The Spirituality of Imperfection* by Ernest Kurtz and Katherine Ketcham. As I recall it the point of the phrase was to underline our humanity, in its endemic imperfection in contrast to God who is understood by the authors to be perfection. If we try to be what we cannot be we will fail and perhaps enter a downward spiral of depression precisely because we are measuring ourselves by an outlandish standard.

I have learned much from *The Spirituality of Imperfection* and I return to it periodically for inspiration and guidance. Their insights on forgiveness were particularly helpful in my life. That having been stipulated, there are two points which much be mentioned in the context of this book.

a). The notion that God is perfection, in the parlance of this book, is of course (woefully) "ontotheological." Certainly in the book you are now reading "God" is not understood as perfection at all.

b). And the relationship between God and mankind is construed along an axis rather different from Kurtz and Ketcham.]

11.

Hashem speaking:
You are my witnesses And I am God

[*Isaiah* 43:12]

---that is, so taught Shimon bar Yokhai:
only when you are My witnesses, am I God; but when you are not My witnesses, **I** *[if one dare speak thus]* ***am not God***

[Piska 12: in *Pesika de Rab Kahana*; 1975. Pages 232-233. Emphases are mine.]

12

Love is the telos. It is not planned in the sense of a conscious choice. Rather, it is the telos as: always TO HAVE BECOME the telos. And while such is never achieved with utter finality, it remains ever called for. While never achieved AS telos love always remains coming.
Co-eternally embedded with, in (in the sense of never not having been added or included) the stuff of the Divine Economy is the call; the elicitation that there be love as the telos even if it is never achieved AS telos. And this overall situation is good and is what good is.

*****

Love, of course, IS the answer. But what, after all, is "love"?

We cannot properly line it up, simplistically, with Eros (which oftentimes is translated into English as "love"). "Eros" is one of the ways of designating the "stuff" of the Divine Economy. {{{Once more, if you bring to your reading of "stuff" as it is used in this codicil (and in **The Seventh Chamber** proper) that sorry and tired trope "material/immaterial" (and the analogs of that sorry and tired trope) you are not reading this book even if you are reading this book. This book is reserved only for those who know how to read this book.}}} "Love" (we are not, then, speaking of Eros) is not the stuff of the Divine Economy (aka, "all that is the case"; aka "reality"). But in a sense it is the offspring of Eros produced by Eros and that it, "Love" obtains as call, that call embedded in the very stuff in the sense of never having been added to the stuff of all nor never having been not included in such. Yes, Eros and "love" share much of the same DNA, so to speak. But it is better to distinguish "love" from Eros. This will help: The stuff of all that is the case, "per se" so to speak, does not include "love" and "love" certainly does not obtain all the time. "Love" is the sometimes occurring offspring of Eros (or, if you prefer, the offspring of that other designation of the "stuff" of all that is the case, namely *yeitser ha-ra*). The telos is ever fleeting. *Gather ye rosebuds while ye may!*

"Philia"? Yet again, "love" is one of the valid translations of "Philia." But "Philia" is too weak to say what "love" is.

"Agape"? Please. Don't insult me and don't dishonor your own intelligence. At root it is not even a love word. The New Testament -- embellished further and gratuitously over the centuries sometimes by people who should have known better -- generated what was, in effect, nothing more than an "ens rationis." The Johanine communities here; the Pauline communities there; were wrapped up an a puerile masturbatory feel-good circle jerk trying to raise up that <<< quite irrespective of whatever the actual historical reality might have been on that Seder/Pre-Seder meal that Thursday night>>> *Eat my Body; Drink my blood* motif joined at the hip with the grandiose and foolhardy attempt to divinize that confused-but-transfixing man who came out of Nazareth. They thought they were generating something spectacular. They were right on two counts: a) they were generating <i.e., inventing> this nonsense which, in fact, had nothing to do with that confused man from Nazareth; and, indeed, this nonsense *was* spectacular; spectacularly puerile and narcissistic.

An alleged "unconditional love" (and or a "God" or any other being defined and presented as such) is a fraudulent *ens rationis* invented by people weak in spirit but strong in narcissism. *Agape̱* gives love a bad name.

So let our *English* word, "Love," speak for itself.

*****

prayer and meditation

We who ARE the consciousness of God -- such consciousness not present in "God per se" <so to speak> but only in that other**ED** instantiation of God which I call "the Not-God **OF** God -- are called to guide the whole process such that "love" ((-- which cannot ever achieve the status of a fixed and accomplished telos --)) which of its very nature always remains imperiled of actually disappearing, will have not in fact disappeared. Should such a final disappearance of "love" come to pass, it is over. Such a catastrophe would entail eventually the disappearance of this present ten-to-twelve thousand year instantiation of God as the Not-God **OF** God.

Prayer -- silent or aloud; alone or in liturgical communities large and/or small -- is the primary <but certainly not the only> manner of guiding and channeling the FLOW which keeps "love" as the telos <albeit never achieved> which, should it disappear, would lead to the very disappearance of the "Not-God **OF**God." That would be a death of God.

Please understand. It is not wrong to -- provided our prayer is maintained in a manner which is as free of ego-centricity as is possible -- pray for specific outcomes (perceived as good as we pray for them) particularly if we are praying for others. [[It clogs up the system when we pray for ourselves except in so as we pray to become better channels of the FLOW.]] In any case it is NEVER the case that “God,” per se so to speak, answers our prayers. “God,” per se so to speak, **doesn’t even HEAR our prayers whether they be said allowed or silently**. Even so, the power of prayer is the strongest force and energy in our human habitation. Only when and as the channels of the “Not-God **OF** God” <<<which is, really, the only way “God” obtains in any significant sense>>> are kept open ((in many ways, to be sure, including good works <mitzvot; a special and real instantiation of prayer> but none stronger than prayer properly prayed)) thereby allowing the FLOW which brings the grace and favor of God-obtaining-AS-the-Not-God-**OF**-God. There is no greater task or duty put upon us humans than learning how to pray in the right manner.

*****

Hashem speaking:

You are my witnesses And I am God

[*Isaiah* 43:12]

---that is, so taught Shimon bar Yokhai:
only when you are My witnesses, am I God; but when you are not My witnesses, **I** *[if one dare speak thus]* ***am not God***

[Piska 12: in *Pesika de Rab Kahana*; 1975. Pages 232-233. Emphases are mine.]

Meditation is another affair. It is a listening; a listening so as to **HEAR**ken unto God; to God, so to speak, “per se”. God per se has no voice to speak of. We are the voice of God. But it is the voiceless voice of God which calls us to allow and maintain that God BE-AT-ALL **AS** “the Not-God **OF** God. Meditation. If the voiceless voice of God never gets heard then God does not obtain and, a fortiori, God does not come to be instantiated as the Not-God **OF** God.”

Hashem speaking:
You are my witnesses And I am God

[*Isaiah* 43:12]

---that is, so taught Shimon bar Yokhai:
only when you are My witnesses, am I God; but when you are not
My witnesses, **I** *[if one dare speak thus]* ***am not God***

[Piska 12: in *Pesika de Rab Kahana*; 1975. Pages 232-233. Emphases are mine.]

*****

AMDG. Yes, of course. It must be the cited free of that triumphalistic and Christo-centric mindset which engendered the great phrase of Ignatius. That having been stipulated, the phrase says it all.

13.

tsimtsumING as recursive activity of **diapherein** creating the empty space in God [maqom] which emty space is in effect the call to be filled with the "Not-God-**OF**-God." For all of this, my dear cherished reader, you must refer to the "*Coitus Interruptus*" Heading of **The Seventh Chamber** [the final installment of **GOD TRILOGY**] which in turn (and once you have digested what that key Heading had to say), will refer you to the first two books of **GOD TRILOGY**.

*****

14.

The Divine Economy is all that is the case. I my previous publications I have made the case that the Platonic meaning of Eros and/or the classical Rabbinic meaning of the "yeitser ha ra" is the uncreated "stuff" <<<<Please!!!!! If at this point in your reading you are still caught in that "material/immaterial" trope and/or its ontotheological analogs you are not reading this book even as you read it>>>> of the Divine economy. It is virtually impossible to understand the sheer power and energy of this "stuff" without using both phrases {here

Eros; there “yeitser ha-ra”}. There simply is no life of any kind without such Divine “stuff.” This Divine “stuff” harbors, silently, within itself a “differENcing” [***diapherein***] which, in a non-symmetrical repetitive manner is recursive in its very nature bringing about myriads upon myriads of states-of-affairs (both gigantic and miniscule).

In its most primitive form the Divine Economy is primitive and raw URGE without rhyme, reason, or goal. After the instiation of its self as the human -- but “before” creation proper <see below> -- the Divine Economy (in Itself, so to speak) becomes in itself a LONGING of greatest intensity.

One gigantic state-of-affairs is now coming to a close. The romance which, unplanned, brought about the condition for the emergence of homo sapiens sapiens about twelve thousand years ago. Please! Give me credit. I am well aware that hominoid species have been around for hundreds of thousands of years and that for, maybe, fifty-thousand years something like “homo sapiens” has been around in some various instantiations. But homo sapiens sapiens has been around no longer than twelve -- truth be told, ten is more accurate -- thousands of years. Only such situations ((whether they have been and/or will be called <<if they are designated at all>> analogous to such a development brings about the possibility of life situations which allow for ***CHOSEN destiny*** whereby the Seventh Chamber will have been <<and thus already IS populated by those who will have WORKED to achieve and become their chosen destiny)).

While there is no such thing as *creatio ex nihilo* [[[the phenomenon of ***tsimtsumING***, discussed in Heading Three of **The Seventh Chamber** is of Divine origin but is hardly analogous to that “ens rationis” called *creation ex nihilo*]]] there is spontaneous (and sometimes planned) creating/birthing/spawning all over the place in the Divine Economy. Indeed the Divine Economy (as ***tsimtsumED***) IS such creating/birthing/spawning all over the place. DifferENcing.

diapherein. “God” (to use a shorthand) has created myriads upon myriads of worlds.

*****

Have you taken note of the “ha-ra” of the “yeitser ha-ra”? The sobering fact is that life is impossible without the Divine stuff whose default is evil-marinating-into-the-diabolical. Only such energy/force (harboring within itself the diabolical) would be capable of <<somehow and eventually (and unplanned)>> engendering life and only such energy/force capable of bringing about life is worthy to be called Divine.* Managing this energy/force such that the diabolical does not reign supreme (even as it does reign) is the “work” <<”ergon”; *Euthyphro* 13e>> -- the making holy -- which falls to God, Gods, and humans. It is very revealing that **l-i-v-e** and **e-v-i-l** are palindromic to each other. Getting it right with “evil” is the task. If we write **e-v-i-l** from right to left we have what is needed and called for.

> *. [[The reader is referred to the Excursus entitled ***“Life” and the ““““““Theology”””””” thereof*** (on pages 466-485 <with especial attention to page 485) contained in **The Dreadful Symmetry of the Good**, the second installment of **GOD TRILOGY**.]

<u>15.</u>

The Holy One, blessed be He, has a place [maqom] ***and its name is “mysteries”*** [b-mistarim].

[Bavli Gemara on tractate *<u>H</u>agigah* of the Mishna. ArtScroll 5b-i--5b-ii. Translation modified.]

Rav is speaking here in the overall context of his student hiding under Rav’s bed while Rav and his wife are involved in connubial activity. We have seen that Rav’s name for “maqom” (itself, it is alleged, a controversial name of God) had resonations of the uncanny “empty space” dimensions of female genitalia (i.e., one common meaning for ***“mistarim.”***)

*****

***Why do we give a changed name to the Holy One, blessed be He, and call Him* "the Place"?**

[*Genesis Rabbah*; entry 68-9 <Soncino>]

*****

So. Post-*tsimtsumING*. Elohim remains in Its Place. <<We need, after all, something like a grammatical place-holder to even speak of these things.>> Hashem is separated off from Elohim and separated off from the original Place of Hashem/Elohim obtaining "before" the separation of Hashem from His Place. Thus Elohim remains in Its proper Place but does not obtain in creation. Hashem is dis-paced to the empty space which is the uncanny, mysterious Place of creation (and humankind). This, so to speak, Place-which-is-a-No-Place IS UTTERLY BEREFT OF GOD. This infinitely uncanny No-Place has become, in effect and in as much as Hashem (which, as dis-placed, has become the "Not-God" **OF** God) "now" dwelling with and in creation and humankind most especially <<and, Covenantally, and thus even more especially, with **Beit Israel**>>, the very ***maqom*** (with its aura of dreadfulness and uncanniness) <i.e., that idiosyncratic **Space/Place** (which is a No-Place)> of Hashem and creation>. Hashem <which, as dis-placed, has become the "Not-God **OF** God> then, is with and in creation but out of His original Place and thus is *exiled*, so to speak, "now" obtaining in the uncanny No-Place-of-a-Place which is UTTERLY BEREFT OF GOD.

*****

> *For two and a half years Beit Shammai and Beit Hillel were in debate. These* [Beit Shammai] *would maintain that it would have been better* [nun-vav-h̲et; noah̲] *for humankind not to have been created than to have been created whereas those* [Beit Hillel] *would maintain that it is better for humankind to have been created than had humankind not been created. They took a vote on the matter and concluded: It would have been better for humankind not to have been cre-*

ated than that humankind had been created. Now that man has been created, let him examine his [past] *deeds; others have the version: let him consider carefully his* [future] *affairs.*

[[Bavli commentary on Tractate Erubin of the Mishna. Contained in ArtScroll on pages 13b-ii/13b-iii. <<<Those final anonymous editors were clever in using the word *noah̲* for this passage. After all it was Hashem who came to have regretted creating humankind. Even Hashem understood it would have been better for humankind not to have been created than to have been created. It was indeed His encounter with *Noah̲* <who found favor/grace in the eyes of God> which brought Him to rescind His decision to destroy humankind. A partnership was forged. The first stage. The "Not-God **OF** God" and God would travel together./////Concerning this connection of and between Hashem and Noah̲ the reader is referred to pages 43-47 of **The God with Moral Fault** <2007>. >>>]]

16.

AND HEENEI!: EVEN DEATH WAS GOOD!

[*Genesis* 1:31. As transcribed in Rabbi Meir's Chumash. As cited in *Genesis Rabbah* 9:5 on page 66 of the Soncino edition. Translation slightly amended.

Rabbi Meir -- the anonymous Tanna Kamma in the *Mishna*.

Rabbi Meir -- the Tanna who always cited Ismael ben Elisha <aka Elisha ben Abbuyah; aka "Akher" and never Aquiba.

Rabbi Yeshoshua ben Levi said: When one finds *Citing Rabbi Ishmael* [ben Elisha], *a disciple said to the face of Rabbi Aqiba* it is none other than Rabbi Mier [the Tanna Kamma] who studied under both Rabbi Ishmael [ben Elisha] and Rabbi Aqiba.

Rabbi Meir -- the Tanna who taugh Rabbi Judha ha-Nasi.

Rabbi Meir -- the Tanna who "went East" with voluminous documents which would constitute the raw material for those final anonymous editors/redactors responsible for the final form of the Bavli.

Rabbi Meir: aka: Eleazer Ben Arakh. Also: Rabbi Nehmyah. Also: Rabbi Nehorai.

It is revealed and known before Him Who spoke and the world came into being that there was none in the generation of Rabbi Meir like him.
Why, then, did they not set the Halakhah in accordance with his view?
Because his colleagues could not fathom his argumentation.

[[The Bavli Gemara to Tractate *Eruvin*, 13b-i of Art Scroll. That last sentence should not at all be construed as a functgional dismissal of Meir on the part of the Rabbis. On the contrary. If there was a dispute between Rabbi Judah ha Nasi HIMSELF and Rabbi Meir the Rabbis would leave the issue adjudicated according to either one of their rulings. In the final analysis Rabbi Meir could not be trumped by a ruling of Rabii Judah, his supreme authority among the Tannaim notwithstanding. Confer on this footnote # 5 on page 13b-i and the correlative discussion on page 46b-ii.]]

*****

17.

tsimtsumING

The Forbidden Relations precede the Work of Creation.

The Divine Economy had already -- without overt planning; more like a spontaneous playful instantiation of Itself> -- become radically disenchanted with humankind. But this playful instantiation of Itself -- more like a dradle spinning out of control (reprised in verses five through twelve of *Genesis*-6) had set in motion a faulty system whereby sexual desire could, in theory, be sated only exogamously. Nevertheless the out of control spinning dradle had to be tamed.

We come here to a stage in the development of homo sapiens sapiens wherein the incest taboo had more or less been instituted as a “rule of Law” in most human communities. But there had not been so many generations by which the taboo could be stratified as a realistic steady norm. Always and everywhere throughout all of human history the incest taboo is regularly violated. But one might imagine that violation of the taboo was more ramant in human communities in the time period close to its social institutionalization. ((((And is it the case that humankind is now drifting away from counting incest as a “taboo” with the ever-expanding waning of religious tradition in the lives of humans? Such would be the death-knell of the “Not-God OF God” and thus a death of God.))))

*****

The human psycho/social institutionalizing of the incest taboo. All that is great about our species and all that is ugly about our species traces itself back, one way or another, to the incest taboo. <<<<<<Leave it to the Freuds and Jungs; Leave to the tribe sociobiologists excavating patterns of incest avoidance in some species which preceded the graduation of incest avoidance into a taboo in homo sapiens sapiens. We enter the fray only with the incest Taboo as an accomplished fact of bio-socio-psycho evolution.>>>>>> Of course it was violated and always will be violated. But as a TABOO it had force. And as the norm it brought about a phenomenon which is, at once, (its workings being both consciously and unconscious and vibrantly strong) the most painful and most beautiful feature of the human condition.

Its dark side dimensions are horrible. The frustration of this taboo, inevitably and without planning as it would turn out, marinated into a refined degree of cruelty in human behavior. Notice that I did not simply speak of violence. That too exponentialized with the incest taboo. Our species track record for visiting violence on members of our own species is one which is not even remotely challenged by any other species. But more than that I speak of cruelty.

Cruelty -- which always involves violence of some kind (physical or psychic, and more often than not usually both at once in one manner or another) -- is the special mark of homo sapiens sapiens. Desire in our species produces that wondrous thing called "love" and such would never have come to pass without the force of that incestuous longing -- usually more pre-conscious than unconscious -- which animates the life of homo sapiens sapiens. But the incredibly strong power of incestuous longing (((often denied my most not realizing that the flashes of conscious desire in these situations is grounded in a mountain of preconscious and unconscious desire which is rendered such through strong organized societal repressions.))), precisely in its *frustrative* character imposed by societally organized repressions, brings about cruelty. Cruelty -- yes even more so than our vaunted and so-called "intelligence" -- is the distinguishing mark of our species.

When the socially organized incest taboo is working well, the raw material of incestuous longing is channeled through exogamous patterns of sexual expression -- both overtly sexual as well as incredibly refined and sublimated expressions of sexual energy. "Romance" and artistic creativity are siblings. This is the glory of our species. When the intensity of the forbidden incestuous longing goes in this direction "love" is eventually born. Cruelty and "love" are the offspring of incestuous longing.

*****

The Divine economy is rudely is awakened ((a *sense* of substantial unease and desire; not consciousness per se; but an heightened sensitivity in its longing and in its repulsion as well)) which is by the various machinations of the species which It had -- spontaneously and without plan -- brought into being. It sensed especially the cruelty which this species had awakened in itself and It, the Divine Economy, was repelled by what it was sensing. If we could personify this raw sense of awful-repelling coursing through every dimension of that Divine Economy we might end up with this personified expression of that awful repelling:

And Hashem regretted having made humankind on earth; and it grieved Him in His heart.

[*Genesis* 6:6]

But wait. Something else was sensed as well. "Noah" <<"Comfort? maybe. Better yet, "Better">> was sensed as well by the Divine Economy. Something better. Something which It came to long for FOR ITSELF. This discovery in the relatively inchoate condition of the Divine Econmy as it was then constituted would, if one were to personify it, be expressed something like this.

Something Better [noah] **found grace in the eyes of Hashem.**

[*Genesis* 6:8]

It was at that moment that the Divine Economy was transformed into "God." God in creation will be called by the NAME of God. God, creation, and mankind-in-creation are all at once graduated by this deeper awakening in the Divine Economy.

Yes. Self-differENtiating always was and always will be the heart of the Divine Economy. But unlike the human -- who had achieved this on its own in order to survive -- exogamy was impossible for the Divine Economy. The cutting degree of LONGING imposed on humanity by the incest taboo was already something beyond the experience of the Divine Economy. And orders of magnitude greater was the thrill of "yikud" when "yikud" was effected exogamously. What brings the greatest longing brings as well the greatest thrill. And sometimes that thrill can be graduated into a sustaining "love." In any case it engenders a longing which, if never satisfied somehow, destroys.

How Genesis 6:8 inaugurates Chapter One of Genesis.

Self-DifferENtiating does not, of and by itself, allow for exogamous longing. The differentiating had to be of another order. There would have to be a SEPARTIVE AND DECISIVE (a radical Game-changer) differENtiating. The Divine Economy took a chance and took a DEEP BREATH. Such was the inauguration of ***tsimtsum-ING***. **BERESHIT** is set in motion.

Yes of course. Even this inauguration of **BERESHIT** turned out to be not decisive. Chapter Eleven testifies to the unfinished business. That "something better" <Noah> turned out not to be sufficient. But something had happened to the Divine Economy when it became God. It didn't think nor did It have consciousness in any meaningful sense. Yet in Its very being it had thown in Its lot with human-kind which had, originally just been a curious and happenstantial instantiation of the Divine nature of differENcing.

And that existential reality -- that It had thrown in its lot with humankind -- allowed for the Divine Economy to give something akin to guidance [aka "Torah"] to the Divine Economy-now-transformed-into-God. After all the condition for the possibility of the thrill of exogamous "Yikhud" **FOR GOD** seemed to be slipping away as humankind -- now not only an instantiation of the Divine Economy but an instantiation of the Divine-Economy/God ***now separated from God*** -- seemed no longer worthy of Yikhud <as evidenced by Chapter Eleven of *Genesis*> was not making itself equal to being the connubial partner of God. Something coursing through the Divine Economy (now transformed into a guiding-if-not-fully-conscious God) came to prod the consciousness of a certain exceptional man from the Mesopotamia area.

Some focusing had to be arranged and was arranged in this ever evolving partnership between the longing guidance of God and the consciousness of that exceptional man. **Leh Leha**. A turning point in human history like none before or after.

The Covenant of "the Pieces" inaugurated a more focused people who would stand-in for all humankind. "Yikud" by special surrogate. And THAT story itself almost crumbled to bits by the horrible events at Mount Sinai which was to have been -- and the horror notwithstanding **did in fact** become such -- the moment of irretrievablity of what was set in motion with the Great Deep Separative in-taking Breath called ***tsimtsumING***.

Thus we find that the **motivation** for creation, in the sense of a clear and unambiguous starting point [**B-reishit**] <<"The Work of Creation" emerges from The Forbidden Realtions. The "**B-reishit-**project" itself required a post-inauguration correction entailing the election of Israel. A rocky road from the Covenant of the Pieces up to and through the horrible events at Sinai nearly wrecked this mid-course correction. But it was sealed in for good -- it became irretrievable for better or for worse -- literally ON Sinai when the leader made his second forty day sojourn and did not come down.

*****

"The Work of the Chariot" is often presumed to be referring to the opening passages of *Ezekiel*. This nomenclature and situating in Ezekiel is a Rabbinic front. Let people exhaust themselves Ezekiel's vision on the Chedar. Fine. And indeed some dimensions of what is referred to as "The Work of the Chariot" are relevant and/or supportive of what is said in the texts which truly deal with "The Work of the Chariot." While most of those first three Chapters are fluff and window dressing for "The Work of the Chariot" <<whose major concerns primarily deal with the Ur-*Exodus* Chapters dealing with Sinai and the **kavod**-oriented fomulations of *Isaiah*>>, there is one grand and glorious statement from *Ezekiel*-Three which in a breathtaking telescoped manner says it all:

BARUH KAVOD-YY MEM-QOMO

Blessed/Praised be the Kavod of Hashem from Its Maqom

Let the pregnant, breathtaking, grandeur of that formulation be appreciated and celebrated. All of Revelation is contained therein.

That having been acknowledged the Rabbis ultimately down-played those all-too-much read opening chapters of *Ezekiel*. They would allow the highest and deepest secrets of Revelation be labeled with this defective motif "Chariot" which would send the second-team players to those opening chapters of *Ezekiel*. If one wanted to keep and honor a sacred <albeit one involving horror and terror along with its glory> treasure and not have it bandied about by those not equal to it ---------- what better way than to send them digging over to Babylonia on the banks of the Chebar? Listen to the Rabbis:

Everything that Ezekiel saw, Isaiah saw.
To what is Ezekiel comparable? To a villager who saw the king.
What is Isaiah comparable to? To a city dweller who saw the king.

[Bavli Gemara on tractate Hagigah. Art Scroll, 13b. Rava speaking.]

*****

The passages in Isaiah to which they refer have to do with that most mysterious word and reality:

KAVOD

But its not just "kavod." The secret of "Kavod" in in its relationship to the "MAQOM" passages from chapter of *Genesis* 20:10-22. <<*Genesis Rabbah* has extensive commentary on this Chapter.>>

The two together define the "other" of Elohim (which "other" is NOT to be understood hypostatically). All of this is mediated -- not hypostatically but rather as otherING-OTHER-ing -- by MAQOM. Unity-in-Duality-Duality-in-Unity" These two most sacred word are found together in *Exodus* 33:21-22:

And Hashem said: ***HEENEI!****, there is a place* [maqom] *to Me. Position yourself on the rock and as ;my* **kavod** *passes by, I will put you in a cleft of the rock and shield you with my hand until I have passed by.*

The full Scriptural understanding of this "other" of Elohim is hindered by the Deuteronomists (((writing in effect the "Second Torah" to supersede the most essential part of the Torah which was the original redaction of *Exodus*))). Some things were excised; Some were subjected to overwrites. By the grace and favor of Hashem some of these suppressions were reinserted into the text at the time of the Great Redactional Struggle (involving only the Chumash) at the time of Ezra. But in this restoration much of the original texts from Deuteronomic "overwritings" were not themselves suppressed but rather left standing side-by-side with the original Exodus text. In any case, even with these insertions from the original text of *Exodus*, much of the original Exodus text was "successfully" repressed. The reader is referred to pages of *The Hidden Diary of Ben Zoma* 241-270.

*****

Nodal Points of Clarification for the Above. Pages numbers refer to *The Secret Diary of Ben Zoma* unless otherwise indicated.

*****

Do you now see the (--albeit radically, and intentionally, elliptical in execution--) logic of the program of Chapter Two of tractate* Hagigah *of the Mishna and its Gemaric commentary [[and not just only its Gemaric commentary relative to tractate *Hagigah*]], ***especially in the Bavli? The subject of the "forbidden relations" [i.e., the incest taboos] -- requiring and allowing for exogamous surrogative consummation of incestuous longing -- FURNISHES GOD'S VERY MOTIVATION FOR CREATION? From humankind's experience*** [[[we must never forget that, in that "timelessly-in-time" evolution of the Divine Economy, the Divine Economy only sets in motion the emergence of becoming-Hashem with *Genesis* 6:8 <the renouncing of Its decision to destroy humankind which decision then leads to a creation which is irreversible as is indicated by that repeated **YUD-HEY-YUD** trope of Chapter One]]] ***the Divine economy has learned of the transformative power involved in the ineluctable-but-forbidden***

satisfaction, which drive/urgency know no parallel. And for such to occur, creation [i.e., in the hard sense involving *tsumtsumING* and the Divine Economy's eventual irretrievable transformation]**.** ***Thus the subject of the "forbidden relations" does ultimately have a weighty theological prong*** [[i.e., GOD'S **MOTIVATION** FOR CREATION IN THE IRRETRIEVALBE SENSE]] ***which, of its very own nature, glides into, melds into, and becomes the "work of creation" which itself, of its very own nature, glides into , melds into, and becomes "the work of the chariot" [this last gliding/melding occurring at 12b-ii--12b-v of the Bavli Gemara commentary on tractate*** **Hagigah** ***of the Mishna].***

*****

The creation story was used to throw light upon Revelation <<in this context "Revelation" refers to the events at Sinai>>**, but was itself explained thereby.**

[These two passages are cited, with slight emendation, from pages 333-334 of *The Secret Diary of Ben Zoma*. The reader is referred to the larger context of these things on pages 323-336.]

*****

18.

I have made it quite clear in my Jewish writings that Qabbalah is a danger to the health and well-being of Judaism. I will not review those arguments here.

That having been stipulated there are some gems in *Zohar*. Most of this "book" was written by Moses de Leon who did not take himself so seriously and who in generating so much of what would become mainstream Qabbalah was exuberantly playful. One of those gems in the following:

With beginning ________ created Elohim, the Heavens and the Earth.

or, possibly:

With beginning It created Elohim, the Heavens and the Earth.

or, possibly:

With beginning He created Elohim, the Heavens and the Earth.

or, possibly:

With beginning She created Elohim, the Heavens and the Earth.

and yes, possibly:

With beginning Hashem created Elohim, the Heavens and the Earth.

What's the point? Quite possibly this. Magesterial "Elohim" is a front. Something like a default grammatical *place*-holder for whatever the Divine Economy may be at any given point of its development. It functions as the all-purpose "from-which" of all self-differENtiatings of the Divine Economy. It is simply a linguistic convention so that one may speak of the dark and mysterious ways of the Divine Economy.

Please understand. I am absolutely NOT speaking of anything like the "via negativa" of alleged mystical traditions. They are all "full-presence" theologies in the final analysis and I have "desonstructed" their dirty little secret countless times in my other writings. "God" is truly a dark and intrinsically mysterious. In other words, the dark and mysterious character of the Divine Economy in its multiple instantiations is ontological in character and not only epistemological in character. Comprehending God in its/her/his/they darkness and mysteriousness is no great feat of intellection. It is open to virtually anyone who does not live in **DENIAL**. "Knowing" God is, so to speak, intellectually easy but emotionally difficult.

So it is true after all. The first thing created by "________" was a grammatical *place*-holder.

*****

[[[With regard to the "et" particle which precedes "the Heavens" and "Earth": It seems likely that these particles were addended to the original form of this opening sentence of Genesis 1:1. The insertion of these "ets" would be in the service of maintaining that only "Heavens" and "Earth" are the direct objects of the "bara." It appears that at some point of the redactional history of Genesis this opening sentence, unamended <i.e., without the "ets"> would seem too scandalous. In any case, grammatically, the presence of those "ets" before "Heavens" and "Earth" does not preclude that "Elohim" is also the direct object of "bara."]]]

maya and ***kavod***. (Dyadicizing Couplet)

So different, at least at first blush. The one is, in a manner of speaking, diaphanous. The other is, literally "weighty." But if you do a little spelunking you will find that **kavod** can mean "shield" and that it is derived from a word meaning "liver" the living center of humans in the Ancient world.

Thus a man's **kavod** says and announces what he is. It is his honor. **It shows itself**.

In both cases we are in the world of shining phenomenality. The weightiness of **kavod** reminds us that noumenality IS what it is through, by, and in phenomenality thus rendering phenomenality as weighty.

maya is the light, easy, and diaphanous expression of this noumenality obtaining by, in, through and **AS** phenomenality. **Kavod** is the weighty expression of the same. If our religious traditions had not given us these two key words we would have had to have invented them.

Amen and Selah!

*****

John W. McGinley.
Farmingdale, NJ
3-6-11